THE FAMILY AT RISK

SOCIAL PROBLEMS AND SOCIAL ISSUES
Leon Ginsberg, Editor

THE FAMILY AT RISK

ISSUES AND TRENDS IN
FAMILY PRESERVATION SERVICES

Marianne Berry

UNIVERSITY OF SOUTH CAROLINA PRESS

Published in Columbia, South Carolina, by the
University of South Carolina Press

Manufactured in the United States of America

01 00 99 98 97   5 4 3 2 1

Portions of chapter 8 appeared in Marianne Berry, *Keeping Families Together*
(1994), New York: Garland. They are reprinted here with permission.

Library of Congress Cataloging-in-Publication Data

Berry, Marianne, 1960-
   The family at risk : issues and trends in family preservation
services / Marianne Berry.
      p. cm. -- (Social problems and social issues)
   Includes bibliographical references (p.) and index.
   ISBN 1-57003-163-0 (pbk.)
   1. Family social work--United States. 2. Home-based family
services--United States. 3. Problem families--United States.
4. Child welfare--United States. I. Title. II. Series: Social
problems and social issues (Columbia, S.C.)
HV699.B49 1997
362.82'8'0973--dc21   97-4722

To George Stephanopoulos

CONTENTS

EDITOR'S PREFACE

This series of books is written for workers in the human services and for others who have an interest in human services programs. The books are designed to help social workers, psychologists, nurses, educators, and the many other professionals in the human services field improve their knowledge and skills so that they might better discharge their responsibilities and improve the lives of others. Board members of social agencies, public officials, and other groups that have authority over or special interests in the human services are also among the audiences for this series.

Marianne Berry's book represents a new direction for this series. It deals with the subject of family preservation, a concept that is both popular and controversial in the human services field. Family preservation is critically important because the family is the basic institution of every society. People's lives are molded by families; care and nurturing are provided through families; and much of human learning occurs in families. The social values of a society emanate from and are preserved by families.

The family is also the basic economic institution of society. People are provided with support through families. Therefore, the maintenance and enhancement of family life is the top priority of every government on earth.

However, societies also discover that not everyone lives in a nurturing family environment, and not every family is able to discharge its responsibilities to its members, especially to its youngest and most vulnerable members, children. Therefore, over the years, societies have developed alternatives to families, such as orphanages (as they were originally known), or (in the modern terminology) group child care facilities; there is also adoption, for those who cannot live with their biological families, and foster care, for those who must be at least temporarily removed from their homes.

However, societies have learned through centuries of experience that those alternatives to family life are expensive in both economic and human terms.

The amount that U.S. citizens pay for the very few children in foster care is great. And the children, although they may be better cared for in their foster homes than with their biological families, often suffer from psychological and even physical difficulties because of their removal and placement with alternative families. Even the process of placing children with adoptive parents is costly to the society at large and, often, to the children who are placed.

Of course, none of this means that all children can live with their biological families or that all biological families are able to care for their children. Numerically only a few, but in terms of gross numbers, many children must be removed from their biological homes and placed in temporary alternative care.

However, it has always been public policy, especially within child protective services programs and public social services agencies, to keep families together whenever possible. Counseling, financial assistance, and other kinds of interventions and support traditionally have all been geared to maintaining the family unit.

The more recent concept of family preservation is another step on the road to maintaining families, so long as maintenance is possible. Family preservation recognizes the need for many services that can be effective in maintaining families and keeping children with their biological parents. But family preservation goes a step beyond the counseling and referral and economic assistance programs that have been the tradition in the human services and child welfare field.

In family preservation, as Professor Berry shows so ably, intensive services by family preservation workers who serve only a limited number of families employ a variety of models of helping. Family preservation workers are ready, on short notice, to help the families at any time of day or night to prevent or resolve problems that might otherwise tear them apart.

Family preservation programs are costly. They require much more intense involvement of family members with human services workers than do traditional services. However, the cost of family preservation workers and the services they provide are minor, in every case, to the costs that are incurred in both the long and short term when a family is not preserved. The best interests of children and their families, as well as the social and economic interests of society, are well served by programs of family preservation, and that is why so many state and local governments, so many federal social policies and so much federal financing are devoted to family preservation activities.

Berry's book is an excellent analysis of the family preservation ideology and movement, as well as a clear description of several family preservation programs. Those programs continue to develop and evolve in ways designed to improve the lives of children and the families of which they are a part.

Marianne Berry is one of the pioneer experts in studying and writing about family preservation. Her book is a welcome addition to this series.

—Leon Ginsberg

PREFACE

Family preservation services are a relatively new form of service delivery system based on a fundamental social work principle: to be effective, services must build on family strengths and family-defined needs. These services, provided to families who are at imminent risk of child removal, therefore include a flexible range of resources and therapies to improve family functioning and keep families together.

The goal and form of services to preserve families are hotly debated topics in the current political and social arenas. Politicians, practitioners, and public citizens alike are not convinced of the wisdom or the effectiveness of preserving families that are experiencing extreme poverty, chaotic or dangerous environments, or abusive or erratic parenting of children. The debate is thus particularly charged because the preservation of families is argued on both philosophical/emotional grounds and methodological/rational grounds.

The term *family preservation* reflects both a philosophy and a set of methods used in working with families. Family preservation as a philosophy emphasizes the importance of families to children and to society and the value of strengthening families as a first strategy in crisis. It also refers to a set of social work services and practices that are fairly clearly delineated as a new way to work with families toward the goal of keeping them together and safe. This text will present each domain of family preservation separately, attempting to keep the philosophical and rational grounds of family preservation clear and distinct.

The development of many intensive family preservation services programs over the past decade is thus the result of two complementary forces and reflects a shift in philosophy and practices. The first force was a compelling demonstration in the 1970s by the Alameda Project in Oakland, California, later bolstered by the success of the Homebuilders program in Tacoma, Washington, * that

---

*Homebuilders™ is a registered trademark of the Behavioral Science Institute, Tacoma, Washington. Subsequent references to Homebuilders throughout the book should be regarded as implicitly carrying the trademark.

short-term services provided in a timely and intensive fashion could be both effective in keeping families together and efficient at saving program and foster care dollars. This form of service to families was a radical departure from the usual practice of placing mistreated children in foster care and delivering services to children and parents separately toward the goal of rehabilitation and reunification. The second catalyst was federal legislation in 1980, built on the success of the Alameda Project and others, that called for making reasonable efforts to preserve families before a child could be placed into foster care.

Family preservation programs are therefore family-centered rather than child- or parent-centered; they are provided primarily in the home rather than at an office; and services focus on a strengths model rather than a deficits model of family functioning. Based on these fundamental tenets, such programs have proliferated across the United States at breakneck speed. This growth has come at the expense of careful elucidation and construction of program models and despite mixed evaluative findings regarding their efficiency and effectiveness.

Family preservation programs are labor-intensive, incorporate a client- and family-centered definition of problems, and are intended to begin with a clear definition of the risks present in the family and to end when those risks have been reduced. These principles of family preservation programs are often at odds with the philosophy and constraints of the larger public child welfare and child protective services systems within which they are embedded. The rush to implement family preservation services as reasonable efforts to keep families together has taken place without a full understanding of these principles or their ramifications for the larger system.

After approximately twenty years since the introduction of the Homebuilders model and ten years of development of other home-based family preservation programs across the country, it is worthwhile to take stock and to assess critically the promise and problems in intensive family preservation services. In describing the development of family preservation services in the child welfare system, this text will examine the evolution of the philosophy of family preservation, the basic practice innovations that support service models, the research and evaluation base that has informed these models, and the resulting service innovations and policy directives that are beginning to emerge on a national scale. Chapters 1 and 2 will present the philosophy of family preservation and its evolution within the child welfare policy framework in the United States, including its relationship to permanency planning. Beginning in chapter 3, the principles and methods of family preservation services are presented, illuminating this most recent and widespread form of permanency planning. This chapter will clarify the distinction between family preservation as a philosophy and an approach to families and intensive family preservation services as a clearly defined set of principles and services to families. In chapter 4 the Homebuilders model of services and other clearly defined service models will be presented and compared. Chapters 5 through 8 discuss the controversial and undetermined issues facing the field of family preservation, including concerns about program effectiveness, administrative and organizational issues, risk assessment and service targeting, and the efficacy of service components. Finally, chapters 9 and 10 offer both practical and abstract analyses of the emerging issues in family preservation, with recommendations for greater use of research tools in practice and attention to community issues surrounding programs and families.

The following critical analysis of the existing state of knowledge about family preservation services will delineate the successes and limits of this form of services to families. More than that, however, it will provide an understanding of the interplay between innovations in practice, evolution of research, and development of policy in social work. One cannot proceed wisely without the others, and the family preservation movement is a timely microcosm of that interdependence.

ACKNOWLEDGMENTS

Many people had a loving and critical hand in the development of this manuscript, and I am deeply appreciative of their efforts and care. I would like to thank Dean Dorcas Bowles, Associate Dean Shirley King, and Judy Birmingham for creating a supportive and stimulating environment at the University of Texas at Arlington School of Social Work and Center for Child Welfare. I am lucky to work in a place where I feel challenged and loved.

I would also like to thank Leon Ginsberg for his support of my work on this book. I have been the grateful recipient of his gentle guidance and a free rein in the book's development and completion. I count my collaboration with him as one of the most enjoyable in my career. I am grateful as well to Professor Barbara A. Pine who, at Professor Ginsberg's request, provided comprehensive, detailed criticism of an earlier draft of the book and gave me complicated ideas with which to wrestle.

I also enjoy the insights of many wise scholars and practitioners in family preservation in Texas and across the country, whose contributions to my understanding of services to children and families are evident in these pages. These colleagues include Sharon Alpert, Martha Dore, Jere Fenton, Mark Fraser, Roger Friedman, Eileen Gambrill, Charlie Johnson, Michael Lankford, Duncan Lindsey, June Lloyd, Ruth McRoy, Pat Newlin, Peter Pecora, John Ronnau, Twila Ross, Alvin Sallee, and Ray Worsham. Of course, there are many others, too numerous to name, whose influences are obvious or subtle and are deeply appreciated.

I thank several individuals who had a direct hand in the production of the manuscript; who made sure I had my facts straight, my spelling correct, my references complete; who omitted half of my commas and prepositional phrases. These beacons of patience, humor, and intelligence include Scottye Cash, Carole Kahler, Angela Pack, Artie Williams, and Melissa Wilson. I thank my mother, Rae Ann Hopkins Berry, who read the first several chapters for clarity and made suggestions and comments with a loving hand.

I extend my deepest appreciation to Jo Ann Stevenson, who supports my professional and personal life with measured enthusiasm, concern, wisdom, and humor. Jo Ann is a secretary and colleague nonpareil; I have learned more about life and work from watching and listening to her than she will ever know.

Finally, I would like to thank Debora Cavazos Dylla. Debbie Dylla is a doctoral candidate in the UTA School of Social Work and is a valued co-author, co-researcher, and friend. She provided a jump start to two chapters that were going nowhere and made them better than I ever could. She helped me focus on the issues when I needed to and distracted me when I needed diversion. Most important, she forgave me my inevitable transgressions in the process. She has been a wonderful sounding board, cheerleader, and center of gravity throughout our friendship, and I hope she ever will be.

Part I

THE PHILOSOPHY OF FAMILY PRESERVATION

Chapter 1

THE CALL TO PRESERVE FAMILIES

Family preservation services are being heralded by many as the latest force to ensure the well-being of children. Support for these services is based on social, legal, and economic rationales that children do best in families, that family life contributes to their healthy and productive development. Like all practice and policy arguments, these rationales are not fixed but are influenced by social and political environments, by national and world events, and by the successes or failures of the practice and policy directives of the day (Antler and Antler 1979; Franklin 1990; Sarri and Finn 1992).

Attention to the welfare of children and families is nothing new, of course. American government involvement in this area, however, is relatively new; public support of families and parenting responsibilities began only in the twentieth century (Breul and Diner 1980; Leff 1973). In the late nineteenth century private organizations such as hospitals and churches attended to the needs of children, primarily through orphanages.

In the interests of the welfare of children, there is always a tension between children's rights to nurturance and protection and parents' rights to raise children free from unnecessary intrusion from government. The tension has stretched along this continuum over the past century or so as professional child welfare services have developed and evolved. The services given to children and families over the past hundred years, however, have not always held the preservation of families as their ultimate goal. A brief overview of the history of services in the interest of children will illustrate the shifting focus and goals of American practice and policy during this period.

THE BEGINNINGS OF SERVICES TO CHILDREN

Although social workers have provided supportive and protective services to children and families since the beginning of the profession, the goal of family preservation has not always been of foremost importance. The first efforts for children served the dual purposes of protecting them from adversity and protecting society from certain children. The humble beginnings of American child welfare services were in response to the many abandoned and orphaned children in the large cities during and after the Civil War. In defining the problem of street waifs in New York City in 1872, Charles Loring Brace wrote:

> Among a million people, such as compose the population of this city and its suburbs, there will always be a great number of misfortunes; fathers die, and leave their children unprovided for; parents drink, and abuse their little ones, and they float away on the currents of the street; step-mothers or step-fathers drive out, by neglect and ill-treatment, their sons from home. Thousands are the children of poor foreigners, who have permitted them to grow up without school, education or religion. All the neglect and bad education and evil example of a poor class tend to form others, who as they mature, swell the ranks of ruffians and criminals. So, at length, a great multitude of ignorant, untrained, passionate, irreligious boys and young men are formed, who become the "dangerous class" of our city. (28)

Prior to the formation of formal child welfare service agencies—and to the public recognition of child mistreatment, for that matter—private benevolent charitable groups responded to the problems of incorrigible children and street waifs through orphanages, industrial schools, and "orphan trains." Orphan trains, organized by charitable organizations such as Brace's Children's Aid Society, transported many children from the dangerous streets of large urban areas to the farms and ranches of the Midwest, West, and Southwest to be reared by rural families there, away from the misfortunes of the big cities (Anderson 1989; Holt 1992).

Scientific Philanthropy

Brace's response to the problem of the "dangerous class" was framed in the ideology of the Charity Organization Societies of the day, philanthropic groups which emphasized hard work and individual initiative as the solutions to poverty. The Charity Organization Societies in the large cities were characterized by the motto "Not alms but a friend" (Bremner 1956, 170) and were a primary element of the scientific philanthropy movement of the era. The scientific philanthropists stressed that alms were as dangerous as drugs and that the poor could become dependent on financial assistance to the detriment of individual initiative. The underlying assumption was that anyone who did not have to work would not and that many would receive alms through fraud, reducing the amount of resources available for the "truly needy" (Bremner 1956).

4

In their insistence that alms and other assistance were not the answer, Charity Organization Societies promoted cooperation and coordination among relief agencies to prevent the dispensation of aid to undeserving cases so that adequate resources could be maintained for deserving ones (Bremner 1956). Toward this end, philanthropic agencies and charities had to become more scientific in their investigation and determination of who was truly needy and deserving of assistance and who was an imposter. This focus on a scientific approach to solving individual problems was best exemplified in the book *Social Diagnosis* by Mary Richmond (1917), which elaborated on individualized services following a detailed assessment of the client's situation.

Over time, the Charity Organization Societies and other scientific philanthropists developed a base of knowledge on the living conditions of low-income families and introduced more individualized assessments of these families rather than relying on stereotypes and guesswork (Bremner 1956). The scientific philanthropists produced detailed accounts of the correlates of poverty through their investigations of the poor, which then contributed to greater societal awareness of the necessary evils of the industrial revolution and urban life. For the scientific philanthropists, however, the path out of poverty always involved hard work and individual initiative.

As a result of the scientific philanthropy movement, then, "the old charity had but one way of expression; the new charity has a thousand channels" (Peabody 1894, 22). The practiced solutions to the problem of the "dangerous classes," rather than charitable donations and alms, included industrial schools, institutions, lodging houses, and perhaps most famous, the orphan trains that took street waifs to rural homes in Ohio, Michigan, Illinois, and many other western states. Many children were removed from the dangerous influences of urban life and sent to live with farm families, where they could benefit from country life, hard work, and a religious upbringing. Some evidence indicates, however, that poor families unable to care for their children were encouraged to surrender them for the promise of a better life in the country (Holt 1992) and that most children so transported were, in fact, *not* orphans.

Brace reported in 1872 that up to 24,000 children had already been placed in this way and that the effort was an "unmingled blessing," as evidenced by "the immense, practically unlimited demand by Western communities for the services of these children" (242). He went on to say, "The lives of poor children in these homes seem like the annals of great States in this, that when they make no report and pass in silence, then we may be sure happiness and virtue are the rule" (242–43). These orphan trains continued to take children to Western families until 1929, relocating an estimated 100,000 to 150,000 individuals (Holt 1992).

The Settlement Movement

The public provision of services to children and families began around the turn of the century, although social welfare was still "a local affair handled at the municipal, town or county level" (Mohl 1973, 7–8). For example, it was not until 1899 that the first county juvenile court was established in Illinois (Breul and Diner 1980). Federal or even state involvement in the welfare of children and families was minimal.

One of the most widespread forms of social service provision at the local level was through the settlement houses established in large cities. The recent family preservation movement, while focused on child and family welfare, takes much of its philosophy and its founding principles from the settlement movement. Settlement houses such as Hull House in Chicago and Andover House in Boston, and settlement workers including Jane Addams, Sophinisba Breckenridge, Edith Abbott, and Julia Lathrop, laid the groundwork for current social work and social welfare considerations of the physical, social, and political environments as key factors in the well-being of individuals.

Settlement houses, the precursors of present-day neighborhood centers, were established in working-class and low-income neighborhoods, many of them populated primarily by immigrant families. Settlement workers concentrated on identifying community needs and strengths *as defined by the community itself.*

The essence of the settlement idea was "residence." This implied the cultivation of permanent neighborly contacts with those who lived in the vicinity of the houses and the development . . . of that "sense of identification with others" (Tucker 1893, 362), which comes from living among them. Moreover, settlement workers were eager to adapt their services to community needs and, by utilizing the inherent resources of the groups with which they were in daily association, they endeavored to encourage democratic participation and self-help. It was at least their intention to base their activities not upon preconceived ideas, but upon the careful study of the life of the neighborhood (White 1959).

In sum, then, the settlement movement posited an ideology of identifying, celebrating, and building on individually defined strengths through the democratic ideal of participation by all. Through the process of identifying the needs and strengths of the communities in which the houses and workers were located, the movement also served to provide systematic and detailed information on the living conditions of economically deprived groups such as blacks and immigrants (Diner 1970; White 1959). This collection of information provided a basis for establishing an association between poverty and family and individual stress and the role of the social environment in contributing to or ameliorating that stress.

6

Like Charles Loring Brace and his colleagues in the Charity Organization Societies, the settlement workers were troubled by the number of children and youth on the streets. Through "friendly visiting" with their neighbors, settlement workers talked with community residents and discovered that the problems of poverty and social isolation contributed to a schism between parents and their children, particularly among immigrant families (White 1959).

One of the best-known examples of a settlement-based solution to community need was the establishment of community parks and recreation centers. The first model playground in America opened at Hull House in Chicago on May Day, 1894 (McArthur 1975). Neighborhood playgrounds, field houses, and recreation centers were seen as important components in improving the quality of urban life and fostering community spirit by serving as places for sports and social activities.

This solution, unlike Brace's emphasis on hard work and individual initiative, looked to family and community identity and integrity as the basis of family strength and of improved quality of life for children and families. Schools were also seen as an important basis for community integrity. Settlement workers "believed that the school should be the focal point for neighborhood life . . . opened to the entire community when classes were not in session" (White 1959, 64). Settlement workers looked to schools, rather than to churches or other private charitable institutions, as having extended public and municipal responsibility for the quality of urban life.

In addition to emphasizing the importance of the social environment, settlement workers "proposed to expand the role of government . . . to decrease economic dependency" (Breul and Diner 1980, 180). They were instrumental in establishing, in 1907, the Juvenile Protective Association, an umbrella agency that "investigated cases of alleged mistreatment, supervised areas where youth congregated, employed probation officers in the Juvenile Courts, and studied the causes of juvenile delinquency" (Diner 1970, 397).

Settlement workers were also instrumental in the regulation of child labor in many cities (Gordon 1977). A reform movement led by Jane Addams, Florence Kelley, and Elizabeth Morgan secured almost unanimous passage of the Illinois Factory Inspection Bill of 1893, which stated that no child under the age of fourteen could work in a factory and that females and children could work no more than eight hours a day or forty-eight hours a week. Such child labor laws were the first state assertions of children's rights as transcending parental rights (Gordon 1977).

Thus settlement houses were an important step in the definition of family integrity as rooted in community stability, and settlement workers played an important role in documenting the needs of these communities and their inhabitants in an individualized and specific way. Settlement workers strove to provide not only parenting education but also parks and recreational opportunities and governmental protections for women and children. And they achieved these things not by dictating to communities and individuals but by working cooperatively with them to identify community and individual goals and the best means of achieving these goals.

Mothers' Pensions: Scientific Philanthropy versus Settlement Work

At the beginning of the twentieth century, "home visitors" provided counseling and information to mothers on issues of parenting and poverty (Richmond 1917). These emissaries from the charities approached mothers with the goals of "moral education" and helping them to see the importance of taking moral responsibility for their children. The "friendly visitors" from the settlement houses also visited with mothers, but their goals were to identify cultural mores of immigrant families and help these parents and their first-generation children communicate as the children became socialized in American schools.

As settlement workers began to document the connection between poverty and poor outcomes for children, the question brought to public debate was whether or not to use state funds to support mothers (most notably widows with children). The 1909 Conference on the Care of Dependent Children debated the question of public versus private relief for the widow with children and came to the following resolution:

Home life is the highest and finest product of civilization. It is the great molding force of mind and of character. Children should not be deprived of it except for urgent and compelling reasons. Children of parents of worthy character, suffering from temporary misfortune, and children of reasonably efficient and deserving mothers who are without the support of the normal breadwinner, should, as a rule, be kept with their parents, such aid being given as may be necessary to maintain suitable homes for the rearing of the children. This aid should be given by such methods and from such sources as may be determined by the general relief policy of each community, preferably in the form of private charity, rather than of public relief. Except in unusual circumstances, the home should not be broken up for reasons of poverty, but only for considerations of inefficiency or immorality. (U.S. Congress 1909, 9–10)

Thus began one of the most notable demonstrations of the conflict between the scientific philanthropy movement, exemplified by the Charity Organization Societies, and the settlement movement: the question of mothers' pensions or cash payments to mothers for children with employable fathers (which later became Aid to Dependent Children [ADC] and Aid to Families with Dependent Children [AFDC]). Woods and Kennedy (1922) noted that "the social service profession polarized over what has been called 'the universal disagreement' between settlements and organized charity on the question of widows' pensions" (380). Nowhere was this better illustrated than in New York City, "where every major private charity in the state opposed the 1913 Widows' Pension Bill, while the Association of Neighborhood Workers, which represented the settlement houses of New York City, publicly favored it (Leff 1973, 402).

Although the White House Conference in 1909 stated a preference for private relief, its force "catalyzed the drive for public legislation" (Leff 1973, 400). Mothers' pension legislation followed with "wildfire spread" (Bullock 1915, 87), although it was limited to local funding and administration by juvenile courts. Almost every "statute established a maximum allowable monthly pension, which ranged from nine dollars to fifteen dollars a month for the first child and four dollars to ten dollars a month for additional children. To be eligible to receive this pension, a mother had to be a proper person, physically, mentally and morally fit to bring up her children (Children's Bureau 1914, 22; Leff 1973, 401). The mother's role of caring for her children was held as a service to society, worthy of public support: "He is paid for his work; she for hers. And she should be paid by those for whom she does it—all the citizens of the state, not the subscribers to the charities" (Hard 1915, 108).

The provision of mothers' pensions dealt a blow to the private charities and scientific philanthropy, moving responsibility for child and family welfare more firmly into the public sector (Leff 1973). Because the basis for this public relief was the principle that mothers should be supported in bringing up their children "as right-thinking, right-minded, useful American citizens" (U.S. Congress 1926, 85), however, the moral standards espoused by the charities and scientific philanthropists found their way into legal and administrative guidelines for the pensions (Leff 1973).

Around this same time, Mary Richmond's *Social Diagnosis* (1917) proposed a detailed description of social casework building on a systematic investigation and diagnosis of the client *in the social environment*. Because problems occurred in a social environment, Richmond believed that they were probably best solved by treating individuals in small groups, in which caseworkers could make "expert observations of the normal reactions of two or more persons to one another" (Richmond 1920, 256). She proposed that casework thus bridge the gap between individual and community approaches: "Halfway between individual psychology and studies of neighborhoods . . . there is a field almost as yet unexplored . . . I have neither the time nor the equipment for such an excursion" (1920, 256). Richmond focused social work on the need for a scientific and social diagnosis, but social caseworkers were at a loss in developing an appropriate scientific treatment to respond to such a diagnosis once they had made one. Richmond lamented that caseworkers' energies were greatest for diagnosis and that "the treatment seems to drop to a lower level almost as suddenly as though it went over a cliff" (1920, 254).

Thus "friendly visiting" as practiced by the settlement workers evolved into "home visiting" by administrators of the mothers' pensions, and the advice these home visitors gave was often directed toward the removal of incapacitated husbands or male boarders (Leff 1973) and correction of other "moral transgressions." Public social services, then, were still based on the notions of motherhood and virtuous living that their private benevolent charitable counterparts had espoused. While administrators of mothers' pensions were "family friends" who would "educate the mothers more and supervise them less" (Howe and Howe 1915), offering "only kindness, help, and advice" (Appo 1912), the chief probation officer of the Cook County Juvenile Court in Chicago (1913) is quoted as saying, "For the children of mothers with right motives and willingness to accept and follow kindly and intelligent advice, the system has been of great benefit" (73).

PUBLIC CHILD WELFARE SERVICES

These early local systems of services to children and their mothers were focused primarily on the needs of orphans and incorrigible children in urban settings. The focus of child welfare services began to change as the population of orphans declined. In 1920 there were 38 million children in the United States, and 750,000 of these were "orphans" (see figure 1). Ten years later there were 450,000 children classified as orphans, and the number decreased to 60,000 in the mid-1950s (Pelton 1989).

Despite this decrease in the number of orphans, the population of children in foster family and institutional care increased over the same period. The primary agencies involved in the foster care of children continued to be private institutions and organizations such as Children's Aid Societies. No longer was placing children primarily intended for orphans, however; the emphasis on the role of the parent as "a proper person, physically, mentally, and morally fit to

Figure 1

U.S. Children Out of Home, 1910–1978

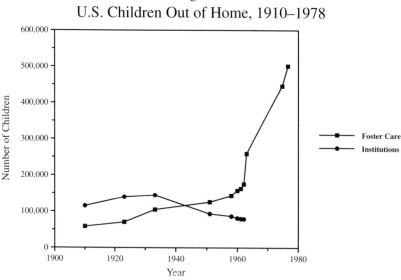

SOURCES: Wolins and Piliavin (1964); Pelton (1989).

bring up children" (Children's Bureau 1914, 22) resulted in children's being removed from families who were "too poor or too vicious" to care for them (Clement 1978). Children could be returned to their families when their mothers had proved they were physically, mentally, morally, and financially able to take care of them.

The public sector began to take responsibility for the welfare of children as a result of the New Deal and the Social Security Act of 1935, which gave grants to states for the provision of financial assistance to families with dependent children. As Lindsey (1994) explains, "By the time the Social Security Act was passed in 1935, the child welfare system had been defined as being for the protection and care of homeless, dependent and neglected children and children in danger of becoming delinquent" (95). The decade after World War II witnessed the rapid emergence of the public child welfare system, of which foster family care was the linchpin (Lindsey 1994).

The Emergence of a Research Base in Child Welfare

Public child welfare professionals in the 1940s and 1950s were guided by "common sense, energy and practicality" (Lindsey 1994, 7) because there was a dearth of empirical studies of the needs of dependent children and/or their families, outcomes for children placed into foster care or institutions, and the effectiveness of casework services in preventing placement or returning children to their families. Science and technological advances during and after World War II, however, brought a public interest in the effectiveness of services and a demand for a sound study of this issue.

After World War II, the increased activity of the scientific and medical professions influenced social work dramatically. The work of Sigmund Freud and others in the fields of psychiatry and psychoanalysis greatly forwarded the view of individual well-being along the medical and scientific continuum of disease and health. As a result, the "cure" for an individual's problems was believed to arise from a careful and systematic investigation and diagnosis of the problems and to require individual rather than social efforts to eradicate them. Such efforts often involved looking inward to discover the "intrapsychic" determinants of difficulties and eliminating or overcoming those determinants through self-awareness.

Research on the welfare of children during this era centered on child development and contributors to developmental problems. John Bowlby (1958) studied infants and children in institutions and found that children who did not have a consistent caregiver or much one-on-one interaction with caregivers failed to develop healthy attachments to others and that this resulted in a variety of developmental and social problems. Bowlby's finding led to a greater acceptance of foster family care as a healthier alternative for abused and neglected children because foster homes were less restrictive and more familylike than impersonal institutions. This shift, in addition to the declining number of orphans in the United States, caused the child population in foster care to increase while that in institutions decreased.

While psychiatry and psychoanalysis were the firm domain of the medical profession, social caseworkers also began to follow the scientific model of treatment, as much as possible without practicing psychiatry (Specht 1990; Specht and Courtney 1994). Menninger (1948) wrote, "The social worker rarely attempts to change the structure of personality. Rather does he help the individual to live with his personality" (33). He said further that social workers' therapy "is directed toward helping the individual accept the situation, modifying external factors insofar as this is possible" (33).

Specht (1990) writes that over the past century, because of their inability to break into the psychiatric and medical domains, social workers became reliant on the more American humanistic and client-centered therapies (for example, the approach of Carl Rogers), becoming "secular priests in the church of individual repair" (356) and moving away from concerns outside the self, including those of communities. Children were thus removed to foster care, and treatment often focused on helping them accept their situations and not blame themselves. Treatment for biological parents also required either psychiatry (not within the domain of social work) or other client-centered approaches. The pendulum shifted during this era back to a focus on the individual, and again, treatment focused on the child rather than on the parent. The treatment of choice for dependent and neglected children was foster care.

Research on Foster Care. Foster family care was first studied in detail in the late 1950s. Henry Maas and Richard Engler (1959) conducted a large study of children in foster care in four communities entitled *Children in Need of Parents,* in which they found that children placed into foster care (most often because of neglect, abandonment, parental illness, and poverty) too seldom went home; rather they "lingered" in foster care with no plan for a return home. They spent an average of three years in care, and 28 percent of them were in care more than five years. A subsequent study by Helen Jeter (1960) at the Children's Bureau, in which she examined child welfare agencies in forty-two states, found a comparable length of care for foster children across the nation, with 27 percent in care for more than five years.

These studies found that, although the purpose of foster care was to provide a temporary home for children and casework services to their parents to enable their children's return, services to parents were often lacking, and in many cases agencies did not judge parental improvement sufficient for children's return. Maas and Engler (1959) reported that 70 percent of the parents of children in care had either no relationship with the agency or an erratic one, and Jeter (1963) found that 35 percent of the families in her national study received no casework services. Maas noted that "agency relationships with most fathers and mothers of the children in care are such that, if parental conditions are to be modified, the process will have to be one of self-healing without any assistance of casework services" (Maas 1959, 5).

The population of children in foster care was thus beginning to grow in the late 1950s because of the many new entries into the system and the diminishing likelihood that those in the system would return home within a short period of time. The social work community had been alerted to the likelihood of this increase, and it began to formulate a response to the problem. In the early 1960s, however, another scientific development would increase the foster population even more.

Battered Child Syndrome. In 1962 Henry Kempe and his colleagues published "The Battered-Child Syndrome" in the *Journal of the American Medical Association,* outlining the identification of child abuse of infants and young children when they were presented to medical doctors with unusual injuries, broken bones, or injuries that were inadequately explained. Building on previous scientific reports of correlates of child abuse published in medical journals (Caffey 1946; Lis and Frauenberger 1950; Wooley and Evans 1955), this article brought child abuse, a greater threat than the perils of disease, war, or urban life, firmly into the domain of child welfare services. Kempe and others recommended that physicians be required to report child mistreatment, and by 1963 thirteen states had laws mandating them to report suspected child abuse (Lindsey 1994). More states mandated reporting of abuse over the next several years, and in 1974, the federal Child Abuse Prevention and Treatment Act mandated the reporting of suspected child abuse by medical and other professionals in all states.

The 1962 Kempe article galvanized the medical profession and child welfare professionals around a national effort to protect children from abuse, deflecting attention away from the care of dependent and neglected children. This outcry from the medical community and the public over the plight of physically abused children led to some of the highest numbers of children removed from their families and placed in foster care during the twentieth century.

THE EMERGENCE OF PERMANENCY PLANNING

These several studies of foster care in the 1950s and 1960s were consistent in their findings that temporary foster care was in practice a long-term placement for large numbers of children; that it was very difficult for families to be reunited with their children; and that once children entered foster care, they often "drifted" from one foster placement to another. Research in the 1970s began to focus on the service element of casework with children and their families before and after placement.

Many studies in the 1970s, like those in the 1950s and 1960s, found that services to biological families were lacking (Emlen 1975; Fanshel and Shinn 1978; Gambrill and Wiltse 1974; Gruber 1973). The Carnegie Council on Children (Kenniston and the Council 1977) reported that large numbers of children were in foster care with no plans to return home because of a prevailing view of child neglect as the result of a pathological condition of parents, for which there was little hope of remediation. Viewing human behavior in terms of pathology is an obstacle to helping people. When child neglect is viewed in pathological terms, it is "regarded as a willful act of uncaring parents for which removal of the child is just punishment" (Kenniston and the Council 1977, 188–89). The flaw in this rationale, of course, is that not only is the parent punished, but so are children and the society that must care for them.

Most studies of service provision to families and children served by the child welfare system found that the child was the primary recipient of services (Brieland, Watson, Hovda, Fanshel, and Carey 1968; Jones 1977), often being referred to "talk therapy" to work out his or her feelings about the mistreatment that had occurred or the placement into foster care. Many of these studies also found that there often was no case plan for the child in care and that the child's proposed length of stay in care was often undetermined (Emlen 1975; Fanshel and Grundy 1975; Festinger 1975; Sherman, Neuman, and Shyne 1974). Emlen (1975) looked at cases from fifteen counties in Oregon and reported that 50 percent had no case plans; Sherman, Neuman, and Shyne (1974) reported that between 62 percent and 77 percent of children had no case plans.

Studies also found that parents' receipt of services was directly affected by whether or not the child was removed from the home. Duncan Lindsey (1991) conducted a secondary analysis of the 1978 National Study of Services to Children and their Families by Shyne and Schroeder and found that when the child was removed from the home, biological parents received fewer services from the agency and fewer resources from community agencies than they did when the child remained in the home. Such services included counseling, employment help, financial assistance, health services, homemaker services, and transportation. Gruber (1973) found that 83 percent of the children in care in Massachusetts had never had a trial visit home and that 31 percent of the biological parents never saw a social worker.

Fanshel and Shinn (1978), upon concluding their longitudinal investigation of children in foster care, wrote:

> For all of the vast experience of child welfare agencies in dealing with failing parents, the professional literature with respect to diagnosis and treatment that has emerged from this area of practice is relatively meager. This is another indication that service to parents of children in placement is the manifest and blatant area of failure in service delivery that one can find as one reviews the foster care phenomenon. (486)

The Role of Community Resources

By 1970 many researchers had determined that child welfare families had often established a "track record" with community agencies before coming to the attention of the child welfare agency (Birt 1956; Boehm 1964; Brieland et al. 1968). In fact, the first documented family-centered program began in St. Paul, Minnesota (Birt 1956), in response to the proposal that the city make an accounting of all families served by governmental and voluntary agencies in Ramsey County, Minnesota. The resulting study found that a small percentage of families received a disproportionately large share of social welfare services, with some families receiving multiple services from numerous agencies in a piecemeal fashion. A pilot project grew out of this study; it was aimed at identifying these "'hard-core' families in the making" (Birt 1956, 42) and giving them family-centered treatment through the coordinated efforts of public and voluntary casework agencies.

Researchers (Stein, Gambrill, and Wiltse 1978, for example) acknowledged that community resources play a part in the placement decisions of social workers. In a study by Ann Shyne (1969), social workers were queried about their "ideal" decisions about placement as compared to actual outcomes in child welfare cases. Shyne found that the availability of resources in the community influenced the correlation between the actual and the ideal outcomes; in other words, a child's needs were often determined by what resources were available. Other studies also found that the unavailability of some relatively inexpensive and unintrusive community resources such as day care could account for the removal of many children from their homes (Jenkins and Sauber 1966; Wolins and Piliavin 1964).

Research had also brought into question the role of other community resources such as external mental health professionals in private or public agencies. Gambrill and Wiltse (1974) raised the concern that social workers exhibited a "mystical reliance" (14) on the healing powers of mental health professionals. And Stein, Gambrill, and Wiltse (1978) stated that "workers are over reliant on resources such as mental health professionals when they do exist, and fail to have mental health agencies share responsibility for making decisions" (12). A failure to coordinate services between agencies and service providers was common:

> The mental health worker decides what to work on in what period of time, and any reports that may be given to the social worker are usually in vague language, such as "Mrs. T is making progress." Rarely does the mental health worker focus on the natural mother's parenting abilities or upon the areas that seem even slightly related to them. In fact, when asked how parenting abilities may be changing, the mental health worker may say that he is not working on that area at all, and furthermore, that the social worker should

not place any pressure on the mother. This divergence of interests between the child welfare worker and the mental health professional was so frequently noted as to be of major concern. (Gambrill and Wiltse 1974, 14)

This problem also existed for the St. Paul project (Birt 1956). Because caseworkers worked for a variety of organizations, there was confusion over responsibility for treatment. Maintenance of cohesion between workers and supervisors and among various agencies was a continual struggle. Much work had to be done regarding coordination between agencies and definitions of responsibilities in a common treatment plan (Horejsi 1981).

These studies were the first systematic examinations of what happened to children and families receiving child welfare services, shifting again to a consideration of the community, if only in terms of linkages with other client-centered agencies and therapies. A study by Jones, Neuman, and Shyne (1976) examined the services provided to 549 families at risk of having a child placed in foster care and found that families who received more intensive services were more likely to retain their children (93 percent versus 82 percent after one year and 92 percent versus 77 percent after eighteen months), as were families who had received hard services (such as those pertaining to health and housing). Fanshel and Shinn's (1978) longitudinal study of foster care at this same time found that high levels of parental visiting and casework activity correlated with children's return home. Of the family changes that allowed for a child's return home, an improvement in the parents' health was most prominent.

Coupled with the concurrent research on the importance of attachments and continuity to children's psychological health, these studies led to the development of model programs and demonstration projects to prevent placement into foster care and to shorten children's length of stay in foster care.

Demonstration Projects

Several demonstration projects were undertaken in the 1970s to try new approaches to keeping children out of foster care. The best-known of these projects were one conducted in Alameda County (Oakland), California, in 1974–75 by Theodore Stein, Eileen Gambrill, and Kermit Wiltse (1978) of the University of California; another that took place in Oregon in the mid-1970s (Lahti, Green, Emlen, Zadny, Clarkson, Kuehnel, and Casciato 1978); and the Homebuilders Project in Tacoma, Washington (Kinney, Madsen, Fleming, and Haapala 1977).

The Alameda Project. Based on the premises that actions were often taken for the child from a moralistic rather than a scientific point of view and that a moralistic approach encourages "discretionary decision making based upon personal value judgments and opinions" (Stein, Gambrill, and Wiltse 1978, 5), the Alameda Project sought to establish a more scientific framework for decision making in services to children and their families.

The Alameda Project studied 428 children and their families, with 227 children in the experimental group and 201 in the control group. The children in the experimental group, unlike those in the control group, were served by a pair of professionals: a county worker, who served both the child and his/her foster parents, and a project worker, who served the biological parents. These project workers used more behavioral methods than were used with the control group: they had written treatment contracts, identified reinforcers (incentives) that parents could obtain when they met intermediate or incremental goals, and tracked parents' progress toward meeting contract objectives. Parents who met contract objectives then had their children restored to them.

The Alameda Project found that 79 percent of the children in the experimental group were out of foster care or headed out by the project's end, compared to 40 percent of the children in the control group (Stein, Gambrill, and Wiltse 1978). At the end of the project, 60 children in the experimental group were restored to their families, compared to 38 of the control group. Another 29 children in the experimental group and 11 children in the control group had been adopted or were well along in the process of being adopted. Fifteen children in the experimental group and 3 in the control group were in guardianships.

What contributed to the difference in outcomes? Workers spent close to the same amount of time on experimental and control cases. What varied was the clients workers served: those in the experimental group spent the bulk of their time with biological parents, while those in the control group split their time between foster parents and children. The control group caseworkers were much more likely to engage in "exploration"—seeking information about the past or present situation to gain knowledge and allow for airing of emotion-laden subject matter (Stein, Gambrill, and Wiltse 1978, 67)—and much less likely to use behavioral techniques.

The Oregon Project. A similar demonstration project, the Oregon Project (Lahti et al. 1978), found that 66 percent of the study children (all deemed by caseworkers to be unlikely to return home) were in permanent placements at the end of the study: a full 40 percent of the children were in adoption, and 26 percent were returned home. Almost all of those placed in adoptive homes were still in those homes eighteen months later, compared to 80 percent of those returned home. Children who returned to foster care after being reunified with their families were older and had had fewer visits with their biological families prior to their reunification.

The Homebuilders Project. Homebuilders was a quiet project in Tacoma, Washington, funded by the National Institute of Mental Health. Based on their review of innovations and evaluations of services to families with severe family disturbance, Kinney et al. (1977) designed the Homebuilders program to include six weeks of service, around-the-clock availability of workers, and a home-based and family-focused model of treatment. This model will be discussed in more detail in chapter 4.

In an evaluation in 1977 following the first sixteen months of the program (Kinney et al. 1977), the primary presenting problems of the 80 families served were shown to include truancy, incorrigibility, and running away among the children and emotional exhaustion on the part of parents. The evaluators reported that 97 percent of the children served (primarily adolescents) avoided institutional placement. Although the evaluation findings were fairly limited in scope and rigor, this project gathered support and attention throughout the 1970s and 1980s.

Demonstration Projects' Aims and Shortcomings

In sum, the objective of these demonstration projects was to determine how to keep children from entering foster care and how to return children in foster care to the biological home as quickly as possible. Only a few of the studies looked at measures of children's adjustment in their respective placements, and fewer still looked at long-term adjustment. The primary goal was the avoidance of foster placement, and outcome measures reflected this orientation. A few follow-up studies, such as the Oregon Project, did look at longer-term outcomes for children and thus countered Charles Loring Brace's assertion a century earlier that "the lives of poor children in these homes seem like the annals of great States in this, that when they make no report and pass in silence, then we may be sure happiness and virtue are the rule" (Brace 1872, 242–43).

Responses to Demonstration Projects

These and other studies and demonstration projects led to a new hope that if services were provided efficiently and correctly, children could remain at home, children in foster care could be restored to their families expeditiously, and children unable to go home could find new permanent families quickly. Research indicated that effective services needed to focus more intensively on biological parents; to be more behavioral and observable; and to address more directly concerns of health, housing, and the parent-child relationship.

Another result of this research was an increase in adoptions of older children. These studies found that if parents could not make improvements in needed areas in a reasonable length of time, children needed to be freed for adoption to avoid the likelihood of long-term foster care and drift. The demonstration projects used adoption as the primary permanent home for children much more than had been done in previous decades. The number of noninfant children in adoptive homes increased substantially in the 1970s as a result. Many children were interracially adopted because a disproportionately large number of the children in foster care were black, and the majority of adopting parents were white. Concerned with an overreliance on and overuse of transracial adoption, the National Association of Black Social Workers issued a position statement against this practice in 1972 (NABSW, 1972).

With the emerging research base and demonstration projects and the increased political activity of social workers and others during the 1960s and 1970s, the stage was set for the passage of federal legislation in 1980, the Adoption Assistance and Child Welfare Act of 1980, which mandated that preservation of the family would be the fundamental activity of child welfare services.

REFERENCES

Anderson, Paul G. (1989). The origin, emergence and professional recognition of child protection. *Social Service Review* 61: 222–24.

Antler, Joyce, and Stephen Antler. (1979). From child rescue to family protection. *Children and Youth Services Review* 1: 177–204.

Appo, Alice M. (1912, August). House Bill No. 626. *Collier's* 49: 20–21.

Birt, Charles J. (1956). The family-centered project of St. Paul. *Social Work* 1 (4): 41–47.

Boehm, Berniece. (1964). The community and social agency define neglect. *Child Welfare* 43: 453–64.

Bowlby, John. (1958). The nature of the child's tie to his mother. *International Journal of Psychoanalysis* 39: 350–73.

Brace, Charles Loring. (1872). *The dangerous classes of New York, and twenty years' work among them.* New York: Wynkoop and Hallenbeck.

(Republished 1973, Silver Spring, MD: National Association of Social Workers.)

Bremner, Robert H. (1956). Scientific philanthropy, 1873–93. *Social Service Review* 30: 168–73.

Breul, Frank R., and Steven J. Diner. (Eds.). (1980). *Compassion and responsibility.* Chicago: University of Chicago Press.

Brieland, Donald, Kenneth Watson, Philip Hovda, David Fanshel, and John J. Carey. (1968). *Differential use of manpower: A team model for foster care.* New York: Child Welfare League of America.

Bullock, Edna D. (1915). Wildfire spread of mothers' pensions. In Edna D. Bullock (ed.), *Selected articles on mothers' pensions,* 87–89. White Plains, NY: H. W. Wilson.

Caffey, J. (1946, August). Multiple fractures in the long bones of infants suffering from chronic subdural hematoma. *American Journal of Roentgenology* 56: 163–73.

Children's Bureau, U.S. Department of Labor. (1914). *Laws relating to mothers' pensions in the United States, Denmark, and New Zealand.* Children's Bureau Publication no. 7. Washington, DC: Government Printing Office.

Clement, P. F. (1978). Families in foster care: Philadelphia in the late nineteenth century. *Social Service Review* 53: 406–20.

Cook County, IL, Family Court. (1913). *Report of the chief probation officer, annual report.* Chicago: Cook County Family Court.

Diner, Steven J. (1970). Chicago social workers and blacks in the Progressive Era. *Social Service Review* 44: 393–410.

Emlen, Arthur C. (1975). *Freeing children for permanent placement.* Portland, OR: Regional Research Institute for Human Services, Portland State University.

Fanshel, David, and John F. Grundy. (1975). *Child Welfare Information Services Report.* New York: Child Welfare Information Services.

Fanshel, David, and Eugene Shinn. (1978). *Children in foster care: A longitudinal investigation.* New York: Columbia University Press.

Festinger, Trudy. (1975). The New York court review of children in foster care. *Child Welfare* 54: 217.

Franklin, Donna L. (1990). The cycles of social work practice: Social action vs. individual interest. *Journal of Progressive Human Services* 1 (2): 59–80.

Gambrill, Eileen D., and Kermit Wiltse. (1974). Foster care: Plans and activities. *Public Welfare* 32: 12–21.

Gordon, Lynn. (1977). Women and the anti-child labor movement in Illinois, 1890–1920. *Social Service Review* 51: 228–48.

Gruber, Alan. (1973). *Foster home care in Massachusetts*. Boston: Governor's Commission on Adoption and Foster Care.

Hard, William. (1915). Moral necessity of state funds to mothers. In Edna D. Bullock (ed.), *Selected articles on mother's pensions,* 98–108. White Plains, NY: H. W. Wilson.

Holt, Marilyn I. (1992). *The orphan trains: Placing out in America*. Lincoln: University of Nebraska Press.

Horejsi, Charles. (1981). The St. Paul family-centered project revisited: Exploring an old gold mine. In Marvin Bryce and June Lloyd (eds.), *Treating families in the home*. Springfield, IL: Charles C. Thomas.

Howe, Frederic, and Marie Howe. (1915). Pensioning the widow and the fatherless. In Edna D. Bullock (ed.), *Selected articles on mother's pensions,* 118–39. White Plains, NY: H. W. Wilson.

Jenkins, Shirley, and Mignon Sauber. (1966). *Paths to child placement*. New York: Community Council of New York.

Jeter, Helen R. (1960). *Children who receive services from public child welfare agencies*. Washington, DC: Children's Bureau.

Jeter, Helen R. (1963). *Children, problems, and services in child welfare programs*. Washington, DC: Children's Bureau.

Jones, Martha L. (1977). Aggressive adoption: A program's effect on a child welfare agency. *Child Welfare* 56: 401–7.

Jones, Mary A., Renee Neuman, and Ann W. Shyne. (1976). *A second chance for families: Evaluation of a program to reduce foster care*. New York: Child Welfare League of America.

Kempe, C. Henry, Frederic N. Silverman, Brandt F. Steele, William Droegmuller, and Henry K. Silver. (1962). The battered-child syndrome. *Journal of the American Medical Association* 181: 17–24.

Kenniston, Kenneth, and the Carnegie Council on Children. (1977). *The American family under pressure*. New York: Harcourt Brace Jovanovich.

Kinney, Jill M., Barbara Madsen, Thomas Fleming, and David A. Haapala. (1977). Homebuilders: Keeping families together. *Journal of Consulting and Clinical Psychology* 45: 667–73.

Lahti, Janet, Karen Green, Arthur Emlen, Jerry Zadny, Quentin D. Clarkson, Marie Kuehnel, and Jim Casciato. (1978). *A follow-up study of the Oregon Project: A summary*. Portland: Regional Research Institute for Human Services, Portland State University.

Leff, Mark H. (1973). Consensus for reform: The mothers'-pension movement in the Progressive Era. *Social Service Review* 47: 397–417.

Lindsey, Duncan. (1991). Factors affecting the foster care placement decision: An analysis of national survey data. *American Journal of Orthopsychiatry* 61 (2): 272–83.

Lindsey, Duncan. (1994). *The welfare of children.* New York: Oxford University Press.

Lis, E. F., and Frauenberger, G. S. (1950). Multiple fractures associated with subdural hematoma in infancy. *Paediatrics* 6: 890–92.

Maas, Henry. (1959). Highlights of the foster care project: Introduction. *Child Welfare* 38: 5.

Maas, Henry, and Richard Engler. (1959). *Children in need of parents.* New York: Columbia University Press.

McArthur, Benjamin. (1975). The Chicago playground movement: A neglected feature of social justice. *Social Service Review* 49: 376–95.

Menninger, William C. (1948). *Psychiatry: Its evolution and present status.* Ithaca, NY: Cornell University Press.

Mohl, Raymond. (1973, July). Three centuries of American public welfare: 1600–1932. *Current History* 65: 7–8.

National Association of Black Social Workers (1972). *Position statement on transracial adoption.* New York: National Association of Black Social Workers.

Peabody, Francis G. (1894). The problem of charity. In Daniel C. Gilman (ed.), *The organization of charities.* Baltimore, MD: Johns Hopkins University Press.

Pelton, Leroy. (1989). *For reasons of poverty: A critical analysis of the public child welfare system in the United States.* New York: Praeger.

Richmond, Mary. (1917). *Social diagnosis.* Chicago: University of Chicago Press.

Richmond, Mary. (1920). Some next steps in social treatment. In *Proceedings of the National Conference of Social Work, 1920.* Chicago: University of Chicago Press.

Sarri, Rosemary, and Janet Finn. (1992). Child welfare policy and practice: Rethinking the history of our certainties. *Children and Youth Services Review* 14: 219–36.

Sherman, Edmund A., Renee Neuman, and Ann W. Shyne. (1974). *Children adrift in foster care: A study of alternative approaches.* New York: Child Welfare League of America.

Shyne, Ann W. (1969). *The need for foster care.* New York: Child Welfare League of America.

Specht, Harry. (1990). Social work and the popular psychotherapies. *Social Service Review:* 345–57.

Specht, Harry, and Mark Courtney. 1994. *Unfaithful angels.* New York: Free Press.

Stein, Theodore J., Eileen D. Gambrill, and Kermit T. Wiltse. (1978). *Children in foster homes: Achieving continuity of care.* New York: Praeger.

Tucker, W. J. (1893, March). The work of the Andover House in Boston. *Scribner's Magazine* 13: 362.

U.S. Congress. (1909). *Conference on the care of dependent children: Proceedings.* 60th Congress, 2d session, 1909, S. Doc. 721.

U.S. Congress House of Representatives. (1926). *Congressional Record, 69th Congress, 1st Session* 67: 3566.

White, George C. (1959). Social settlements and immigrant neighbors, 1886–1914. *Social Service Review* 33: 55–66.

Wolins, Martin, and Irving Piliavin. (1964). *Institution or foster family: A century of debate.* New York: Child Welfare League of America.

Woods, Robert A., and Albert J. Kennedy. (1922). *The settlement horizon.* New York: Russell Sage Foundation.

Wooley, Paul V., and William A. Evans. (1955). Significance of skeletal lesions in infants resembling those of traumatic origin. *Journal of the American Medical Association* 58 (7): 539–43.

Chapter 2

THE POLICY FRAMEWORK OF PERMANENCY PLANNING AND FAMILY PRESERVATION

Prior to the passage of the Adoption Assistance and Child Welfare Act of 1980, tales abounded of children lost in foster care and drifting from one foster home to another with no plan for return to their biological homes or for placement in any other permanent homes. Following the demonstration projects of the 1970s, there was a general recognition of the importance of treatment within the family environment, and maintaining children in their own homes became preferable to placing them in foster care and then making efforts to reunify affected families. In response to these changes in philosophy and practice, federal legislation shifted to emphasize placement prevention over the benefits of foster care. The 1980 legislation sought to keep children in their homes by mandating "reasonable efforts" and providing fiscal incentives to prevent foster placement and promote permanency planning.

Maluccio, Fein, and Olmstead (1986) have defined permanency planning as "the systematic process of carrying out, within a brief time-limited period, a set of goal-directed activities designed to help children live in families that offer continuity of relationships with nurturing parents or caretakers and the opportunity to establish life-time relationships" (5). Stein and Gambrill (1985) note the lack of firm empirical underpinnings for preserving families, but they acknowledge that "permanency planning supports the value that our society places on family life and the best interests of the child, which we assume are best served within a family unit" (38).

The federal permanency planning legislation in 1980, which was supported by subsequent state laws enacted during the 1980s, thus set forth the primary philosophy and goal of preserving families. Alternative placement outcomes are prioritized in this law by their degree of permanency: adoption, followed by guardianship, followed by long-term foster care. Federal legislation more specifically focusing on family preservation services and methods was implemented in 1993. This chapter will explore the goals of permanency for children and preservation of families within the policy framework of these two major laws.

PL 96–272: THE ADOPTION ASSISTANCE AND CHILD WELFARE ACT OF 1980

The Adoption Assistance and Child Welfare Act of 1980, PL 96–272, put permanency planning into policy. It was based on the tenets that children are best cared for in a permanent, secure, and safe environment and best served by planful practice directed toward this goal. It was built on the shoulders of a number of demonstration projects and informed testimony by social workers and other experts.

Mandates of PL 96–272

This legislation set forth a prioritized list of potential outcomes for children served by child welfare agencies. According to its mandates, the most preferable outcome for children is to remain at home with their biological families. According to the law, "reasonable efforts" to keep children with their families safely must be expended by the agency before it determines that children must be removed to foster care. If a child must be placed in foster care, he or she should be returned to the biological family as expediently as possible. If family preservation or reunification is not possible, adoption is the next most preferable outcome because it provides a permanent home and lifelong family for the child. After return to the biological family or adoption, guardianship is the next preferred outcome because of its potential to preserve family ties. The least preferred placement option is long-term foster care.

The 1980 act broadened the scope of child welfare services funded by Title IV-B to include the prevention of family breakup and the unnecessary separation of children from their families. Thus Title IV-B funds would cover the services meeting the "reasonable efforts" mandate of the legislation. The act also shifted foster care payments to a new Title IV-E of the Social Security Act providing matching funds to states for foster care at a rate of 75 percent of expenditures. And it required states to provide adoption assistance for special-needs children who could not return home.

To be eligible for the extra Title IV-B appropriations, a state had to do the following four things to track and serve foster children (Sullivan 1993):

(1) conduct an inventory of children in foster care longer than six months;
(2) establish a statewide information system on children in foster care;
(3) conduct periodic case reviews for each child in foster care at six months and a dispositional hearing at eighteen months; and
(4) implement a reunification program.

The Senate Report accompanying PL 96–272 explained that the purpose of the Adoption Assistance and Child Welfare Act of 1980 was to provide states with fiscal incentives "to lessen the emphasis on foster care placement and to encourage greater efforts to find permanent homes for children either by making it possible for them to return to their own families or by placing them in adoptive homes." Senator Alan Cranston of California emphasized the legislation's focus on provision of services *in the home:*

In the past, foster care has often been the first option selected when a family is in trouble: the new provisions will require states to examine alternatives and provide, wherever feasible, home-based services that will keep families together. . . . Of course, state child protective service agencies will continue to have authority to remove immediately children from dangerous situations, but where removal can be prevented through the provision of home-based services, these agencies will be required to provide such services before removing the child and turning to foster care. (125 Congressional Record 1980, 14767)

Reasonable Efforts. A clause of PL 96–272 requiring that reasonable efforts be made to maintain family integrity and keep the child in the home resulted in greater emphasis in policy and practice on continuity and family ties for children and refocused attention on home-based services. These emphases, in turn, led to a growth in family preservation programs, higher family preservation and family reunification rates across the country (see figure 2), and increased efforts to maintain family ties during foster care and even adoption.

Specifically, the law provided that "in each case, reasonable efforts will be made (a) prior to the placement of a child in foster care, to prevent or eliminate the need for removal of a child from his home, and (b) to make it possible for the child to return to his home" (42 U.S.C. 671 [a][15], 1986). In addition, for any child entering placement after October 1, 1983, there must be a judicial determination that reasonable efforts to prevent placement had been made (42 U.S.C. 672, 1986).

Figure 2
National Trends in Foster Care Entries
Related to Abuse Reports

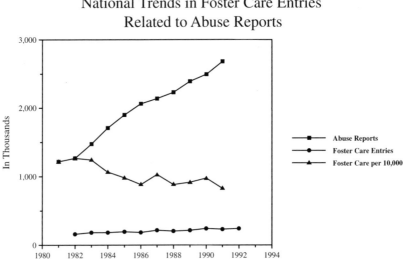

SOURCES: American Humane Association (1990); Tatara (1994).

In the 1960s and 1970s, agencies had removed the child first and asked questions later. This provision forced them to come up with placement prevention services that judges would deem sufficient (or "active and reasonable"). Using as models the demonstration projects in Alameda County, California (Stein, Gambrill, and Wiltse 1978), and in Oregon (Emlen, Lahti, Downs, McKay, and Downs 1978; Lahti, Green, Emlen, Zadny, Clarkson, Kuehnel, and Casciato 1978), practitioners and judges looked to home-based, goal-directed, behavioral interventions; and many such programs, like Homebuilders, were thus born during this period (Kinney, Madsen, Fleming, and Haapala 1977).

Many of these family preservation programs met criteria of reasonable efforts. First, program advocates insisted that intensive family preservation services be provided only to families at "imminent risk" of child placement (Feldman 1990; Nelson 1990). This required a specific and accurate assessment of the risk factors or problems contributing to the likelihood of placement (for a more thorough description of risk and risk assessment, a technique that developed substantially in the 1980s, see chapter 7). To establish the relevance of services to specified problems, family preservation programs became family-centered, meaning that services were intended to do "whatever it takes" to keep a family together. A service plan detailing the relevance of services was to follow from the risk factors and the family strengths identified in the initial assessment. Finally, family preservation programs often used service contracts in case planning and documentation. Both the social worker and the family member(s) specified the tasks and activities to be covered in service, signed an agreement to perform these tasks and activities, and documented their completion.

Temporary Foster Placement of Children. According to the terms of the law, if reasonable efforts have been made and a child is at risk of further abuse in the home, the child is removed and placed in protective care, usually a foster home. This is a drastic step and should not be taken unless the risks outweigh the benefits of remaining at home. The separation of a child from the biological family has detrimental effects, not least of which may be a loss of parental commitment to the permanence of family ties. Impermanence undermines children's chances of learning the lessons they should learn in family life, lessening their ability to form healthy, lasting relationships and weakening their economic and social bases in future life. The more quickly a permanent home is restored (through reunification, adoption, or guardianship), the less detrimental the removal of the child is likely to be.

While a child is in foster care, efforts are made to treat and educate the biological parents so the child can return to the family with reduced and manageable risk of abuse or neglect. At the same time, the child often receives treatment for the physical and psychological wounds from the abuse as well as those caused by the separation from the family. In this manner, the parents and child are rehabilitated separately and then reunited, or reunified, with the hope that their individual gains from treatment will help them to form a better-functioning and safer family union. However, this "separate treatment" methodology is known to be weak (Kadushin and Martin 1988; Stein, Gambrill, and Wiltse 1978).

Family Reunification. For a child and his or her parents to "fit" together in a family, they must be "glued back together" in tandem. Separate and individual treatment does not take into account the important interactional practice of new behaviors that must occur. Theoretically, the ideal is family maintenance, in which the child never leaves the home, rather than family reunification, in which relationships must be reestablished and prosocial behavior newly established. Of course, family reunification is preferable to family maintenance if the child is at risk of further harm in the home.

Duncan Lindsey (1994) has proposed that the American child welfare system adopt the term *safety home,* used in Great Britain in place of *foster home,* to emphasize that a foster home is intended to serve as a safe place for a child but not intended to replace the child's family or family life. Foster care is intended to provide safety for the child, and foster parents have the role of working with the child *and with the biological parents* in hopes of the child's eventual return home. They can do this through nurturing the child; informing the biological parents of the child's ongoing behavior and needs; facilitating contact and communication between parent and child; and discussing parenting, nutrition, games and play, and the like with the biological parents (Maluccio and Whittaker 1988).

Many studies have established that visiting between the biological parent(s) and the child in foster care is associated with the child's return home (Fanshel and Shinn, 1978; Stein, Gambrill, and Wiltse, 1978). However, James Whittaker (1981) proposes that there are numerous obstacles to parental involvement in foster care, including a lack of resources to provide services (transportation, financial help, etc . . .) to biological parents; placement of children in foster homes that are long distances away from their biological homes; cultural, class, and ethnic differences between foster and biological parents; limited roles for the involvement of birth parents (in decision making around the child's day-to-day activities); biological parents' feelings of guilt and failure; and other family problems such as financial and legal difficulties.

Adoption. The Adoption Assistance and Child Welfare Act of 1980 established in policy that adoption is the second choice of a permanent home for a child if the biological family cannot be preserved. The periodic case review provision, discussed below, mandated a periodic review of all children in care so that they would not be lost in the system or drift through foster care without a plan for their ultimate permanent placement. Therefore, to move quickly in making permanent decisions for children and families and avoid contributing to their sense of uncertainty and drift, reasonable efforts need to be made expeditiously and determinations of their success or failure established. If families are successful in maintaining safety and adequate care, children can be maintained in them or returned to them. In decisions about family preservation and child removal, the burden is on the agency and the state to show why the family should not be preserved rather than on the parent to show why it should. By the provisions of the law, agencies are given a brief period of time (the dispositional hearing for a child in care is at eighteen months) either to make improvements in the family situation and close the case or to determine that improvements are insufficient and free the child for another permanent home. The intent is to avoid repeated continuances of the case in the hope that conditions will improve, while denying the children permanence and certainty of their family status. These time limits were intended to reduce drift and ensure that children achieve permanency with as little uncertainty and upheaval as possible.

For children who cannot return home, adoption provides a set of "lifetime relationships" (Fein, Maluccio, Hamilton, and Ward 1983) and a family to grow up in and to call on both in the transition to adulthood and during adulthood. PL 96–272 recognized the benefits of adoption over long-term foster care and provided subsidies to parents to enable them to adopt children with physical, mental, or emotional needs that necessitate special care and children with other characteristics that make them hard to adopt, such as being one of a set of siblings that must be adopted together. Adoption subsidies have allowed many foster parents to adopt their foster children without risking financial hardship and have thus helped to provide lifelong families for many former foster children who were unable to return home.

Long-Term Foster Care. Long-term foster care is the least preferred option for children served by the child welfare system precisely because of its failure to provide them permanency. Research on foster care prior to PL 96–272 revealed that replacement, or movement from one foster home to another, was very likely for foster children, particularly as they got older (Maas and Engler 1959; Stein, Gambrill, and Wiltse 1978). Research also showed that the length of time a child spent in foster care was related to how long the child had already been in foster care, which meant that the longer a child had been in foster care, the less likely he or she was to return home (Fanshel and Shinn 1978; Fein et al. 1983).

Case Reviews. The permanency planning movement and PL 96–272 called for increased emphasis on goal-directed practice, mandated plans of service, time limits, and court reviews for all children served. The act requires that each child in care have a detailed case plan, periodic case reviews every six months, and a dispositional hearing within eighteen months of placement. Stein and Gambrill (1985), two early pioneers in the permanency planning movement through the Alameda Project, have warned that judicial implementation is crucial to its success. "Whether workers are developing case plans in accordance with the guidelines described in the law, whether case reviews are substantive or whether reviewers are merely rubber-stamping plans made, whether administrators are utilizing the data from information management systems to facilitate planning for children are only some of the issues that must be addressed if the intent of the law is to be realized" (91–92).

Actual Outcomes of the Adoption Assistance and Child Welfare Act of 1980

Permanency planning was successful to the extent that it could be, considering that the reforms and requirements set forth in the 1980 legislation were not backed up by the promised funding and were funded in directions that were contrary to the law's intent. The primary shortcoming in PL 96–272 was that Congress failed during the 1980s to appropriate IV-B funds (for family preservation, placement prevention, and reunification services) up to the authorized levels, while Title IV-E allocations (for foster care) steadily rose throughout the decade (Kamerman and Kahn 1990). While these funding allocations, which gave short shrift to family preservation services while favoring foster placement, were in direct opposition to the intent of the federal legislation, they were in accord with societal changes and demands arising from increasing poverty and homelessness rates and rising numbers of child abuse reports.

Outcomes have been the chief indicators of the effectiveness of PL 96–272 because of the relative ease with which they can be generated (English and Tritz 1992; Jimenez 1990; Lewit 1993; Pelton 1994). This is too simplistic a means of evaluation, however. The Alameda Project and other demonstration projects viewed permanency planning as more than certain outcomes for children; it is important to remember that permanency planning is defined as a process by which to work toward these outcomes. Without reliable national-level statistics on a variety of measures of the well-being of children and families, it is difficult to assess the overall effectiveness of permanency planning in the United States in terms any more revealing than placement rates and placement outcomes. The U.S. Congress has called for data collection from the states' Title IV-E programs in numerous acts, including the Child Abuse Prevention and Treatment Act of 1974 (PL 95–266) and the Adoption Assistance and Child Welfare Act of 1980 (PL 96–272). None of the mandates produced the desired data collection, however, so the Office of Human Development Services of the Department of Health and Human Services provided funds to the American Public Welfare Association in 1982 to establish the Voluntary Cooperative Information System (VCIS) to collect information from state welfare agencies about children in substitute care and special-needs adoptions (Sullivan 1993). Through this system, federal tracking of state data on child placement rates, adoptive placements, and other indicators of permanency have been performed for the past decade, with difficulties arising from disparate state definitions and categorizations of substitute care, units of analysis (children versus families), and other key variables. For example, according to one account, "in 1985 states used 21 different definitions for foster care and 14 different definitions for adoption" (Bussiere 1990, 78).

The full potential of permanency planning was not attained. The requirements for reasonable efforts to be extended to all families experiencing child abuse or neglect, following on the heels of the 1974 federal legislation mandating reporting of child abuse and neglect, resulted in what has been called the Child Welfare Paradox (Jimenez 1990). The 1980s saw dramatic increases in the numbers of families served and the mandated provision of increased services to these families. During this same period, agencies were faced with serving these families with no increased funding for family preservation or placement prevention services, while funding was increased for foster placements. Foster care, as a result, remained the placement of choice in many cases (see figure 2).

Still, certain key elements of the Adoption Assistance and Child Welfare Act of 1980 were implemented that allow the assertion that the basic intents and purposes of permanency planning are met, including increases in the likelihood of permanency for many children and the introduction of plans and periodic reviews of the progress on plans for children with an emphasis on permanency.

Family Preservation Outcomes. Family preservation and family reunification are central tenets of permanency planning. Rates of both in proportion to the number of child abuse reports increased during the 1980s as a result of PL 96–272. As illustrated in figure 2, the number of children reported to be abused increased from 1,154,000 in 1980 to 2,178,000 in 1987 (an 89 percent increase), while the number of children in foster care rose only 19 percent (from 302,000 to 360,000) from 1980 to 1989 (Barth and Berry 1990). Thus foster placement did decrease as the initial service response for many children, and efforts to preserve the family were a primary contributor.

Barth and Berry conducted the review "Outcomes of Child Welfare Services under Permanency Planning" in 1990 and found that after the passage of permanency planning legislation, more children were returned home from foster care, and children who previously would have entered foster care were instead maintained in their homes. Many children who could not return home were freed for adoption. However, as noted by Cohn and Daro (1987) and others, the placements or returns were often effected without sufficient knowledge or resources to preserve families or promote successful reunifications or adoptions. As a result, many of the children who were returned home or maintained in the home remained at risk of abuse or neglect and often came back into the system later (Barth and Berry 1990). Toward the end of the 1980s, many critics complained that the child welfare system had become a revolving door; service time limits, overwhelming caseloads, and concerns about helping the family expediently and moving on resulted in short-term or minimal gains that precipitated recurrent breakdown.

Although the number of children in foster care did decrease after permanency planning legislation in 1980 (from 302,000 nationally in 1980 to 270,000 in 1984), foster care numbers rebounded in the second half of the decade (Barth and Berry 1990). While returning children who might be drifting through foster care to their original homes was a worthwhile and just action, reunifying these children with families who were not adequately prepared or supported set the children and families up for yet more crises, possibly resulting in further abuse, neglect, or even death. In fact, studies found that children who were reunified with their families were most poorly served under permanency planning services (Barth and Berry 1987). These children were often reabused at rates reported from 22 percent (Jones 1983) to 25 percent (Runyan and Gould 1985). Children returned home from foster care were also not guaranteed permanence in their homes. As many as 20 percent (Lahti et al. 1978) to 32 percent (Fein et al. 1983) of these children returned to foster care. In many states, reunification services were mandated to last no more than six months (Barth 1986) and, on average, ended after only three months (Barth and Berry 1990).

Adoption Outcomes. As a component of permanency planning, the increased use of adoption became a key contributor to reductions in the number of children in long-term foster care (Fein, Maluccio, Hamilton, and Ward 1983). The Adoption Assistance and Child Welfare Act of 1980 increased federal and state support of adoption, stated that no child is unadoptable, changed policies that had ruled out foster parents as adoptive parents, and provided for adoption subsidies. Without federal-level data on the number of children who were adopted, it is difficult to know exactly how successfully this was implemented. Based largely on state data on the number of adoptions and federal data on the provision of adoption subsidies, it appears that special-needs adoptions have increased substantially since the passage of PL 96–272. For example, in California, relinquishment adoptions increased 34 percent between 1981 and 1987 (Barth and Berry 1988). Federal adoption subsidies increased from $442,000 in 1981 to $132 million in 1990 (U.S. Senate Committee on Finance 1990). Despite an increase in the number of special-needs adoptions, there does not appear to be an accompanying rise in the adoption disruption (or breakdown) rate (Barth and Berry 1988).

In addition to placement outcomes, the satisfaction of children and families is another indicator of whether permanency planning has been successful. Many intensive family preservation programs report high levels of family satisfaction with services, particularly relating to the ability to keep families together and parents' self-reports of improvement in managing child behavior and life circumstances (Fraser, Pecora, and Haapala 1990). In the Oregon permanency planning demonstration project (Lahti et al. 1978), all but one of the children who returned home preferred their biological homes to their foster homes. Children who do not return home rate the permanency and security of adoptive homes highly also (Barth and Berry 1990; Lahti et al. 1978).

Issues in Implementing PL 96–272

Many practitioners and analysts complained that "reasonable efforts" was never adequately defined in PL 96–272 (Ratterman, Dodson, and Hardin 1987; Seaberg 1986). The job of defining this point of the law was left to individual states, and the phrase was interpreted in varying ways. According to Seaberg (1986), documentation of reasonable efforts should consist of three primary elements: (1) verification of the accuracy of case assessment—that is, that the problems specified are actually the reasons the child is in foster care or at risk of entering foster care; (2) a procedure for establishing the relevance of specific services to the problems identified in the case; and (3) a fully documented sustained level of activity in facilitating use of those services by the appropriate parties in the case.

Various groups investigated the use and interpretation of reasonable efforts by judges and social workers (Hunner 1986a, 1986b; Ratterman 1986; Ratterman, Dodson, and Hardin 1987). Debra Ratterman (1986) and her colleagues at the American Bar Association (Ratterman, Dodson, and Hardin 1987) reported that judicial review of reasonable efforts was more firmly established regarding re-unification efforts than regarding preplacement prevention efforts. However, social workers they interviewed emphasized that complete and accurate documentation of efforts made to prevent placement and parents' responses to those efforts comprised important evidence at hearings on termination of parental rights (Ratterman 1986).

Hunner (1986a) offered two reasons that reasonable efforts were not provided at optimal rates: fear of liability and making the wrong decision, she said, led social workers to remove the child to reduce the risk of harm; and family maintenance services had not been adequately proven to make a difference. In situations of suspected child abuse, where tension is high and the risks to the child may be substantial, the question of whether to use maintenance resources that have proven effective in some cases or to remove the child is often decided in favor of the latter as offering the most protection to the child.

In addition, the extent of the provision of reasonable efforts was partially determined by the availability of services (Hunner 1986a; Seaberg 1986). The availability of home-based, family-centered services throughout the community that are aimed at the preservation of families and the prevention of placement is crucial to the expenditure of reasonable efforts to prevent placement.

Where appropriate services are not available, the provision of reasonable efforts is thwarted. For example, Kamerman and Kahn (1990), in their investigation of how various states adapted to the evolution of child welfare problems and legislation, found that in one two-month period in Los Angeles in 1988, more than 3,000 mothers were referred to court-mandated drug treatment as part of their reasonable efforts to be reunited with their children in foster care, but there were only 1,750 treatment slots in such programs in the entire city during the same period.

A decision by the Supreme Court in 1992 (Kopels and Rycraft 1993) determined in the case of *Suter v. Artist M 1992* that "because Congress had provided no other statutory guidance regarding how reasonable efforts were to be measured, the requirement was intended only as a directive whose meaning would vary with the individual case" (402), and individuals could not bring a lawsuit to ensure the provision of reasonable efforts. This ruling will, of course, have a direct impact on states' service delivery since this legal course of action to ensure work to preserve families has been eliminated (and there are many related class-action suits now pending). The impact of this decision on the availability of family preservation services has yet to be determined, but its impact on the balance between parental rights and the protection of children has clearly shifted to child removal (Kopels and Rycraft 1993).

While hard data on the impact of permanency planning on placement outcomes are uneven, shifts in the focus of practice from child rescue to family support, with a commitment to family ties and continuity for children, are evident throughout the practice and research literature. These shifts are demonstrated in a variety of other outcomes: increased emphasis on visiting and contacts between parents and children while children are in out-of-home care; increased use of foster adoption, in which foster parents adopt their foster child (preventing another separation for the child); and a growth in the practice of open adoption, wherein the biological and adoptive parents of a child remain in contact as the child grows up.

Hard data on the extent of the implementation of case planning requirements are even less readily available than on placement outcomes. Hardin's (1990) review of implementation of PL 96–272 by the courts finds that, while court implementation has been variable, improvements are "powerful and positive" (52): these include the reduction of state involvement in nonserious cases and more serious placement prevention efforts by agencies because they know that courts would review the extent of their reasonable efforts to prevent placement. Hardin also reports that because of the increased number of court reviews, which are tied to federal funding incentives, "continuing foster placement is no longer the path of least resistance that it was prior to PL 96–272. That is, judicial review has made it harder for workers to leave a child in care and thereby encourages them to achieve another permanent placement" (53). Hardin notes too that joint struggles by agencies and courts to implement PL 96–272 have resulted in more coordinated decision making and planning for children.

Successes and Failures of PL 96–272; Resulting Further Legislation

Permanency planning succeeded in that it brought about greater efforts to preserve family ties and permanence for children and families, and these were effective. Growth in programs and practice models to maintain family integrity, and increased efforts to find "forever families" (Barth and Berry 1988) through adoption for children previously considered unadoptable, are two primary and tangible indicators of its success.

Intensive family preservation programs have proliferated over the past decade. These programs have the common goal of doing whatever it takes to reduce risk of maltreatment and improve family functioning so that children at risk can remain safely at home. The increase in the number of family maintenance and preservation programs is thus another indicator of the success of a shift from child rescue to family support.

Where permanency planning was not successful or was not fully realized, two significant trends during the 1980s were influential. First, the requirements of permanency planning were implemented in varying degrees from state to state (Kamerman and Kahn 1990) because the federal law put the responsibility for interpretation and implementation on the states, and the support of key policy makers and advocates varied from state to state (Samantrai 1992).

Figure 3 illustrates the dramatic differences in child welfare indicators in four large states between 1980 and 1992. Legal definitions of child abuse and neglect are determined by state law; and community norms, state cultures, and state legislatures vary in how they balance child protection and family autonomy. For example, California and New York have higher rates of child abuse and neglect reports and higher proportions of children in foster care than Texas does, even though Texas has a somewhat higher rate of child poverty (23.3 percent versus 21.4 percent), higher low-birthweight rates (6.9 percent versus 6.0 percent), and higher unemployment rates (21.8 percent versus 15.7 percent) (1990 figures; Children's Defense Fund 1990), all common correlates of child maltreatment. California's definitions of what constitutes abuse and neglect and what warrants state intervention are much more inclusive than those of Texas, which means that (1) abuse and neglect

Figure 3
Abuse Reports by State, 1980–1992

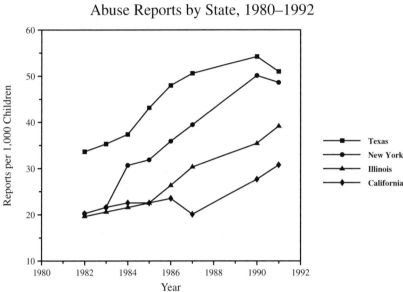

SOURCE: American Humane Association (1993).

misleadingly *appear* to be less common in Texas than in California; and (2) California child welfare agencies serve a much higher proportion of their child population than Texas agencies.

Narrowing definitions of abuse and reducing preventive services are two ways in which many states responded to the rise in child abuse reports (Kalichman and Brosig 1992; Kamerman and Kahn 1990; Pecora, Whittaker, and Maluccio 1994). These developments had devastating effects on the ability of state child welfare agencies to provide adequate services within a family-focused framework.

Second, demographic, social, and economic trends since 1980 have intensified the need for state child welfare agencies to perform the mandates of permanency planning legislation, but without concomitant increases in societal support and funding. The drug epidemic of the 1980s, increases in child poverty, and reductions in family support programs have created a social environment of increased hostility to family integrity. Growing caseloads of stressed families and troubled children are thus straining agencies' abilities to provide permanence-oriented services.

THE FAMILY PRESERVATION ACT OF 1993

By the end of the 1980s, many practitioners and scholars had taken stock of the outcomes of PL 96–272 (Barth and Berry 1990; Kamerman and Kahn 1990) and were making recommendations for new legislation to build on its strengths and clarify its vagaries. These recommendations coalesced around an emphasis on communities and supports for families rooted in the community.

In 1991, the U.S. Advisory Board on Child Abuse and Neglect issued a report entitled *Creating Caring Communities: Blueprint for Effective Federal Policy on Child Abuse and Neglect.* In this report the board made many recommendations, all based on a framework of preventive services in the community and intensive services best provided in the home to the entire family. One of the two recommendations it identified as crucial was a national voluntary neonatal home-visitation program. The other was the establishment of a national policy on child protection. This report echoed the sentiment of many analysts that child welfare agencies are in crisis and unable to adequately serve all children and families in need without federal-level support and the addition of preventive and universal supportive community services for all American families.

Beginning in 1990, legislation was introduced in Congress to strengthen the Title IV-B components of services to children. The Family Preservation Act of 1990, the Family Preservation Act of 1991, and the Family Preservation Act of 1992 were all defeated, the last passing both chambers of Congress but being vetoed by President George Bush on November 4, 1992. Bush had campaigned for the presidency on a platform plank of "family values," which were also espoused by Wade Horn, his commissioner of the Administration for Children, Youth and Families in the Department of Health and Human Services. Horn stated that "the Government can and should play a crucial role in the reform of child welfare services, by enabling families to function effectively without the need for direct and ongoing intervention of the Government. . . . The Government's job is to structure policies and programs in a way that strengthens America's families, building upon [the] concept of the 'culture of character'" (U.S. House of Representatives 1992, 124, 127).

At the same time, the National Commission on Children was at work on the problem. This body had been formed in 1987 under PL 100–203. It was chaired by John D. Rockefeller IV and included among its members Marian Wright Edelman of the Children's Defense Fund; Bill Clinton, who was governor of Arkansas when the commission was formed; and T. Berry Brazelton of Harvard University. The commission produced a report, *Beyond Rhetoric: A New American Agenda for Children and Families* (1991), which documented that families had lost ground during the 1980s: child poverty rates had increased, neighborhood violence was on the upswing, foster care rates were getting higher, and so on. One of the recommendations of the commission (although some members dissented) was to change Title IV-B to an entitlement, with equal availability of funding for family preservation services and foster care.

On August 10, 1993, President Clinton signed the Omnibus Budget Reconciliation Act of 1993, which contained the Family Preservation and Family Support Act of 1993 (PL 103–66), incorporating many of the provisions of the three earlier family preservation acts and influenced by the recommendations of the National Commission on Children and the U.S. Advisory Board on Child Abuse and Neglect. This legislation is said to be the most sweeping reform of the child welfare system since the Adoption Assistance and Child Welfare Act of 1980 (Sullivan 1993). It creates a new Subpart 2 of Title IV-B for family preservation and support services. Under this legislation, family preservation services include

services designed: (1) to help children, where appropriate, return to their families or to be placed for adoption, with a legal guardian, or in some other permanent living situation; (2) to provide preplacement preventive services; (3) to provide follow-up care to families to whom a child has been returned after foster care; (4) to provide temporary relief through respite care of children for parents or other caretakers (including foster parents); and (5) to improve parenting skills with respect to child development, family budgeting, coping with stress, health and nutrition. (Sullivan 1993, 27)

Family support services are "community-based service designed to promote the well-being of children and families by increasing the strength and stability of families (including foster families and extended families), parents' confidence and competence in their parenting abilities, and a stable and supportive family environment for children and by otherwise enhancing child development" (Sullivan 1993, 28). Included in this act are grants for state reviews to assess the effectiveness of courts in implementing the requirements of Titles IV-B and IV-E, determining the appropriateness of foster placement, termination of parental rights, and other court decisions.

In the introduction to the Family Preservation and Support Act of 1993, Olivia Golden of the Commission of the Administration on Children, Youth and Families remarked, "Because the multiple needs of these vulnerable children and families cannot be addressed adequately through categorical programs and fragmented service delivery systems, we encourage states to use the new program as a catalyst for establishing a continuum of coordinated and integrated, culturally relevant, family-focused services for children and families" (quoted in Allen, Kakavas, and Zalenski 1994, 1). It is clear in this legislation that family preservation services are still intended for families at risk of child placement, but the addition of family support services directed toward all families should strengthen a continuum of preventive and crisis-level community-based services.

This sweeping legislation is not without its critics, however. In contrast to its push for supporting families from the community level, some policy makers, concerned about the number of children entering foster care, are calling for a return to orphanages (Kroll 1994). Governor Jim Edgar of Illinois called for the opening of orphanages in February, 1994. An Illinois state senator Judy Baer Topinka has called orphanages "an idea whose time has come. . . . The issue is not whether there will be orphanages in Illinois. The question is how and in what manner" (quoted in Hunter 1994, 4). The Menninger Foundation offered to establish several new group-care facilities for foster children in Minnesota. Five such homes opened there in 1993 at a daily cost per child of $114.81 compared to $16.24 for an identical child in family foster care (Kroll 1994).

The Family Preservation and Support Act of 1993, enacted after several years of debate and compromise, follows years of family preservation demonstration programs and calls for child welfare reform and a return to supporting the family. The legislation's funding of family support and community-based programs harks back to the settlement houses' strengthening of the culture of neighborhood and tradition. But its path will not be smooth: effective implementation must rely on community shaping of the program, accurate information on the critical elements and format of effective family preservation practice, and sensitive and ongoing evaluation of whether family preservation programs are achieving gains with families and their children.

REFERENCES

Allen, Marcia, Amy Kakavas, and John Zalenski. (1994, Spring). Family preservation and support services: Omnibus Budget Reconciliation Act of 1993. *The Prevention Report:* 1–3.

American Humane Association. (1993). *Highlights of official child abuse and neglect reporting.* Denver, CO: American Humane Association.

Barth, Richard P. (1986). Time limits in permanency planning: The child welfare worker's perspective. *Children and Youth Services Review* 8: 133–44.

Barth, Richard P., and Marianne Berry. (1987). Outcomes of child welfare services under permanency planning. *Social Service Review* 60: 71–90.

Barth, Richard P., and Marianne Berry. (1988). *Adoption and disruption: Rates, risks and responses.* Hawthorne, NY: Aldine de Gruyter.

Barth, Richard P., and Marianne Berry. (1990). A decade later: Outcomes of permanency planning. In Joe Kroll (ed.), *The Adoption Assistance and Child Welfare Act of 1980: The first ten years.* pp 7–39. St. Paul, MN: North American Council on Adoptable Children.

Bussiere, Alice. (1990). Implementation of PL 96–272: Adoption assistance. In Joe Kroll (ed.), *The Adoption Assistance and Child Welfare Act of 1980: The first ten years,* 75–86. St. Paul, MN: North American Council on Adoptable Children.

Children's Defense Fund. (1990). *S.O.S. America: A children's defense budget.* Washington, DC: Children's Defense Fund.

Cohn, Anne H., and Deborah Daro. (1987). Is treatment too late?: What ten years of evaluative research tell us. *Child Abuse and Neglect* 11: 433–42.

Emlen, Arthur, Janet Lahti, Glen Downs, Alec McKay, and Susan Downs. (1978). *Overcoming barriers to planning for children in foster care.* Portland, OR: Regional Research Institute for Human Services, Portland State University.

English, Jeanine L., and Michael R. Tritz. (1992). In support of the family: Family preservation as an alternative to foster care. *Stanford Law and Policy Review* 4: 183–91.

Fanshel, David, and Eugene B. Shinn. (1978). *Children in foster care: A longitudinal investigation.* New York: Columbia University Press.

Fein, Edith, Anthony N. Maluccio, V. Jane Hamilton, and Derryl Ward. (1983). After foster care: Outcomes of permanency planning. *Child Welfare* 62: 485–560.

Feldman, Leonard. (1990). Target population definition. In Ying-Ying Yuan and Michele Rivest (eds.), *Preserving families: Evaluation resources for practitioners and policy makers,* 47–71. Newbury Park, CA: Sage.

Fraser, Mark W., Peter J. Pecora, and David A. Haapala. (1990). *Families in crisis: The impact of intensive family preservation services.* Hawthorne, NY: Aldine de Gruyter.

Hardin, Mark. (1990). Ten years later: Implementation of Public Law 96–272 by the courts. In Joe Kroll (ed.), *The Adoption Assistance and Child Welfare Act of 1980: The first ten years,* 51–74. St. Paul, MN: North American Council on Adoptable Children.

Hunner, Robert J. (1986a). *Active and reasonable efforts to preserve families: A guide for delivering services in compliance with the Indian Child Welfare Act of 1978 and the Adoption Assistance and Child Welfare Act of 1980.* Seattle: Northwest Resource Associates.

Hunner, Robert J. (1986b). Defining active and reasonable efforts to preserve families. *Children Today* 15 (6): 27–30.

Hunter, Kimberly. (1994, Spring). The misguided call for orphanages. *Adoptalk:* 4–5.

Jimenez, Mary Ann. (1990, September). Permanency planning and the Child Abuse Prevention and Treatment Act: The paradox of child welfare policy. *Journal of Sociology and Social Welfare* 17: 55–72.

Jones, Mary Ann. (1983). *A second chance for families—five years later: Follow-up of a program to prevent foster care.* New York: Child Welfare League of America.

Kadushin, Alfred, and Judith Martin. (1988). *Child welfare services.* 4th ed. New York: Macmillan.

Kalichman, Seth C., and Cheryl L. Brosig. (1992). The effects of statutory requirements on child maltreatment reporting: A comparison of two state laws. *American Journal of Orthopsychiatry* 62: 284–96.

Kamerman, Sheila B., and Alfred J. Kahn. (1990). Social services for children, youth, and families in the United States. *Children and Youth Services Review* 12 (special issue).

Kinney, Jill M., Barbara Madsen, Thomas Fleming, and David A. Haapala. (1977). Homebuilders: Keeping families together. *Journal of Consulting and Clinical Psychology* 45: 667–73.

Kopels, Sandra, and Joan R. Rycraft. (1993). The U.S. Supreme Court rules on reasonable efforts: A blow to child advocacy. *Child Welfare* 72: 397–406.

Kroll, Joe. (1994, Spring). Invest in families. *Adoptalk:* 1–2.

Lahti, Janet, Karen Green, Arthur Emlen, Jerry Zadny, Quentin D. Clarkson, Marie Kuehnel, and Jim Casciato. (1978). *A follow-up study of the Oregon Project.* Portland: Regional Research Institute for Human Services, Portland State University.

Lewit, Eugene M. (1993). Children in foster care. *The Future of Children* 3: 192–200.

Lindsey, Duncan. (1994). *The welfare of children.* New York: Oxford University Press.

Maas, Henry, and Richard Engler. (1959). *Children in need of parents.* New York: Columbia University Press.

Maluccio, Anthony N., Edith Fein, and K. A. Olmstead. (1986). *Permanency planning for children: Concepts and methods.* London: Routledge, Chapman, and Hall.

Maluccio, Anthony N., and James K. Whittaker. (1988). Helping the biological families of children in out-of-home placement. In W. W. Nunnaly, C. S. Chilman, and F. M. Cox (eds.), *Troubled relationships: Families in trouble,* vol. 3, 205–17. Newbury Park, CA: Sage.

National Commission on Children. (1991). *Beyond rhetoric: A new American agenda for children and families.* Washington, DC: National Commission on Children.

Nelson, Douglas. (1990). Recognizing and realizing the potential of "family preservation." In James K. Whittaker, Jill Kinney, Elizabeth M. Tracy, and Charlotte Booth (eds.), *Reaching high-risk families: Intensive family preservation in human services,* 13–30. Hawthorne, NY: Aldine de Gruyter.

Pecora, Peter J., James K. Whittaker, and Anthony Maluccio. (1992). *The child welfare challenge.* Hawthorne, NY: Aldine de Gruyter.

Pelton, Leroy. (1994). Has permanency planning been successful? No. In Eileen Gambrill and Theodore Stein (eds.), *Controversial issues in child welfare,* 268–74. Newbury Park, CA: Sage.

Ratterman, Debra. (1986). Judicial determination of reasonable efforts. *Children Today* 15 (6): 26, 30–32.

Ratterman, Debra, G. Diane Dodson, and Mark A. Hardin. (1987). *Reasonable efforts to prevent foster placement: A guide to implementation.* Washington, DC: American Bar Association.

Remy, Linda, and Stuart Hanson. (1983). *Evaluation of the emergency family care program: Final report.* San Francisco: Children's Home Society of California.

Runyan, Desmond K., and Carolyn L. Gould. (1985). Foster care for child maltreatment: Impact on delinquent behavior. *Pediatrics* 75: 562–68.

Samantrai, Krishna. (1992). To prevent unnecessary separation of children and families: Public Law 96–272—Policy and practice. *Social Work* 37 (4): 295–302.

Seaburg, James R. (1986). "Reasonable efforts:" Toward implementation in permanency planning. *Child Welfare* 65: 469–79.

Stein, Theodore J., and Eileen D. Gambrill. (1985). Permanency planning for children: The past and present. *Children and Youth Services Review* 7: 83–94.

Stein, Theodore, Eileen Gambrill, and Kermit Wiltse. (1978). *Children in foster homes: Achieving continuity of care.* New York: Praeger.

Sullivan, H. Patrick. (1993). *Provisions for child welfare, family preservation, and family support in the Omnibus Reconciliation Act of 1993.* Austin: Texas Department of Protective and Regulatory Services.

Tatara, Toshio. (1994). *Voluntary Cooperative Information System.* Washington, DC: APWA.

U.S. Advisory Board on Child Abuse and Neglect. (1991). *Creating caring communities: Blueprint for effective federal policy on child abuse and neglect.* Washington, DC: U.S. Advisory Board on Child Abuse and Neglect, Department of Health and Human Services.

U.S. Congress. (1980). *125th Congressional Record,* 14767, June 13, 1980.

U.S. House of Representatives. (1992). *Hearing before the Subcommittee on Human Resources of the Committee on Ways and Means on the Family Preservation Act of 1991.* 102d Congress, 1st Session, June 11–12, Serial 102–42, 123–27. Washington, DC.: U.S. Congress.

U.S. Senate. (1980). *Adoption Assistance and Child Welfare Act of 1980.* Washington, DC: Senate Report number 96–336, 1.

U.S. Senate Committee on Finance. (1990). *Foster care, adoption assistance, and child welfare services.* Washington, DC: Government Printing Office.

Whittaker, James K. (1981). Family involvement in residential child care: A support system for biological parents. In Anthony N. Maluccio and Paula A. Sinanoglu (eds.), *The challenge of partnership: Working with parents in foster care,* 67–88. New York: Child Welfare League of America.

Part II

FAMILY PRESERVATION PRACTICE METHODS

Chapter 3

THE EMPIRICAL BASE FOR FAMILY PRESERVATION PRINCIPLES

The child welfare system, which is responsible for the protection of children, works to support and maintain families while optimizing children's development. Services are intended to support and not replace family life unless absolutely necessary. This intent is reflected in the dual goals of family preservation services: keeping the family together while keeping the child(ren) safe. A child is removed from the home and placed in substitute care only if he or she is deemed to be abused or neglected and if services are not able to ensure safety in the home.

Recent child welfare policy has attempted to remove the value-laden motives that have plagued services to children and families, and it strives to maintain the child in the biological home. The philosophy of family preservation programs embodies the settlement-house approach in a new era, calling on families to use their communities and extended families for support and exhorting social workers to advocate for families and operate from a strengths perspective rather than from a problem-diagnosis approach. Along these lines, child welfare services are becoming more client- and family-centered, with clients determining the objectives of service, in keeping with the overall goals of the prevention of child abuse and child removal, and social workers applying their scientific and practical knowledge toward helping clients and families achieve those goals. This is a basic tenet of home-based and family-centered services.

This chapter will examine the principles underlying family preservation services and describe how those principles frame treatment. Principles common to most programs include a values system based in client empowerment and a home-based and family-centered focus. These principles are based on the ecological paradigm of service to promote the well-being of children and families (described below). In the perspective of this paradigm, this chapter will discuss the basic treatment goals of the family preservation philosophy, such as prevention of placement, increasing parenting skills, improving parent-child relationships, enhancing the social support network, and improving developmental outcomes for children. It will also establish the empirical basis for program components.

WHY PRESERVE FAMILIES?

Why save the family rather than the child? For several reasons that we have learned over the past century:

Keeping families together is more humane. Children and families are traumatized by the separation of foster placement and the subsequent uncertainty of whether or not the child can return home. Placement increases parental "ambivalence" toward family integrity, which in turn decreases the likelihood of successful return home (Hess and Folaron 1991). Placement also increases difficulties for children in forming relationships (Werner and Smith 1992). Charles Gershenson, chief of research funded by the Children's Bureau, U.S. Department of Health and Human Services, has commented that "research over the past 40 years says that if you remove the child from the home, you traumatize the child more than he is already hurt. You inflict a subsequent injury, especially on a young child who can't understand why he's been removed from his family. They feel they did something bad, and that it is their fault, or they view it as a kidnapping" (quoted in Kagan 1991, 16).

A recent and ongoing longitudinal study of children born into a variety of risk factors (Werner and Smith 1992) has found so far that disruption of the home, including foster child placement, is highly correlated with subsequent disruptions in adult life including divorce, unemployment, and other difficulties. Additionally, national research on young adults reveals that disproportionate numbers of homeless teens and young adults in prison were former foster children (Callahan 1992). More than a third of runaway and homeless youths in a recent national study had been in foster care in the year before they ran away (Bass 1993).

Services aimed at the family should be more efficient. By spending money on services for a family, the agency incurs one cost that is intended to have an impact on the whole family. If services are focused on one child at a time, costs escalate with increased family size.

Foster care is especially expensive. Costs for individual children in foster care include foster care payments to care providers and therapy and medical costs. Many foster care service dollars are spent on individual therapy for children to help them deal with the traumas of separation as well as acting-out

50

behavior, poor self-esteem, learning and developmental difficulties, and other such problems. These dollars spent on individual therapy multiply if more than one child is removed from a family.

Services aimed at the family should be more effective. A focus on a family solution is more effective because many problems subsist not in one family member but in the interactions among family members. Family relations, which are at the core of child welfare interventions, cannot be effectively improved by only one person's actions.

Ann Hartman (1990), former dean of the Smith College School of Social Work and a past editor of *Social Work,* has said she now considers it unethical practice for social workers to treat an individual without involving some other member or members of his or her self-defined family system. If social work practice aims to improve the transactions between the person and the environment, practice must focus on both the person *and* the environment, including the family, the community, and the larger social environment.

Family preservation is consonant with "family values." In interviews with family preservation workers in Illinois, Littell and colleagues at the University of Chicago (Littell, Howard, Rzepnicki, Budde, and Pellowe 1992) identified an important message that family preservation workers impart to children, families, and society as stated by a family preservation worker:

> Children learn behaviors by what's going on around them. A family is in place to serve as a support. They are the child's first introduction to support. If a family isn't functioning or a worker tries to separate them before working to keep them together, it's going to make kids feel unsafe and insecure. Children can learn to work through difficulties and not just split. That's what's important about trying to keep families together in the midst of difficulties. Teaching children about what's supportive, that you don't just give up. (6)

Family preservation thus fits very well into larger American objectives such as making divorces harder to get and promoting greater involvement of fathers in the economic, physical, and emotional care of children. Both of these objectives are aimed at maintaining the sanctity of the family and the well-being of its members.

Intensive family preservation services strive to preserve the family because the family is considered the optimal environment for children's growth and development. Services that involve the whole family should be more effective and longer lasting, and services that can keep families safely together should be cost-efficient in the long run. To provide the services that will most effectively and efficiently help families, program goals and services must arise from a clear understanding of the problems and strengths families bring to the program and the services that most effectively address their problems.

AN ECOLOGICAL PERSPECTIVE ON FAMILY AND CHILD WELL-BEING

The ecological paradigm is often used in social work practice to examine the interplay between an individual and his or her environment (Garbarino 1977, 1981; Polansky and Gaudin 1983). The ecological paradigm recognizes that behavior is a function of the person and the environment (Lewin 1951), and it is thus a natural theoretical basis for an examination of social intervention in individual and family behavior. Application of this paradigm to family preservation services is a logical progression.

The ecological paradigm forces interventionists to go beyond theories that consider the family as the whole environment in which children are socialized (Miller 1983) and to realize that the family itself also exists in the larger societal environment. This element is often ignored in theories of individual adjustment. There are layers of interaction within ever-widening circles of the environment, much like the layers of an onion, and effective social intervention will assess the contribution of each layer to a situation and attempt to bolster or influence each layer. An ecological framework "stresses that the focus of intervention is the family unit in the context of its environment. Professional intervention is addressed not to the child or parents as separate entities, but to the total family constellation as an open dynamic system, and to the ongoing transactions with the impinging environment" (Maluccio 1981, 23). Such a framework clarifies the role of the environment and the formal and informal supports it offers in preventing child abuse and child placement. Family preservation services recognize and use the societal resources and networks in the environment that can help stabilize and maximize family functioning.

Families under Stress

Families in which children are abused or neglected are families under stress. Stress is defined as "a relationship between the person and environment that is appraised by the person as relevant to his or her well-being and in which the person's resources are taxed or exceeded" (Folkman and Lazarus 1985, 152).

Responding well to any stressor in the environment—an unruly child, for example—requires resources. These resources could include, in this example, a spouse or grandparent who can take the child to the park, a book or magazine article containing helpful hints for dealing with unruly children, a history of personal experience in dealing with children, money to give the child for a ticket to the movies, a wealth of patience, and so on. As a person deals with a stressor in any variety of ways, these resources may be depleted. Also, ineffective or maladaptive coping (often seen in abusive and neglectful families) can increase stress rather than decrease it. For example, maladaptive coping strategies might include using drugs, leaving the child unsupervised, or physically abusing the child.

All individuals and families experience stress and respond by coping to some degree. What distinguishes families functioning effectively from families that are overwhelmed is the extent to which they experience stressors and cope with them effectively (McCubbin and Patterson 1983). The more stressors in the environment (such as an impoverished or dangerous neighborhood, violence in the home, and financial difficulties), the more quickly resources are used up and the more resources are required for daily living (Lazarus and Folkman 1984).

An ecological analysis of stress and coping highlights the environmental and societal stressors that contribute to or exacerbate the stress of parenting and growing up. "While no one maintains that the maltreatment of children is limited to poor people, the 'myth of classlessness' (Pelton 1981) regarding child abuse has allowed ignorance of the severity of the consequences of poverty for children. . . . Higher levels of deprivation and frustration combine with fewer resources available to deal with those stressors and the result is maltreatment" (Young and Gately 1988, 241).

The ecological approach to dealing with child abuse and neglect thus looks beyond personal and "intrapsychic" determinants of abuse and recognizes the effect the environment, both within the family and within the larger political, economic, and social spheres, has on behavior. "It directs our attention to personally impoverished families clustered in socially impoverished places: high-risk families and high-risk neighborhoods" (Garbarino 1981, 237).

Thus the social and physical community is potentially a source of both stress and support, but it is consistently lacking in supports in urban America. "Cross-cultural evidence reinforces the conclusion [that parents must be supported in caring for children] in that the occurrence of child maltreatment in other cultures is related to the availability of multiple caregivers and the extent to which there is an acceptance of collective responsibility for children's welfare" (Young and Gately 1988, 242).

The most unequivocal empirical evidence of the relationship between environmental conditions and family stress is found in Fred Wulczyn's 1991 report, "The Community Dimension of Permanency Planning." Wulczyn examined a variety of indicators of family well-being for New York City on a household-by-household basis and, using census tract mapping, found that high percentages of families experiencing poverty, teen pregnancies, infant mortality, and child removals clustered in the same neighborhoods and communities around the city. What is especially striking is his finding that, in some communities, more than 12 percent of all infants were placed in foster care before their first birthday.

Wulczyn captures in this report the ecological view of communities as sources of stress or support: "Just as parents are important to a child's sense of self-esteem, communities are an important source of esteem for families. If parents need supportive services to develop or sustain the capacity to nurture children, then service availability within local communities yields multiple benefits. Children are raised in their natural families, and parents learn that their communities are supportive environments" (2).

Resources as Mediators of Stress

Resources can be many things. Obvious family resources are money and material goods such as housing and food. These help families respond to routine demands or stressors. If they are not adequately resolved or managed, stressors can accumulate over time to produce great family stress, which is often a precursor of abuse. An individual who is sufficiently fed, housed, and provided for is generally not overwhelmed by other problems such as a child with a minor illness. A parent who has a phone and enough money can call a clinic or a grandparent. However, without these resources, the situation can quickly become a panic-laden crisis.

Resources are not only monetary or material. Equally important are nontangible resources, including those external to the person (such as love and affection, information and education, and social support) and internal resources (for example, self-esteem, patience, motivation, and ability). Resources tend to multiply, just as stressors tend to multiply. For example, an adequate income can strengthen self-esteem, and information and education usually add to one's ability to cope. Similarly, proficiency at childrearing, for example, bolsters a parent's patience and motivation while helping to diffuse stressful parent-child interactions. On the other hand, the stress and rejection of unemployment may be accompanied by the stressors of disconnected utilities, loss of self-esteem, the difficulties of job-hunting and uncertainty of finding another job, and having less money for food, housing, and other essentials. This dynamic interplay of resources and stressors characterizes everyday life for individuals and families. Stressors are demands, and individuals need resources to manage them. Resources used must be replenished (through financial, social, or emotional support systems) for individuals to avoid being overtaxed and moving into a crisis state.

Like individuals, families respond to stressors, and the better their arsenal of resources, the better their ability to cope. In addition to the resources of individual members, families can also use the resources of family integrity and cohesiveness and adaptability (McCubbin and Patterson 1983; Olson, McCubbin, Barnes, Larsen, Muxen, and Wilson 1983). Individuals in families with these characteristics know that family members will support each other, that the family will not disintegrate under stress, and that the actions of one member will not be condemned by the rest. This knowledge is an important resource when individuals in a family have their own interests and demands because it helps to keep the family from becoming overwhelmed by these. Families without integrity, cohesiveness, and adaptability are easily undone by a difficult child or an alcoholic parent, for example.

The process of preserving families is illustrated in figure 4. Family preservation programs are viewed as a mediating influence between family stress and family breakdown (as evidenced by child placement). Ecological family preservation programs assess family stressors and resources and help to bolster and increase the family's resources to such a point that stressors associated with risk of placement can be ameliorated.

Figure 4 is an adaptation of Hill's 1958 ABCX Model of Family Crisis with an additional intervention component. Hill asserts that stressors (the A component in his model) and crisis-meeting resources (the B component) are typically in balance in day-to-day family life but that an imbalance between A and B leads to crisis (the C component), which then leads directly to the family's resolution of the crisis or its level of adaptation to it (X). Our model of family stress and coping incorporates the intervention strategies used in family preservation programs between the crisis component and the resulting adaptation to that crisis, or the outcome, to include the family preservation response to crisis as a mediator of adaptation.

Stress and coping theorists (Lazarus and Folkman 1984) and family stress theorists (Imig and Imig 1986; Olson et al. 1983) postulate that the experience of stress in the individual or in the family is a reflection of the transaction between the person and the environment (including other family members) when the stressor outweighs the resources the person has to deal with it. Every inter-

55

Figure 4

An Ecological Model of Family Preservation

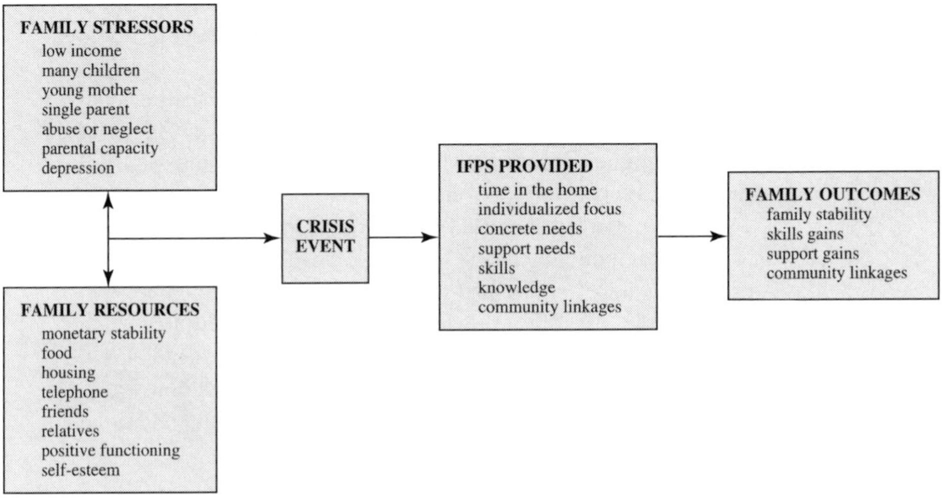

FAMILY STRESSORS
low income
many children
young mother
single parent
abuse or neglect
parental capacity
depression

FAMILY RESOURCES
monetary stability
food
housing
telephone
friends
relatives
positive functioning
self-esteem

CRISIS EVENT

IFPS PROVIDED
time in the home
individualized focus
concrete needs
support needs
skills
knowledge
community linkages

FAMILY OUTCOMES
family stability
skills gains
support gains
community linkages

Adapted from Hill (1958).

action in the family is potentially stressful or challenging and can either increase or deplete resources. For example, depending on the entire transaction, a child's compliance with a parent's demand could increase the parent's self-esteem or feelings of efficacy, increase the child's self-esteem or pride, and/or help to create a history of shared cooperation and positive regard. It could also increase the child's sense of helplessness or anger and/or increase the parent's feelings of power. Thus every interaction has the potential for a positive or negative outcome. Internal and external resources increase the possibility of a positive outcome and contribute to a belief on the part of family members that they can handle such situations (and thus decrease stress).Because every interaction calls upon a person to use his or her resources to meet the stressor, an interaction can thus deplete a resource or help to replenish a resource and even create new resources. For example, social isolation, a key correlate of child abuse and neglect, can prevent the creation or replenishment of key resources for effective and adaptive parenting. Social interaction with friends, neighbors, and relatives can help to create or replenish a variety of resources necessary to parenting and family life. Talking and being with others gives a parent an opportunity to vent frustrations, discuss and learn more about norms of child development (such as the wide range of ages during which children may be toilet trained), laugh and talk about issues other than parenting, have fun with other adults, mobilize resources such as baby-sitting or help with car repairs, and so on.

Daily life in the family system, therefore, is a constant management of transactional stressors and challenges, and the responses to these may vary according to a family's resources, which in turn may fluctuate. In most families, the stressors and resources stay enough in balance to avert crisis or resolve it quickly. However, when resources are not frequently replenished, families can be in "perpetual crisis" (Kagan and Schlosberg 1989), and child abuse or other maladaptive outcomes are likely.

This theory of family stress and crisis helps workers and families identify both the targets of an intervention (the reduction of specific stressors and the enhancement of specific internal and external resources) and the desired outcomes, or goals, of intervention (clear examples of more positive interactions and transactions within the family and its community rather than simply the prevention of placement). For example, if the crisis of child abuse is seen to rise out of an imbalance between the stressors of caring for a medically fragile child and the family's skills and resources to meet the child's needs, then intervention will necessarily focus on bolstering the skills and resources required to meet the medical needs of the child while enhancing the parents' feelings of efficacy as parents and decision makers.

Such a perspective also helps family preservation workers understand the delicate interplay and necessary balance between family stressors and strengths. Employing a strengths perspective within such a theoretical model, therefore, does not mean simply identifying the strengths of a family; the worker must identify those strengths and resources that are influential in the family's response to its situational, environmental, and relational stressors. Such a specific assessment of risks and resources, or stressors and strengths, naturally leads to a clear delineation of the strategies that will comprise the intervention and to a clear explication of goals and expected outcomes.

CORRELATES OF CHILD ABUSE AND NEGLECT

Families with abused or neglected children are often referred to as multiproblem families or families out of control (Garbarino 1977). Instead of viewing abuse and neglect as conditions associated with the psychopathology of parents (Spinetta and Rigler 1972), professionals must understand these phenomena as part of a more general phenomenon of maltreatment of children (Garbarino 1977; Gil 1973) that should be addressed as a product of the interplay between individual behavior and the societal environment surrounding children and families (Friedman, 1976; Polansky, DeSaix and Sharlin 1972).

There is a wealth of empirical research on the correlates of child mistreatment. Child abuse has been associated with parenting stressors such as spending great amounts of time with children (Johnson and L'Esperance 1984), level of parenting skills (Johnson and L'Esperance 1984), illness of the mother (Sherrod, Altmeier, O'Conner, and Vietze 1984), youth (under 25) of the mother (Young and Gately 1988), and the presence of many children in the home (Johnson and L'Esperance 1984). Child characteristics that have been associated with abuse and neglect include illness or abnormalities (Sherrod et al. 1984), difficult temperament (Sherrod et al. 1984), and provocative or difficult behavior (Paulson, Afifi, Chaleff, Liu, and Thomason 1975).

Parents who abuse or neglect their children have histories of deprivation, mental illness, and low self-esteem (Gaines, Sandgrund, Green, and Power 1978; Garbarino 1976; Paulson et al. 1975; Shapiro 1980) and are often, though not always, from a lower socioeconomic group (Garbarino 1976; Shapiro 1980). They are also likely to experience marital difficulties, unemployment, unwanted pregnancy, and crowded living conditions (Parke and Collmer 1975).

Research on child abuse and neglect indicates that maltreating parents are likely to have few and/or weak coping resources (Johnson and L'Esperance 1984; McClelland 1973), particularly social support (Paulson et al. 1975; Weintraub and Wolf 1983). They are isolated from social networks and other sources of modeling and support (Polansky and Gaudin 1983). Their resource deficits and stressors contribute to family tension and a way of life that promotes antisocial and aggressive behavior (Patterson 1982).

Social support has been identified by several researchers as a buffer between parenting stress and parenting behavior (Cochran and Brassard 1979; Corse, Schmid, and Trickett 1990; Rodgers 1993). Though the term *social support* can encompass many kinds of help, it is generally used to indicate both emotional and practical support from friends, family, and professionals that may include giving advice, listening, providing respite care, sharing jokes, and so on. Researchers have found, however, that some people who are in a position to act as social supporters may drain resources rather than provide or boost them (Fiore, Becker, and Coppel 1983; Rook 1984; Van Meter, Haynes, and Kropp 1987). In "The Negative Social Network: When Friends Are Foes," which reports on a study of 248 families with children in foster care, Van Meter, Haynes, and Kropp (1987) found that the best predictors of a child's return home were fewer people in the household and a higher number of contacts with people in the neighborhood. These findings and others on the nature of social support and social systems bolster the ecological view that interventions must focus not only on changing individual behavior but also on the social systems in which the individual behaves.

Given that parenting is often the primary responsibility of mothers (whether in single- or dual-parent households), it is not surprising that child abuse is one area of violence in which women are as often the perpetrators as men are (Breines and Gordon 1983; Young and Gately 1988). Research has shown that mothers in abusive families and socially isolated families have fewer than average positive exchanges within their families to reinforce prosocial behavior and more than average negative and coercive exchanges (Patterson 1982). Over time these patterns provide a stressful and demanding family environment and decrease mothers' positive interactions and resources (Patterson 1980).

Wahler and Dumas (1984) determined that abuse occurs in families with "insular" mothers. They described insularity as being evident in "a specific pattern of social contacts within the community that are characterized by a high level of negatively perceived coercive interchanges with relatives and/or helping agency representatives and by a low level of positively perceived supportive interchanges with friends" (387). Children with insular mothers are at risk of abuse because these mothers have limited opportunities to diffuse stress and also have few models of positive interaction. Helping these mothers develop and increase supportive networks can aid them in diffusing stress and managing it without abusing their children.

The importance of attending to the community as an element of social support is evidenced in a recent study that examined the problems reported by 226 children and their families in a child guidance clinic in a children's hospital (Proctor, Vosler, and Sirles 1993). The study found that, on average, families reported two familial and two environmental problems. It found also that significantly more environmental difficulties such as school problems, unsafe neighborhoods, and housing problems were experienced by minority families, those receiving financial assistance, and those with lower incomes. More than half of all families coming for counseling services had money problems, and one in four had problems with either employment or housing. Low income is also related specifically to trouble with extended family members and child sexual problems or child abuse.

When questions center on community and neighborhood supports and stressors, answers necessarily focus on remedies to structural inequalities, which have increased in recent years. Cotton (1989) reports that between 1967 and 1987, African American income fell from 59 cents to 56 cents per dollar of Caucasian family income. Many researchers have identified declines in neighborhood safety and increases in child neglect rates linked to housing deterioration and the rise of poverty (Coulton, Pandey, and Chow 1990; Hartman 1987; Zuravin 1985).

In a recent study of all families referred for child neglect in Pittsburgh from 1986 to 1989, Saunders, Nelson, and Landsman (1993) found that African American families were judged to have child neglect problems of a more chronic nature, had a significantly lower per capita income, were more likely to live in substandard housing and dangerous neighborhoods, and reported a higher number of health problems than their Caucasian counterparts; but they were less likely to display anxiety. The researchers conclude that "the child welfare system is less responsive to the needs of African American families than the needs of Caucasian families: (1) in delaying intervention until their problems are perceived as chronic, and (2) in failing to address the most pressing problems faced by African American families: poverty, ill health, poor housing, and unsafe neighborhoods" (Saunders, Nelson, and Landsman 1993, 351).

Young and Gately (1988) examined the relationship between social stress, social support, and child maltreatment at the community level by gathering data in the 155 neighborhoods of El Paso, Texas, on median income, unemployment rate, percentage of female-headed households, percentage of females in the labor force with children under age six, and proportion of new residents to the neighborhood. They found that the primary correlate of child maltreatment was the percentage of new residents in the neighborhood, indicating a low level of neighborhood cohesiveness. Beyond this, the researchers found large gender differences in child abuse, with the most important contributor to abuse by females being the lack of female inclusion in the workforce. These researchers concluded that "a purposeful social policy toward families that responds to the embeddedness of family relations in the structured inequalities of society is necessary to solve the problem of child maltreatment" (Young and Gately 1988, 252).

CORRELATES OF CHILD PLACEMENT IN FOSTER CARE

Correlates of child removal sometimes differ from the empirically established correlates of abuse and neglect. Some different populations or families with particular problems are more likely to experience child removal. Family preservation, which aims to prevent both child maltreatment and child placement, must be aware of the risk factors associated with each (assessment of these risk factors will be more fully discussed in chapter 7).

Duncan Lindsey (1991), in his secondary analysis of the 1978 National Study of Children in Substitute Care (Shyne and Schroeder 1978), looked at three variables in predicting whether a child reported as abused or neglected was served in the home or placed into foster care: family income (indicated by whether or not the family was receiving welfare), referral source (self-referral or referral by a professional, an agency, legal sources, or informal sources), and reason for referral (neglect, abuse, parent problem, or child behavior problem). Lindsey found that the primary predictive variable in whether a child would receive in-home services or be placed into foster care was the family's income, and being on welfare was the best predictor of a child's placement into foster care, over and above the reason for referral or the source of the referral.

The Proceedings of the 1909 White House Conference on the Care of Dependent Children said that "the home should not be broken up for reasons of poverty, but only for considerations of inefficiency or immorality" (U.S. Congress 1909, 9–10). It may be true that in many instances children are not placed for poverty alone, because an ecological perspective makes clear that poverty seldom exists alone. Poverty is linked with lower educational attainment, poor prenatal care, living in dangerous neighborhoods, low self-esteem, poor health outcomes, and other such factors (Dore 1993; Ronnau and Marlow 1993), which exacerbate the stress of parenting and daily living.

In a study of failed reunifications—40 children returned home from foster care were put back in foster care within eighteen months—Hess and Folaron (1991) found that some parents were ambivalent about their children's return home, that parental ambivalence about reunification was associated with reunification failure, and that this ambivalence was confounded by poverty.

> The multiple stresses of living in poverty also reinforce parents' conflicting emotions about reunification. Over two-thirds of the ambivalent parents relied on some form of financial assistance. It must be emphasized that family income reflected not only the parents' personal difficulties in locating and maintaining employment, but also the fact that a single parent's reliance on public assistance to care for the children inevitably results in living in poverty. Consequently, their struggle to access and retain the resources necessary to provide care for their children, such as housing, was constant. (413)

Thus child placement is often linked to a complex set of circumstances, with poverty as a contributor. Evidence suggests, however, that sometimes child removal is linked to poverty alone. A recent study of child abuse and child removal looked at child abuse reports made as a result of injuries in children brought to a hospital emergency room (Katz, Hampton, Newberger, Bowles, and Snyder 1986). Physicians and social workers made decisions as to whether injured children would be returned to their families or, if it was determined unsafe for them to return, be placed into foster care. This study found that the removal of the child for placement into foster care was *not* related to the severity of the injury but was most strongly related to the income level of the parents, with children more likely to be placed into foster care when their parents were poor, regardless of the severity of the injury.

Children of minority ethnicity are also overrepresented in the foster care population. Nationally, in 1988, a full 46 percent of children in foster care were African American, more than twice the proportion of African American children in the U.S. population (American Public Welfare Association 1988). A recent two-year study of children in long-term foster care in Connecticut found that 39 percent of the children were African American, compared to 9 percent of the Connecticut population (Fein, Maluccio, and Kluger 1990). Many studies have consistently found that, while abuse rates for minorities do not differ from those in the majority population, minority children are much more likely to be removed to foster care when identified as mistreated (Pinderhughes 1991; Seaberg 1988; Stehno 1982). Minority children enter care at much younger ages than their white counterparts and remain in care longer (McMurtry and Lie 1992; Olsen 1982).

Long stays in foster care, the bane of permanency planning practice and policy, have been linked to a lack of parental visiting while the child is in care (Fanshel 1982; Fanshel and Shinn 1978; Lawder, Poulin, and Andrews 1985; Milner 1987; Sherman, Newman, and Shyne 1973). Research indicates that parents are likely to visit their children in foster care when the agency is responsive to their needs (Aldgate 1980; Maluccio and Whittaker 1988; Milner 1987; Whittaker and Maluccio 1988) and when the parents have social supports available to them (Milner 1987). Research has also found that services to biological parents decrease dramatically once a child is removed from the home (Lindsey 1991, 1994) and that services to minority parents are particularly lacking (Pinderhughes 1993; Stehno 1982). For example, while close proximity between the foster home and the biological home facilitates regular visiting, many children from impoverished neighborhoods are placed across town or even in a different town from that of the biological family (Hess 1988; Whittaker 1981); minority children are often placed with majority foster parents because potential minority foster homes are lacking (Hogan and Siu 1988; National Black Child Development Institute 1989; Olsen 1982).

CORRELATES OF PREVENTION OF CHILD MALTREATMENT

Research on the prevention or treatment of child maltreatment is not as plentiful as that on correlates of abuse or placement. This reflects again an emphasis on diagnosing problems rather than solving them. Nevertheless, evaluations of child abuse prevention and treatment programs have identified several components and frameworks that are correlated with program effectiveness.

Berry (1988) conducted a review of all evaluation research on parent training programs in child welfare services and found that programs to prevent child abuse are much more likely to be didactic than interactive; but the interactive programs were found to be more effective than didactic programs in demonstrating behavior changes in the parents and in producing effects that were still evident at follow-up visits. These interactive and behavioral programs (Forehand and McMahon 1981; Patterson, Chamberlain, and Reid 1982) are based on social learning approaches to parenting and train parents in increasing social rewards to children, giving clear commands, and rewarding compliance.

Dumas (1986) and others (Griest and Forehand 1982; Lovell, Reid, and Richey 1992) have found that socioeconomic stressors and a lack of social support inhibit short-term gains during parent training and minimize long-term longevity of effects. In their article "How Can I Get Any Parent Training Done with All These Other Problems Going On?" Griest and Forehand (1982) reported that child behavior problems were associated with parent adjustment problems, marital problems, and extrafamilial problems and that these problems often interfere with the maintenance of parent-training effects. Similarly, Lovell, Reid, and Richey (1992) found in their training group for abusive parents that "it was not uncommon for parent group members unwittingly to respond to each other with embarrassing and/or inappropriate comments. They appeared genuinely surprised to learn that their remarks were offensive or hurtful to others. . . . In general, mothers appeared unable to give and receive social support" (96).

Both Forehand and colleagues (Forehand and McMahon 1981; Griest and Forehand 1982) and Patterson and colleagues (Patterson 1982; Patterson, Chamberlain, and Reid 1982) have modified their parent training to add a "parent enhancement" component. A parent enhancement component focuses on parents' perceptions and expectations of children's behavior (knowledge of development and milestones, attitudes toward discipline and bad behavior), parents' mood and psychological adjustment, spouse-partner communication, problem solving, and parent interactions outside the family. Wodarski's (1981) review of programs to treat parents who abuse their children concluded that this enhancement component is crucial. "It is logical that a treatment approach to abuse must view the problem as multi-determined and services should be structured in such a manner. . . . Thus, the comprehensive treatment program should consist of the following: (1) child management program, (2) marital enrichment program, (3) vocational skills enrichment program and (4) interpersonal skills enrichment program" (353). Almost ten years ago Cohn and Daro (1987) identified the raison d'être for family preservation services: "(S)uccessful intervention with maltreating families requires a comprehensive package which addresses both the interpersonal and concrete needs of all family members" (437).

More recently, Halpern (1993) echoes the necessity of an ecological approach to treatment: "(W)hen parents and children participate in a particular service, they do not bring only that part of their history, current situation and 'self' that is relevant to that service. They bring everything. . . . Those designing programs to work with young families . . . must decide how much to focus on parenting per se and how much to focus on extrafamilial stressors that impinge both on parenting and on children directly" (165–66).

REFERENCES

Aldgate, Jane. (1980). Identification of factors influencing children's length of stay in care. In John Triseliotis (ed.), *New developments in foster care and adoption.* London: Routledge and Kegan Paul.

American Public Welfare Association. (1988). *Voluntary Cooperative Information System data.* Washington, DC: American Public Welfare Association.

American Public Welfare Association. (1993). *National roundtable on outcome measures in child welfare services.* San Antonio: American Public Welfare Association.

Bass, Deborah. (1993). *1992 update to a national survey of programs for runaway and homeless youths and a model service delivery approach.* Washington, DC.: National Association of Social Workers.

Belle, Deborah. (1982). Social ties and social support. In Deborah Belle (ed.), *Lives in stress: Women and depression.* Beverly Hills: Sage.

Berry, Marianne. (1988). A review of parent training programs in child welfare. *Social Service Review* 62 (2): 302–23.

Breines, Wini, and Linda Gordon. (1983). The new scholarship on family violence. *Signs: Journal of Women in Culture and Society* 8: 490–531.

Callahan, Jean. (1992, February). Foster care at the crossroads. *Parenting:* 70.

Cochran, Moncrief M., and Jane A. Brassard. (1979). Child development and personal social networks. *Child Development* 50: 601–16.

Cohn, Anne H., and Deborah Daro. (1987). Is treatment too late?: What ten years of evaluative research tell us. *Child Abuse and Neglect* 11: 433–42.

Corse, Sara J., Kathleen Schmid, and Penelope K. Trickett. (1990). Social network characteristics of mothers in abusing and nonabusing families and their relationships to parenting beliefs. *Journal of Community Psychology* 18: 44–59.

Cotton, Jeremiah (1989). The declining relative economic status of Black families. *The Review of Black Political Economy* 18: 75–85

Coulton, Claudia, Shanta Pandey, and Julian Chow. (1990). Concentration of poverty and the changing ecology of low-income, urban neighborhoods: An analysis of the Cleveland area. *Social Work Research and Abstracts* 26 (3): 5–16.

Dore, Martha M. (1993, November). Family preservation and poor families: When "homebuilding" is not enough. *Families in Society:* 545–56.

Dumas, Jean E. (1986). Parental perception and treatment outcome in families of aggressive children: A causal model. *Behavior Therapy* 17: 420–32.

Fanshel, David. (1982). *On the road to permanency: An expanded data base for service to children in foster care.* New York: Child Welfare League of America.

Fanshel, David, and Eugene B. Shinn. (1978). *Children in foster care: A longitudinal investigation.* New York: Columbia University Press.

Fein, Edith, Anthony N. Maluccio, and Miriam P. Kluger. (1990). *No more partings: An examination of long-term foster family care.* Washington, DC: Child Welfare League of America.

Fiore, Joan, Joseph Becker, and David B. Coppel. (1983). Social network interactions: A buffer or a stress? *American Journal of Community Psychology* 11: 423–39.

Folkman, Susan, and Richard S. Lazarus. (1985). If it changes it must be a process: Study of emotion and coping during three stages of a college examination. *Journal of Personality and Social Psychology* 48: 150–70.

Forehand, Rex L., and R. J. McMahon. (1981). *Helping the non-compliant child: A clinician's guide to parent training.* New York: Guilford.

Friedman, Roger M. (1976). Child abuse: A review of the psychosocial research. In Herner and Company (eds.), *Four perspectives on the status of child abuse and neglect research.* Washington, DC: National Center on Child Abuse and Neglect.

Gaines, Richard, Alice Sandgrund, Arthur H. Green, and Ernest Power. (1978). Etiological factors in child maltreatment: A multivariate study of abusing, neglecting and normal mothers. *Journal of Abnormal Psychology* 87: 531–40.

Garbarino, James. (1976). A preliminary study of some ecological correlates of child abuse: The impact of socioeconomic stress on mothers. *Child Development* 47: 178–85.

Garbarino, James. (1977). The human ecology of child maltreatment: A conceptual model for research. *Journal of Marriage and the Family* 39: 721–35.

Garbarino, James. (1981). An ecological approach to child maltreatment. In Leroy H. Pelton (ed.), *The social context of child abuse and neglect.* New York: Human Sciences Press.

Gil, David G. (1973). *Violence against children: Physical child abuse in the United States.* Cambridge, MA: Harvard University Press.

Griest, Douglas L., and Rex Forehand. (1982). How can I get any parent training done with all these other problems going on? The role of family variables in child behavior therapy. *Child and Family Behavior Therapy* 4: 73–80.

Halpern, Robert. (1993). The societal context of home visiting and related services for families in poverty. *Future of Children* 3: 158–71.

Hartman, Ann. (1990). Family ties. *Social Work* 35 (3): 195–96.

Hartman, Chester. (1987). The housing part of the homelessness problem. In *Homelessness: Critical issues for policy and practice.* Boston, MA: Boston Foundation.

Hess, Peg. (1988). Case and context: Determinants of planned visit frequency in foster family care. *Child Welfare* 67: 311–26.

Hess, Peg McCartt, and Gail Folaron. (1991). Ambivalences: A challenge to permanency for children. *Child Welfare* 70: 403–24.

Hill, Reuben. (1958). Social stresses on the family: Generic features of families under stress. *Social Casework* 39: 139–50.

Hogan, Patricia T., and Sau-Fong Siu. (1988). Minority children and the child welfare system: An historical perspective. *Social Work* 33: 493–98.

Imig, David R., and Gail L. Imig. (1986). Influences of family management and spousal perceptions on stressor pile-up. *Family Relations* 34: 227–32.

Johnson, Will, and Jill L'Esperance. (1984). Predicting the recurrence of child abuse. *Social Work Research and Abstracts,* 20(2): 21–31.

Kagan, Daniel. (1991, April 29). Saving families fosters hope for America's troubled youth. *Insight on the News:* 16.

Kagan, Richard, and Shirley Schlosberg. (1989). *Families in perpetual crisis.* New York: W. W. Norton.

Katz, Mitchell H., Robert L. Hampton, Eli H. Newberger, Roy T. Bowles, and Jane C. Snyder. (1986). Returning children home: Clinical decision making in cases of child abuse and neglect. *American Journal of Orthopsychiatry* 56: 253–63.

Lawder, Elizabeth A., John E. Poulin, and Roberta G. Andrews. (1986). A study of 185 foster children 5 years after placement. *Child Welfare* 65: 241–51.

Lazarus, Richard S., and Susan Folkman. (1984.) Coping and adaptation. In W. D. Gentry (ed.), *The handbook of behavioral medicine,* 282–325. New York: Guilford.

Lazarus, Richard S., and Susan Folkman. (1984). *Stress, appraisal and coping.* New York: Springer.

Lewin, Kurt. (1951). *Field theory in social science.* New York: Harper and Row.

Lindsey, Duncan. (1991). Factors affecting the foster care placement decision: An analysis of national survey data. *American Journal of Orthopsychiatry* 61 (2): 272–83.

Lindsey, Duncan. (1994). *The welfare of children.* New York: Oxford University Press.

Littell, Julia H., Jeanne Howard, Tina L. Rzepnicki, Stephen Budde, and Diane Pellowe. (1992). *Intervention with families in the Illinois family preservation program.* Chicago: Chapin Hall Center for Children, University of Chicago.

Lovell, Madeline L., Kathy Reid, and Cheryl A. Richey. (1992). Social support training for abusive mothers. In James A. Garland (ed.), *Group work reaching out: People, places and power.* New York: Haworth Press.

Maluccio, Anthony N. (1981). An ecological perspective on practice with parents of children in foster care. In Anthony N. Maluccio and Paula A. Sinanoglu (eds.), *The challenge of partnership: Working with the parents of children in foster care,* (22–35). New York: Child Welfare League of America.

Maluccio, Anthony N., and James K. Whittaker. (1988). Helping the biological families of children in out-of-home placement. In Elam W. Nunnaly, Catherine S. Chilman, and Fred M. Cox (eds.), *Troubled relationships: Families in trouble,* vol. 3, 205–17. Newbury Park, CA: Sage.

McClelland, David. (1973). Testing for competence rather than intelligence. *American Psychologist* 28: 1–14.

McCubbin, Hamilton I., and Joan M. Patterson. (1983). Family transitions: Adaptation to stress. In Hamilton I. McCubbin and Charles R. Figley (eds.), *Stress and the family,* 5–25. New York: Brunner/Mazel.

McMurtry, Steven L., and Gwat-Yong Lie. (1992). Differential exit rates of minority children in foster care. *Social Work Research and Abstracts* 28 (1): 42–48.

Miller, Patricia H. (1983). *Theories of developmental psychology.* San Francisco: W. H. Freeman.

Milner, Jerry L. (1987). An ecological perspective on duration of foster care. *Child Welfare* 66: 113–23.

National Black Child Development Institute. (1989). *Who will care when parents can't?* Washington, DC: National Black Child Development Institute.

Olsen, Lenore. (1982). Services for minority children in out-of-home care. *Social Service Review* 56 (4): 572–85.

Olson, David H., Hamilton I. McCubbin, Howard L. Barnes, Andrea S. Larsen, Marla J. Muxen, and Marc A. Wilson. (1983). *Families.* Beverly Hills: Sage.

Parke, Ross D., and Candace W. Collmer. (1975). Child abuse: An interdisciplinary analysis. In Eileen M. Hetherington (ed.), *Review of child developmental research.* Chicago: University of Chicago Press.

Patterson, Gerald R. (1980). Mothers: The unacknowledged victims. *Monographs of the Society for Research in Child Development* 45 (5): 1–64.

Patterson, Gerald R. (1982). *Coercive family process.* Eugene, OR: Castalia.

Patterson, Gerald R., Patricia Chamberlain, and John B. Reid. (1982). A comparative evaluation of a parent-training program. *Behavior Therapy* 13: 638–50.

Paulson, Morris J., Abdelmonem A. Afifi, Anne Chaleff, Vinnie Y. Liu, and Mary L. Thomason. (1975). A discriminant function procedure for identifying abusive parents. *Suicide* 5: 104–14.

Pelton, Leroy. (1981). Child abuse and neglect: The myth of classlessness. In Leroy Pelton (ed.), *The social context of child abuse and neglect,* 23–38. New York: Human Sciences Press.

Pinderhughes, Ellen E. (1991). The delivery of child welfare services to African American clients. *American Journal of Orthopsychiatry* 61 (4): 599–605.

Polansky, Norman A., Christine DeSaix, and Shlomo A. Sharlin. (1972). *Child neglect: Understanding and reaching the parent.* New York: Child Welfare League of America.

Polansky, Norman A., and James M. Gaudin. (1983). Social distancing of the neglectful family. *Social Service Review* 57: 196–208.

Proctor, Enola K., Nancy R. Vosler, and Elizabeth A. Sirles. (1993). The social-environmental context of child clients: An empirical exploration. *Social Work* 38: 256–62.

Rodgers, Antoinette Y. (1993). The assessment of variables related to the parenting behaviors of mothers with young children. *Children and Youth Services Review* 15: 385–402.

Ronnau, John P., and Christine Marlow. (1993, November). Family preservation, poverty, and the value of diversity. *Families in Society:* 538–44.

Rook, Karen S. (1984). The negative side of social interaction: Impact on psychological well-being. *Journal of Personality and Social Psychology* 46: 1097–1108.

Saunders, Edward J., Kristine Nelson, and Miriam J. Landsman. (1993). Racial inequality and child neglect: Findings in a metropolitan area. *Child Welfare* 72: 341–54.

Seaberg, James R. (1988). Placement in permanency planning: Own home versus foster care. *Social Work Research and Abstracts* 24 (4): 4–7.

Shapiro, Deborah. (1980). A CWLA study of factors involved in child abuse. *Child Welfare* 59: 242–43.

Sherman, Edmund A., Renee Newman, and Ann W. Shyne. (1973). *Children adrift in foster care: A study of alternative approaches.* New York: Child Welfare League of America.

Sherrod, Kathryn B., William A. Altmeier, Susan O'Conner, and Peter M. Vietze. (1984). Early prediction of child maltreatment. *Early Child Development and Care* 13: 335–50.

Shyne, Ann W., and A. G. Schroeder. (1978). *National study of social services to children and their families.* Rockville, MD: Westat.

Spinetta, John J., and David Rigler. (1972). The child-abusing parent: A psychological review. *Psychological Bulletin* 77: 296–304.

Stehno, Sandra M. (1982). Differential treatment of minority children in service systems. *Social Work* 27: 39–45.

U.S. Congress. (1909). *Conference on the care of dependent children: Proceedings.* 60th Congress, 2d Session, 1909, S.Doc. 721.

Van Meter, Mary Jane S., O. Maurice Haynes, and Joseph P. Kropp. (1987). The negative social network: When friends are foes. *Child Welfare* 66 (1): 69–75.

Wahler, Robert G., and Jean E. Dumas. (1984). Changing the observational coding styles of insular and noninsular mothers: A step toward maintenance of parent training effects. In Richard F. Dangel and Richard A. Polster (eds.), *Parent training: Foundations of research and practice,* 379–416. New York: Guilford.

Weintraub, Marsha, and Barbara Wolf. (1983). Effects of stress and social supports on mother-child interactions in single- and two-parent families. *Child Development* 54: 1297–1311.

Werner, Emmy E., and Ruth S. Smith. (1992). *Overcoming the odds: High risk children from birth to adulthood.* Ithaca, NY: Cornell University Press.

Whittaker, James K. (1981). Family involvement in residential child care: A support system for biological parents. In Anthony N. Maluccio and Paula A. Sinanoglu (eds.), *The challenge of partnership: Working with parents in foster care,* 67–88. New York: Child Welfare League of America.

Whittaker, James K., and Anthony N. Maluccio. (1988). Understanding the families of children in foster and residential care. In Elam W. Nunnaly, Catherine S. Chilman, and Fred M. Cox (eds.), *Troubled relationships: Families in trouble,* vol. 3. Newbury Park, CA: Sage.

Whittaker, James K., Steven P. Schinke, and Lewayne D. Gilchrist. (1986). The ecological paradigm in child, youth, and family services: Implications for policy and practice. *Social Service Review* 60: 483–503.

Wodarski, John S. (1981). Treatment of parents who abuse their children: A literature review and implications for professionals. *Child Abuse and Neglect* 5: 351–60.

Wulczyn, Fred. (1991, June 28). *The community dimension of permanency planning.* New York: New York State Department of Social Services, Division of Family and Children Services.

Young, Gay, and Tamra Gately. (1988). Neighborhood impoverishment and child maltreatment: An analysis from the ecological perspective. *Journal of Family Issues* 9 (2): 240–54.

Zuravin, Susan. (1985). Housing and maltreatment: Is there a connection? *Children Today* 14 (6): 8–13.

Chapter 4

Intensive Family
Preservation Service Models

Based on empirical underpinnings of ecologically oriented intervention, most family preservation programs are somewhat similar in their focus, goals, and structure of services. This chapter will present the guiding principles and basic components of intensive family preservation services and discuss different models currently operating in various states and agencies, including program structure, staff qualifications, caseloads, and duration of services.

The effectiveness of these programs can be summarized in terms of a variety of outcomes including maintenance of the child in the home, behavioral improvement of the child, family satisfaction with services, gains in parenting skills, nurturing, attachment, self-esteem, feeling good about one's family, and feeling good about placing one's child if relevant. Any evaluation of a family preservation program must examine more than family preservation as the desired outcome. Because preserving families at the risk of continued abuse is not the best outcome for children, it is important to assess as well whether the risk of abuse or neglect has been reduced (through removing risk factors, improving parenting skills, bolstering other resources, and so on). There will be some families for which placement is the most beneficial outcome. It is also necessary to consider what researchers have learned about the longevity of the programs' effects and what they have found about cost-effectiveness.

GUIDING PRINCIPLES OF FAMILY PRESERVATION SERVICES

Family preservation is both a philosophy and an approach to practice (Ronnau and Sallee 1995). As a *philosophy,* it explicates a values base, values being the basic principles or beliefs on which the movement is built. Family preservation as a philosophy espouses varied definitions of family; the value of diversity and uniqueness among families and communities; and the beliefs that families are the experts on their own lives and that family preservation work is a partnership involving the worker; the family; and the larger systems, such as community agencies, informal helpers, networks, and state administrative agencies. The fundamental underlying value is family self-determination of choices and goals.

Family preservation is also an approach to practice that frames helping behavior. As an *approach to practice,* it involves knowledge, skills, and techniques that grow out of philosophical values and beliefs. Programs frame practice in a strengths-based, family-centered approach aimed at keeping families together and keeping them safe. The fundamental underlying work of family preservation is to help the family become self-sufficient.

Promoting self-determination and self-sufficiency requires an individualized approach to every family and every community. Treatment plans must be individually tailored to meet each family's unique strengths and needs. Thus every plan is different.

The Homebuilders program (Kinney, Haapala, and Booth 1991, 60–67) lists seven guiding principles of respect for clients, all intended to foster a collegial and constructive interventive helping relationship between the caseworker and the family:

1. It is our job to instill hope.
2. We cannot know ahead of time if a situation is hopeless.
3. Clients should have as much power as possible.
4. Clients are our colleagues.
5. Respect is contagious.
6. Not knowing can be valuable.
7. We can do harm.

GOALS OF FAMILY PRESERVATION SERVICES

Family preservation programs have the ultimate goal of preserving families while ensuring the safety of children, and they approach this goal with ecologically-framed objectives. Whittaker, Schinke, and Gilchrist (1986) identify the two essential elements of an ecologically-oriented intervention: "building more supportive, nurturant environments for clients through various forms of environmental helping that are designed to increase social support, and improving clients' competence in dealing with both proximate and distal environments through the teaching of specific life skills" (492). These two objectives reflect the current empirical research base regarding the correlates of abuse and the components of effective treatment for abusive families (as reviewed in chapter 3).

Enrichment of Life Skills

When child abuse and neglect are the results of social isolation and overwhelming stress, the solution is to eliminate or reduce the isolation and stress. Intensive family preservation services are aimed at linking families with resources in their community that they have not previously used and of which they may be unaware. The resources that these programs provide include money, help with housing and food, education on child rearing and job skills, modeling of housecleaning and shopping skills, transportation, and help in improving family communication patterns. Family preservation workers increase skill resources by modeling, training, and helping families rehearse the skills necessary for nonabusive parenting and adaptive family life. Thus they help families acquire and maintain concrete resources such as food and shelter and also train family members in interpersonal skills with each other as well as teachers, doctors, relatives, and other potential supports.

A critical part of effective intervention aimed at family preservation or any other practice goal is engaging the client in the process. Treatment cannot proceed only on the good intentions of the practitioner; it requires a partnership between practitioner and client. This is particularly true in an involuntary or coercive relationship (Rooney 1993), which is often the case in family preservation, since families must participate in treatment or lose their children to foster care or adoption. Therefore, intensive family preservation programs must work to engage family members at the beginning of services.

In keeping with their family-centered and home-based approach, family preservation programs have built services around treating clients as colleagues (Kinney, Haapala, Booth, and Leavitt 1990), working from client-identified problems toward client-centered goals. The family preservation worker spends the first session listening to the client's perception of the problem(s) and the reason for referral. If concrete services such as housecleaning or buying groceries are an immediate need, the worker's ability to roll up his or her sleeves and pitch in on the first day can go a long way toward increasing the family's belief that this set of services will be useful and that the worker won't just prescribe hoops through which the family must jump. Similarly, the provision of such hard services can provide "teachable moments" (Kinney et al. 1990, 46), opportunities for the worker to demonstrate ways to incorporate children into the housecleaning process or to stretch a budget and make healthy choices when shopping for food.

While services are intended to be flexibly matched to the needs and goals of the family, the services most commonly provided in these programs are designed to improve parenting skills and family interaction skills in general. The worker models and teaches active listening, negotiation, and problem-solving skills as ways to avoid conflict, increase positive interactions, and prevent abusive events.

Enrichment of Social Support

As well as originating from individuals' actions, stressors can arise from the social, economic, and political environments in which a family exists. At the same time, coping resources such as social support can be found in that identical environment. "It is the unmanageability of the stress which is the most important factor [in child abuse] and unmanageability is a product of a mismatch between the level of stress and the availability and potency of support systems" (Garbarino 1977, 727). Helping family members interact productively with external systems is just as important as helping them learn to live with each other.

Changes in economic and family structure in the recent past amplify the importance of support for families. The increased mobility of the American family has resulted in a decline in support from extended family. Many families no longer live in the same neighborhood or city as other relatives. Thus they have fewer natural helpers in baby-sitting and child care as well as limits to these kinds of social and recreational opportunities. In a recent experiment with a system of social services in Minnesota, families were provided with vouchers to use for purchasing any social service they desired; they used their vouchers most often for recreational opportunities (Lyle 1993).

Social support in a more formal than informal sense may be needed by multistressed families. Sustaining informal networks may be more stressful than productive to isolated parents (Belle 1982; Fiore, Becker, and Coppel 1983; Rook 1984). Linking such families with more formal services and supports and helping them maintain those links may be more appropriate.

Formal services do not necessarily entail involving a family in such long-term, complicated, and intrusive measures as child protective services. They can be provided by any agency that offers specific kinds of help: the housing bureau, day care centers, schools, and hospitals. Families can be aided in negotiating the maze to apply for the supportive services such agencies offer without having to become permanently enrolled in any particular course of action they provide. In some cases, simply making families aware of these resources for their future use is enough. In others, families may need help accessing and initiating the services to ensure that they understand the process and are supported in their continuing use of services.

THE HOMEBUILDERS MODEL

The first family preservation program to achieve national attention was Homebuilders, which began in Tacoma, Washington, in 1974. Homebuilders is often considered a model program of intensive family preservation services. This program operates in Washington (Behavioral Sciences Institute 1987b; Kinney, Haapala, and Booth 1981) and also recently operated for a time in the Bronx in New York City (Kinney, Haapala, and Booth 1991) and in Maine (Hinckley and Ellis, 1985). Its main components are family therapists who are on call twenty-four hours a day, a flexible limit of about six weeks of service to families, and in-home provision of service.

For families to be eligible for service, at least one family member must be at risk of imminent placement; at least one must express a desire to keep the family together; and there must not be a high potential for danger to the therapist (Kinney, Madsen, Fleming, and Haapala 1977). In Washington, Homebuilders employs twenty-three masters-level family therapists, and each has a caseload of two families (Kinney, Haapala, and Booth 1991).

Small caseloads are an important element of the Homebuilders program. The constraints of twenty-four-hour availability of therapists and the crisis intervention nature of the service limit the accessibility and flexibility of therapists. Serving more than two families at one time would reduce their ability to respond to families that are in a crisis state and need fast, intensive help (Kinney, Haapala, and Booth 1991). Only one therapist serves on a case (although the Maine Homebuilders program uses two cotherapists); this system ameliorates the threatening nature of intervention and the adversarial nature of family therapy (Kinney, Haapala, and Booth 1991). Using only one therapist also increases accountability and decreases costs.

The goal of treatment for Homebuilders is to prevent the need for out-of-home placement. This objective entails the subtasks of resolving immediate crises and teaching skills the family needs to maintain family integrity independently, such as problem solving and communication. Therapists also provide such concrete services as housecleaning and transportation, through which they not only model skills and coping strategies but also demonstrate their commitment to the family. During the provision of such "hard" services, therapists can also observe clients' skills and talk about other problems the family is experiencing. By doing all of these things and being available around the clock, these therapists really are providing intensive and comprehensive family service.

COMMON FEATURES OF FAMILY PRESERVATION PROGRAMS

Intensive family preservation programs go by many names, but all have several common themes and purposes. Like other less intensive home-based and family-centered programs, these programs agree that the home is the best and primary site of service, and the whole family is the client rather than just the child or the parent. This basic tenet affirms the importance of treating the family within its own environment and dealing with family interactional difficulties that precipitate abuse and neglect. These programs are also based on the proposition that services include whatever it takes to improve family relations and keep the family together. Such a commitment requires around-the-clock availability of workers, a wide range of skills and resources, and an ability to work within the family's ecological system, including the community. Most intensive family preservation programs are short-term and labor-intensive, with workers serving only a few families at a time and cases closing within a few months.

Many researchers and writers have discussed the differences between family preservation programs in theoretical framework (Barth 1990; Grigsby 1993), organization (Nelson, Landsman, and Deutelbaum 1990), and delivery of services (Allen 1990; Dore 1991; Nelson, Landsman, and Allen 1991; Soule, Massarene, and Abate 1993). Others have argued that "the competition over approach has infused clinical discussions with a political-ideological tension . . . [resulting in] a loss of breadth of perception" (Friedman 1993, 7). This discussion will focus on the similarities of currently operating family preservation programs. It is followed by a brief delineation of variations from the model.

Family Preservation Services Reflect a Strengths Perspective

Treatment objectives for any particular family are individualized according to family strengths and needs and are set by the caseworker and the family together. This goal setting is at the heart of family preservation practice and purposely moves away from a diagnosis and problem orientation. Family goal setting reflects the client-centered, empowerment, and strengths perspective toward family preservation.

Clients are viewed as colleagues in all stages of treatment including problem definition and problem solving. This approach to, and respect of, clients contributes to the high level of client engagement said to exist in family preservation programs. Problem definition has been described as a battle (Whitaker 1977) between therapist and family. For many clients who have been served by child welfare agencies or in other coercive settings, the problem is usually defined by someone else and may be labeled child abuse, poor parenting skills, child neglect, or lack of parental supervision. The family's or parent's view of the problem could be quite different: lack of child care while the parent is at work, a child who is out of control, and so on.

If the family's definition of the problem is discounted, family members are unlikely to view the therapist's definition of the problem as worthy of their efforts. "The therapist can be leading a charge toward some quickly determined problem only to turn around and find no one behind him/her" (Stewart, Valentine, and Amundson 1991, 102). It is only when the family agrees that something is a problem that it will be invested in doing something to change it.

Kinney and colleagues (1991) assert that "not knowing can be valuable" (66). This echoes the sentiments of the settlement workers earlier in the twentieth century who admitted to not knowing the beliefs, practices, and everyday realities of families in settlement neighborhoods and set about learning them from the inhabitants themselves. Information on the neighborhood families' difficulties, like strategies for change, came from the families themselves. Settlement workers did not approach the neighborhood with an air of authority to prescribe change. Similarly, family preservation workers enter into a partnership with families to help families reach their goals.

In some programs, but not all, goals are set and accomplished through contracting (Rooney 1981, 1993; Tunnard 1988). Contracts were used extensively in the Alameda Project (Stein, Gambrill, and Wiltse 1978) and the Oregon Project (Lahti and Dvorak 1981) and were described by both groups of researchers as critical in helping to rebuild parents' sense of parenthood and their feeling of having the authority to make decisions about their children (Gambrill and Stein 1981). In other words, parents often come into contact with child welfare agencies because of their inability or unwillingness to act responsibly in the care of their children. Contracting, or the process of identifying, delineating, and scheduling the parents' and caseworker's responsibilities for treatment, teaches and rewards responsible and competent behavior.

In programs using contracts, the worker and the family members make service agreements involving tasks that both agree to perform to achieve mutually agreed upon goals. Agreements are written. They specify the task; who will perform it; and where, when, and how often it will be performed. Objectives of service are specified in behavioral terms. For example, an agreement might stipulate that the mother will make an appointment for her child to go to the pediatrician for a well-baby checkup. This would be followed by a task agreement that the mother would take the child to the appointment and that the worker would provide transportation. Everyone signs the agreement when it is acceptable, and workers track progress on tasks. New tasks are typically set at every meeting of family and worker.

Family Preservation Services Are Provided in the Home or Community

Family preservation services are home-based and family-centered. As outlined in chapter 1, home-based services have been in existence since the beginning of the social work profession and the use of home visitors. Home-based services are simply a broad range of services provided to children, parents, and/or families in the home. Thus home-based programs run the gamut from broad educational and informative family support programs aimed at early intervention with infants and their mothers (Halpern 1986) to case management models in child welfare services (Allen 1990) to structural family therapy models incorporating home visits and in-home assessment (Kagan and Schlosberg 1989; Reid, Kagan, and Schlosberg 1988).

Home-based programs emphasize serving the client(s) in the home and their principles have been applied in programs such as Home Start (Collins 1980; Halpern 1984, 1986; O'Keefe 1973), some parent training programs (Hirsch, Gailey, and Schmerl 1976), and other social service provision models (Bloom 1973; Montgomery, Shulman, and Pfenninger 1972). Families and children are served in the home because clients are believed to be better served in the environment in which problems are occurring. Indeed, home-based programs enjoyed a resurgence in the late 1960s and early 1970s, when practitioners realized that many of their clients simply did not always have the resources to come to agencies for treatment and that service provided in the home afforded many benefits to assessment and networking that surpassed those of service provided in the office (Bell 1978; Friedman 1962; Speck 1964; Sperekas 1974).

More recent research has confirmed the contribution of home-based services to the prevention of child abuse (Berry 1992; Johnson 1994). Two separate studies with large samples (367 families and 303 families) and standardized measures each found statistically significant relationships between home visits and positive outcomes for families. Berry's (1992) study of 367 families receiving family preservation services found that no children were removed from the home for up to one year later when more than half of the worker's service time had been spent in the home with the family. The corresponding placement rate was 28 percent for families receiving less than half of their service time in the home. Similarly, Johnson's (1994) study of 303 physical abuse cases found that a recurrence of abuse was significantly less likely for up to two years after the family had received eight or more in-person visits from its caseworker. This same study found that the provision of contracted services, such as counseling or parent training, was not related to the prevention of the recurrence of abuse.

Family Preservation Services Focus on the Whole Family

Family preservation programs are also family-centered. Family-centered services reflect the ecological framework of involving the entire family in treatment. While client-centered, home-based services may be aimed at improving the parenting behaviors of a mother with her preschool-age child, for example, family-centered services will be more likely to focus on communication patterns and interaction in abusive families by working with family members together. Family-centered services are often based on a family therapy model of treatment (Schlachter 1975; Showell, Allen, and Keys 1984), but they can be based on more behavioral methods (Cautley 1980; Patterson, Chamberlain, and Reid 1982; Rooney 1981, 1993; Tunnard 1988).

Family Preservation Services Are Provided to Families in Crisis

Family-centered programs can be viewed as elements of a pyramid that represent services to all families at risk of having a child removed from the home (Norman 1985). The tip of the pyramid contains programs for those families in need of crisis intervention, families who are at risk of imminent placement. The second and somewhat larger level contains services to those families who show signs of risk but are not in immediate danger. The largest segment, the foundation of the pyramid, applies to programs for families in the general population who may have characteristics that are associated with potential for risk. Thus intensive family preservation services are reserved for those families at the tip; less intensive programs and family support programs (including other home-based and family-centered programs) are applied to those families in the middle; and larger, broad-based educational programs are designed for the general population of families.

A crisis event like abuse, child endangerment, or imminent risk of the child's placement into foster care is viewed as a window of opportunity for change in families (Kinney et al. 1990). "Clients in pain are highly motivated to change and try new ways of coping. It is more difficult for them to say they do not need help when one of the family is sobbing, or the children only have T-shirts and the temperature has suddenly dropped 20 degrees" (41).

Family Preservation Services Are Typically Short-Term and Intensive

The Homebuilders program assigns only two families at a time to a worker and serves each family for four to eight weeks, based on the assumption that a better relationship with the family can be formed when the caseworker can spend large amounts of time with the family during the crisis aftermath (Kinney et al. 1990). With intensive service, the caseworker can provide help during the early aftermath, demonstrate a commitment to the family, show the family that he or she believes change can occur in the face of adversity, and practice and build skills with the family in the often slow and incremental steps that are required.

Caseworkers can spend hours each day with a family, particularly at the beginning of service. If family conflict is especially intense during the after-school and dinner hours, the caseworker can join the family in preparing and eating dinner to get a clear picture of family interaction and to model and begin productive interaction skills. This has many obvious benefits over less intensive weekly meetings in conventional child welfare services, in which such family occasions cannot be observed or influenced so intensively.

VARIATIONS IN THE MODEL

Homebuilders is of course not the only family preservation model currently in use, although it may be the most widely emulated. Many programs have implemented the Homebuilders model with variations or have tried other program models wholesale (descriptions of various programs follow this section). Kinney and colleagues (Kinney, Haapala, and Booth 1991) note the interdependence of program components in the formation of a practice model with integrity and effectiveness.

All these aspects of the model—the rapid responses to referrals, the accessibility of workers at home during evenings and weekends, the time available for families, the location of the services, the staffing pattern, the low caseloads, and the brief duration of services—produce a much more powerful intervention than one that utilizes only one or two of these components. It is impossible to have the intensity and flexibility we would like with a large caseload. It is impossible to maintain focus, responsiveness to crisis, and accessibility if the intervention drifts on for too long a period. We urge others considering replication of Homebuilders to try the whole package first and tailor it to their communities if they encounter difficulties. If they eliminate one aspect, such as the short time frame or the low caseload, they are likely to decrease the power of the overall intervention far more than they can realize without first attempting the whole model. (53)

Staffing Varies by Program

Compher (1983) reviewed the various types of home-based social services to children and has classified them as general case management, the comprehensive social worker, the in-house team, and the interagency team. These are listed in ascending order of family needs. General case management in the home setting focuses on the client's contextual needs to strengthen family resources and prevent the need for placement. The comprehensive social worker emphasizes strengthening family functioning through family counseling and facilitates resource development secondarily (this approach is thus the most family-centered of the four types). The in-house team consists of two or three social workers who can develop resources and provide intensive counseling simultaneously. The interagency team has three roles: case manager, clinical family therapist, and family aide.

Kinney et al. (1990) argue against the use of teams such as two therapists per family or a therapist and a paraprofessional for concrete services. They assert that teaming can set up alliances and competition between family members or therapists; that it takes more coordination and planning; that it detracts from trust and a close relationship; and that it minimizes accountability of therapists. A single worker can maximize flexibility and responsiveness to emerging crises or family skills and can capitalize on a trusting relationship with the family and make better use of day-to-day "teachable moments" (Kinney et al. 1990, 46) as they occur.

Lloyd and Bryce (1984) disagree, however. They argue in favor of teaming a clinician with a support worker who provides concrete services. These authors cite the advantages of a team: support between workers; objectivity through dual assessments of families; continuity of service if one member is unavailable; and the benefit of the family's having a common background or rapport with paraprofessionals, particularly if the family has previously had negative experiences with professional services.

Programs May Focus on Specific Populations

Because programs like Homebuilders are flexibly framed, services are usually provided to families at risk of imminent child removal, with no specific orientation to certain age groups or family needs. Some programs, however, have approaches more tailored to specific family problems and may focus on runaway or out-of-control adolescents (AuClaire and Schwartz 1986), children at risk of psychiatric institutionalization (Hinckley and Ellis 1985), or drug-affected families (Jiordano 1990).

Theoretical Orientations Guide Services

Intensive family preservation services involve different foci, with some proponents advocating a structural family therapy approach (AuClaire and Schwartz 1986), others a social learning theory approach (Kinney, Haapala, and Booth 1981; Szykula and Fleischman 1985), and still others an ecological approach (Leeds 1984). The differences in these theoretical approaches can be seen in terms of how they influence practice in various programs currently offered in different states.

Social Learning Practice Models. Intensive family preservation services that are based on social learning theory focus on behaviors and interactions within the family that are causing the risk of placement. These programs may involve parent training, parent consultation, communication training, and problem solving (Barth 1990). They are less concerned that all family members participate simultaneously than they are with improving the interaction patterns of various dyads in the family.

Family Systems Practice Models. Programs that are based on a family systems or structural family therapy approach usually prefer to see all family members simultaneously and concentrate on building trust within the family, establishing the authority of the parent(s), and delineating family boundaries (Barth 1990). The systemic relationships that are maladaptive and are creating the risk are identified, and the family works toward change of the total family system.

Functional Practice Models. Functional theory views client empowerment and client ownership of change and growth as fundamental (Dore 1990). The caseworker demonstrates respect for the client as a colleague in a working relationship and sets a time-limited, structured process for problem solving. Beyond these standard objectives, workers in functionally-oriented programs advocate for the family to change the larger social system in which it exists: to link families with resources; to generate new resources or redistribute other resources; and to promote more effective social policy. These programs thus have a larger social view than other programs, and workers in them take more responsibility for social change (Grigsby 1993). Functional family preservation practice is most commonly found in Australia (O'Brien 1989).

Family Preservation as One Type of Family-Based Program

June Lloyd (Lloyd and Sallee 1994) has conceptualized intensive family preservation as one type of family-based service to families, and she presents a visual depiction of this conceptualization that demonstrates how intensive family preservation programs provide an array of hard and soft services to families, to a greater extent than those provided in other types of family-based services, such as in-office mental health services (see figure 5).

Figure 5
Array of Family Preservation Services

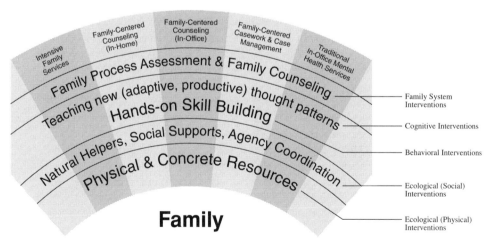

Reprinted with permission from *Protecting Children,* a publication of the American Humane Association, vol. 10 (3), 1994.

The availability of a full array of services, however, is critical to cover the differing needs of families.

The obvious goal of the new array of services is a system designed to provide the mix and intensity of services appropriate to each family's need. Currently, the most frequently provided services are casework or therapy at one hour per week or less and intensive family preservation services at five to fifteen hours per week. A major gap in services lies between these existing levels. . . . We use the term "array of services" rather than "continuum of services" as the term continuum is linear and does not accurately reflect the complexity of most families. We believe that families' needs for family preservation lie scattered through a grid (see figure 5). (Lloyd and Sallee 1994, 4)

REFERENCES

Allen, Marcia. (1990, Spring). Why are we talking about case management again? *Prevention Report:* 1–2.

AuClaire, Philip, and Ira M. Schwartz. (1986). *An evaluation of the effectiveness of intensive home-based services as an alternative to placement for adolescents and their families.* Minneapolis: Hubert H. Humphrey Institute for Public Affairs, University of Minnesota.

Barth, Richard P. (1990). Theories guiding home-based intensive family preservation services. In James K. Whittaker, Jill Kinney, Elizabeth M. Tracy, and Charlotte Booth (eds.), *Reaching high risk families: Intensive family preservation in human services,* 91–13. Hawthorne, NY: Aldine de Gruyter.

Behavioral Sciences Institute. (1987). *Summary of King, Pierce, Snohomish, and Spokane county Homebuilders service, September 1, 1986—August 31, 1987.* Federal Way, WA: Behavioral Sciences Institute.

Bell, John E. (1978). Family context therapy: A model for family change. *Journal of Marriage and Family Counseling* 4: 111–26.

Belle, Deborah (1982). Social ties and social support. In Deborah Belle (ed.), *Lives in stress: Women and depression.* Beverly Hills, CA: Sage.

Berry, Marianne. (1992). An evaluation of family preservation services: Fitting agency services to family needs. *Social Work* 37: 314–21.

Bloom, M. L. (1973). Usefulness of the home visit for diagnosis and treatment. *Social Welfare* 54: 67–75.

Cautley, Patricia W. (1980). Treating dysfunctional families at home. *Social Work* 25: 380–86.

Collins, Raymond C. (1980). Home Start and its implications for family policy. *Children Today* 9 (3): 12–16.

Compher, John V. (1983). Home services to families to prevent child placement. *Social Work* 28: 360–64.

Dore, Martha Morrison. (1990). Functional theory: Its history and influence on contemporary social work practice. *Social Service Review* 64: 358–74.

Dore, Martha Morrison. (1991). Context and the structure of practice: Implications for research. In Kathleen Wells and David E. Biegel (eds.), *Family preservation services: Research and evaluation,* 121–37. Newbury Park, CA: Sage.

Fiore, Joan, Joseph Becker, and David B. Coppel. (1983). Social network interactions: A buffer or a stress. *American Journal of Community Psychology* 11: 423–39.

Friedman, Alfred S. (1962). Family therapy as conducted in the home. *Family Process* 1: 132–40.

Friedman, Roger S. (1993, Spring). Homebuilders, family systems and false dichotomies: Reflections on cross-currents in family preservation thinking and steps toward integration. *Prevention Report:* 7–9.

Gambrill, Eileen D., and Theodore J. Stein. (1981). Decision making and case management: Achieving continuity of care for children in out of home placement. In Anthony N. Maluccio and Paula A. Sinanoglu (eds.), *The challenge of partnership: Working with parents of children in foster care.* New York: Child Welfare League of America.

Garbarino, James. (1977). The human ecology of child maltreatment: A conceptual model for research. *Journal of Marriage and the Family* 39: 721–35.

Grigsby, R. Kevin. (1993). Theories that guide intensive family preservation services. In E. Susan Morton and R. Kevin Grigsby (eds.), *Advancing family preservation practice,* 16–27. Newbury Park, CA: Sage.

Halpern, Robert. (1984). Lack of effects for home-based early intervention? Some possible explanations. *American Journal of Orthopsychiatry* 54: 33–42.

Halpern, Robert. (1986). Home-based early intervention: Dimensions of current practice. *Child Welfare* 65: 387–97.

Hinckley, Edward C., and W. Frank Ellis. (1985). An effective alternative to residential placement: Home-based services. *Journal of Clinical Child Psychology* 14: 209–11.

Hirsch, Josephine S., Jacquelynne Gailey, and Eleanor Schmerl. (1976). A child welfare agency's program of service to children in their own homes. *Child Welfare* 55 (3): 193–205.

Jiordano, Mary. (1990, Spring). Intensive family preservation services to crack-using parents: Hope and help in preserving the family. *Prevention Report:* 4.

Johnson, Will. (1994). *Effects of numbers of in-person visits on rates of child maltreatment recurrence.* Paper presented to the Second Annual Roundtable on Outcome Measures in Child Welfare Services. San Antonio, March 30–April 1, 1994.

Kagan, Richard M., and Shirley B. Schlosberg. (1989). *Families in perpetual crisis.* New York: W. W. Norton.

Kinney, Jill, David A. Haapala, and Charlotte Booth. (1981). *Overview of the Homebuilders program.* Federal Way, WA: Behavioral Sciences Institute.

Kinney, Jill, David A. Haapala, and Charlotte Booth. (1991). Getting off to a good start. In Jill Kinney, David A. Haapala, and Charlotte Booth, *Keeping families together: The Homebuilders model,* 55–70. Hawthorne, NY: Aldine de Gruyter.

Kinney, Jill, David A. Haapala, Charlotte Booth, and Shelley Leavitt. (1990). The Homebuilders model. In James K. Whittaker, Jill Kinney, Elizabeth M. Tracy, and Charlotte Booth (eds.), *Reaching high-risk families: Intensive family preservation in human services,* 31–64. Hawthorne, NY: Aldine de Gruyter.

Kinney, Jill M., Barbara Madsen, Thomas Fleming, and David A. Haapala. (1977). Homebuilders: Keeping families together. *Journal of Consulting and Clinical Psychology* 45: 667–73.

Lahti, Janet, and Jacquelyn Dvorak. (1981). Coming home from foster care. In Anthony N. Maluccio and Paula A. Sinanoglu (eds.), *The challenge of partnership: Working with parents of children in foster care.* New York: Child Welfare League of America.

Leeds, Stephen J. (1984). *Evaluation of Nebraska's intensive services project.* Iowa City: National Resource Center on Family Based Services.

Lloyd, June C., and Marvin E. Bryce. (1984). *Placement prevention and family reunification: A practitioner's handbook.* Iowa City: National Resource Center on Family Based Services.

Lloyd, June C., and Alvin L. Sallee. (1994). The challenge and potential of family preservation services in the public child welfare system. *Protecting Children* 10: 3–6.

Lyle, Charles G. (1993). *Client outcome evaluation in a large public social service agency: The Ramsey County experience.* First Annual Roundtable on Outcome Measures in Child Welfare Services. San Antonio, March 11–13, 1993.

Montgomery, David G., Donald A. Shulman, and George Pfenninger. (1972). Use of social work teams to provide services to children in their own homes. *Child Welfare* 51: 587–97.

Nelson, Kristine E., Miriam J. Landsman, and Marcia S. Allen. (1991). Must family-centered programs be home-based? In David Haapala, Vera O. Pina, and Cecelia Sudia (eds.), *Empowering families: Papers from the fourth annual conference on family-based services.* Riverdale, IA: National Association for Family-Based Services.

Nelson, Kristine E., Miriam J. Landsman, and Wendy Deutelbaum. (1990). Three models of family-centered placement prevention services. *Child Welfare* 69: 3–21.

Norman, Abigail. (1985). *Keeping families together: The case for family preservation.* New York: Edna McConnell Clark Foundation.

O'Brien, Wendy. (1989). Family support work: The Alys Keys family case model. *Australian Child and Family Welfare* 13: 22–26.

O'Keefe, R. A. (1973). Home Start: Partnership with parents. *Children Today* 2 (1): 12–16.

Patterson, Gerald R., Patricia Chamberlain, and John B. Reid. (1982). A comparative evaluation of a parent-training program. *Behavior Therapy* 13: 638–50.

Reid, William J., Richard M. Kagan, and Shirley B. Schlosberg (1988). Prevention of placement: Critical factors in program success. *Child Welfare* 67: 25–36.

Ronnau, John P., and Alvin L. Sallee. (1995). *Theoretical framework for family preservation.* Las Cruces: Family Preservation Institute, New Mexico State University.

Rook, Karen S. (1984). The negative side of social interaction: Impact on psychological well-being. *Journal of Personality and Social Psychology* 46: 1097–1108.

Rooney, Ronald H. (1981). A task-centered reunification model for foster care. In Anthony Maluccio and Paula A. Sinanoglu (eds.), *The challenge of partnership: Working with parents of children in foster care.* New York: Child Welfare League of America.

Rooney, Ronald H. (1993). *Strategies for work with involuntary clients.* New York: Columbia University Press.

Schlachter, Roy H. (1975). Home counseling of adolescents and parents. *Social Work* 20: 427–28, 481.

Showell, William H., Marcia Allen, and Ted Keys. (1984). *The Oregon Intensive Family Services and High Impact family treatment model.* Salem: State of Oregon Children's Services Division.

Soule, Charles R., Kaarina Massarene, and Kathleen Abate. (1993). Clinician-support worker teams in family preservation: Are two heads better than one? In E. Susan Morton and R. Kevin Grigsby (eds.), *Advancing family preservation practice,* 39–55. Newbury Park, CA: Sage.

Speck, Ross V. (1964). Family therapy in the home. *Journal of Marriage and the Family* 26: 72–76.

Sperekas, Nicole B. (1974). Home visiting in family therapy. *Family Therapy* 1: 171–78.

Stein, Theodore J., Eileen D. Gambrill, and Kermit T. Wiltse. (1978). *Children in foster homes: Achieving continuity of care.* New York: Praeger.

Stewart, Kenneth, LaNae Valentine, and Jon Amundson. (1991). Temptations of certainty: The problem with (the problem). In David Haapala, Vera O. Pina, and Cecelia Sudia (eds.), *Empowering families: Papers from the fourth annual conference on family-based services.* Riverdale, IA: National Association for Family-Based Services.

Szykula, S. A., and M. J. Fleischman. (1985). Reducing out-of-home placements of abused children: Two controlled field studies. *Child Abuse and Neglect* 9: 277–83.

Tunnard, Jo. (1988). Using written agreements with families. *Children and Society* 2: 53–67.

Whitaker, C. (1977). Process techniques in family therapy. *Interaction* 1: 4–19.

Whittaker, James K., Stephen P. Schinke, and Lewayne D. Gilchrist. (1986). The ecological paradigm in child, youth, and family services: Implications for policy and practice. *Social Service Review* 60: 483–503.

Part III

PRACTICE AND PROGRAM ISSUES

Chapter 5

FAMILY PRESERVATION PROGRAMS AND THEIR EFFECTIVENESS

There are now a few hundred programs operating across the United States (National Resource Center on Family Based Services, 1994). This section will review the structural components of some of the better-established and better-researched family preservation programs as well as their effectiveness at preventing out-of-home placement of the child and the savings accrued by avoiding placement, when this is known. Obviously effective implementation of a program requires a clear understanding of the program and all its elements: its theoretical approach to families and to help, its structure and delivery of services, its goals and limitations. Such an understanding necessitates a full review of the varying modes and methods of programs. There may perhaps be no perfect package of family preservation services. Indeed, this review will show that many programs achieve less than optimal outcomes. What is more troubling, and results from an incomplete understanding or "a loss of breadth of perception" (Friedman 1993, 7), is that many family preservation programs do not satisfy the most basic defining characteristics of a family preservation model of services.

SPECIFIC PROGRAMS

Homebuilders

Several evaluations have been conducted concerning the Homebuilders program. All have reported the program to be highly successful, although most studies have been done by Homebuilders' own administrators (Haapala 1983; Hinckley 1984; Kinney, Madsen, Fleming, and Haapala 1977). Because the main goal of Homebuilders is to prevent placement, evaluations of the program usually use this criterion as the sole measure of success. One study evaluating the Homebuilders program in the state of Washington (Kinney, Fleming, and Haapala 1977) reported that a full 97 percent of families served had avoided placement at a three-month follow-up point. Families had received a maximum of six weeks of treatment. From 1982 to 1986, the Washington program reported a success rate of 87 percent twelve months after intake (Behavioral Sciences Institute 1987b). The majority of clients responding to a survey said they had found Homebuilders to be very helpful (63 percent) or helpful (18 percent) to their families (Behavioral Sciences Institute 1987b).

In another evaluation of the Homebuilders and other programs (Pecora, Fraser, Haapala, and Bartlomé 1987), the success rate among 216 Homebuilders families at termination was 82 percent, less positive than that found in other Homebuilders evaluations but still impressive. In addition to using family preservation as an indicator of outcome, researchers used other measures of program success, including children's school adjustment, improvement of delinquent behavior, home-related behavior, and cooperation with the agency. Except in the area of cooperation, children made significant improvements from the beginning to the end of service, as rated by service providers. Parents also made significant improvements in supervision of younger children, parenting of older children, their attitudes toward preventing placement, and their knowledge of child care. However, because these ratings were made by the workers providing the services, they may be biased, although some researchers (Pecora, Delewski, Booth, Haapala, and Kinney 1985) have found that workers often underestimate their impact.

Another, more recent, study of Homebuilders, this one by Bath, Richey, and Haapala (1992), examined the case records of all of the 1,506 children served by Homebuilders in Washington from 1985 to 1988. The researchers found placement-avoidance rates in this group similar to those reported in previous Homebuilders evaluations but looked more closely at the characteristics of children and families associated with placement. They found a nonlinear relationship between children's ages and placement: placement was more likely for infants (19 percent were placed) and adolescents (19 percent were placed) than for those in the three- to nine-year-old group (around 11 percent were placed). Among parent characteristics, only parental mental health problems and a low family income (and receipt of public assistance) were associated with child removal.

Beyond these general correlates of placement, the researchers found that other correlates differ with the age of the child. In three multivariate analyses of the three age groups (birth to two, three to nine, and ten to seventeen), the researchers found that

> for infants the predictors consist solely of parental variables [single parent-hood, parental mental health]; for the middle age group predictors relate to the case status or diagnosis [child neglect, developmental disability, child mental health, special education needs, inpatient psychiatric history]; while for older children and youths the predictors are primarily behavioral [family income, male gender of the child, delinquency, previous removal]. (Bath, Richey, and Haapala 1992, 399–400)

Fraser, Pecora, and Haapala (1991) evaluated the Homebuilders programs in Washington and Utah and reported most placement statistics and correlates of program outcomes for each state separately, based on the acknowledgment that, as discussed earlier, public policy about child welfare is primarily determined at the state level rather than the federal level, and there is great variation from state to state in decision making about the placement of children into foster care. Fraser and colleagues concluded that implementation of permanency planning practice and PL 96–272 is much less intensive in Washington than in Utah, and child removal is much more prevalent in Washington because of increased sensitivity to and public outrage about children's deaths and injuries. They caution against state-by-state comparisons "given these differences and the influences that other environmental factors may exert" (Fraser, Pecora, and Haapala 1991, 154).

Fraser, Pecora, and Haapala (1991) found that 92 percent of the families served by the Washington program were still intact at case termination. This study has been the most rigorous evaluation of the Homebuilders program to date, and it provided much specific information on the correlates of success and failure of the program. In Washington, family preservation was more likely when incremental service goals had been attained, when the child was younger than thirteen, when the child had been in the home at intake, when the child had not been removed previously, when the family had not requested child placement at intake, when parental functioning was not impaired by mental illness, when parents could meet the physical needs of the child, and when the child was not involved with alcohol or other drugs. Many of these correlates were substantiated in a more rigorous statistical treatment of the data using event history analysis, except that this more rigorous analysis showed that placement was much less likely among minority children, controlling for other factors (Fraser, Pecora, Popuang, and Haapala 1992).

Homebuilders computes (albeit simplistically) the average cost of serving a family at $2,600 (Behavioral Sciences Institute 1987a). Costs vary with the presenting problem of the family, with higher costs for families in conflict and child abusing or neglecting families and lower costs for families with developmental disabilities. This cost of $2,600 compares well with a cost of $7,186 if the child had entered foster care for an average stay of 19.4 months. Kinney, Haapala, and Booth (1991) revised those dollar amounts to a cost of $2,700 per child in 1991, compared to a cost of $7,813 for 19.4 months of family foster care. The estimated costs of more restrictive foster care placements are of course higher (up to $102,900 for 14 months of long-term psychiatric institutionalization).

Illinois

The Illinois Family First family preservation program was implemented across the state in 1988 through contracts with sixty private child welfare agencies and was evaluated in 1993 (Schuerman, Rzepnicki, Littell, and Chak 1993; Schuerman, Rzepnicki, and Littell 1994). The program was implemented simultaneously across the sixty sites represented by the agencies involved, resulting in significant regional and site variation in the structure and delivery of services. In general, the service model was less behavioral than that of Homebuilders. It used a family systems approach to improving family interaction and parenting skills. Provision of concrete services was an important component of service delivery in most sites, however.

The evaluation of Family First in 1993 (Schuerman et al. 1993; Schuerman, Rzepnicki, and Littell 1994) was the largest randomized experiment of the effect of family preservation services at that time. In six of the sixty agencies, families were randomly assigned to the Family First services or other conventional services. The evaluation showed no difference in placement rates between groups and demonstrated that placement rates were very low for both groups, bringing into question the validity of other programs' reported high placement prevention rates when no comparison group is used. It appears that in many locations, families at "imminent risk" of placement would not really suffer placement in the absence of services (see chapter 7 for a more thorough discussion of the determination of risk). The significant variations among regions and sites led the evaluators to question the consistency of implementation of the program across the sixty agencies. It appears that this evaluation could more accurately be viewed as sixty evaluations of sixty different programs rather than one large evaluation of a program carried out over sixty sites.

Iowa

A version of the Homebuilders model was implemented statewide in Iowa in 1987 and evaluated by Theiman and Dail (1992, 1993). The model was implemented with fidelity to its parent model, Theiman and Dail wrote, in that "caseworkers see families in their own homes, typically maintain a caseload of only two to four cases, and are on call twenty-four hours a day, seven days a week. The average service duration is forty-five days" (1992, 187).

The researchers found that 78 percent of families were intact at termination, and 70 percent were intact twelve months later (Theiman and Dail 1993). Factors associated with child placement included a family history of psychiatric care, out-of-home placement or other use of social services, a family income below $20,000, and having only one caregiver in the home. Using the Child Welfare League of America's Family Risk Scales (Magura, Moses, and Jones 1987), the authors found significant improvement in almost two-thirds of the indicators of family functioning. The researchers note that improvements were commonly found in child-focused areas such as parenting skills, school adjustment, and physical health rather than in family-level indicators such as financial situation or habitability of residence. However, the authors also found that scores on the Family Risk Scales were not predictive of child removal (Theiman and Dail 1992).

Families showing the least improvement in family functioning were those referred for parental dysfunction or chaotic/violent environments. A troubling finding noted in an earlier report (Theiman and Gaskill 1991) concerned service completion: 82 percent of families completed services, but completion was more likely among families whose parents had a high school education and household incomes over $30,000.

Michigan

Family preservation services were implemented as a demonstration project in Michigan in 1988 (Holliday and Cronin 1990). The program, Families First, was based on the Homebuilders model and maintained the staffing and service components of that model. The Michigan program had much stricter criteria for eligibility of families, however: long-term chronic neglect and long-term physical abuse cases were ineligible, as were families who did not appear likely to "respond reasonably or favorably to the service and attempt to make some positive changes to reduce the risk to the minor" (Holliday and Cronin 1990, 304). The exclusion of families with long-term problems or more intractable situations is contrary to the Homebuilders tenet that "we cannot know ahead of time if a situation is hopeless" (see chapter 4).

In an evaluation conducted by University Associates (1993), evaluators found significantly lower child removal rates in families participating in the Families First program compared to a matched group of children returned home from foster care in three sites of program implementation. The question of comparability of groups arises because return home from foster care was a historical condition not entirely present in the treatment group, and was a condition associated with many other outcomes and conditions of children [see Barth and Berry, 1987]). It is unclear too whether the children in the control group also met the eligibility criteria excluding long-term abuse or neglect.

Minnesota

The Hennepin County program of intensive family-based services uses a male-female team of specially trained social workers (AuClaire and Schwartz 1986). This program takes a structural family therapy approach and emphasizes parental empowerment. Treatment is limited to four weeks per family. As in Homebuilders, caseloads in the Hennepin County program consist of two families per worker. Treatment differs from that provided by the Homebuilders model in that only families with adolescents (ages twelve to seventeen) are served, two therapists are assigned to each case, and there is more concern with identification and expression of feelings than in the Homebuilders model.

An evaluation of the effectiveness of this model (AuClaire and Schwartz 1986) showed no difference between the treatment group and a control group in the number of placement episodes. However, groups differed in the type of placement, with children in the intensive family preservation group having a 55 percent success rate and using temporary shelter most when removed from the home. Home-based clients spent 1,500 fewer days in placement and had shorter stays there. Information on the cost of services is unavailable.

Scannapieco (1994) conducted a secondary analysis of data from forty-five families in the Hennepin County program and computed a risk score for each from thirteen risk factors including historical conditions, number of children in the family, and urban residence. She examined the relation of risk to four outcomes of the program: placement prevention, family functioning, program completion, and improvement in problem areas. All risks and outcomes were rated by the workers for the specific families they worked with. There were no significant differences between high-risk and low-risk cases in terms of placement prevention, program completion, or family functioning, but low-risk families were significantly more likely to improve in their problem areas.

The Ramsey County, Minnesota, program of home-based services, like other such programs, has the following characteristics: services are provided in the home, intervention is focused on the entire family, staff providing services function as a team, and services are focused on family functioning and strengths with the intent of preventing family breakup (Lyle and Nelson 1983). A case is deemed ineligible for home-based treatment if it involves mental retardation services, if long-term placement is extremely likely, or if the parents have demonstrated failure in the past to profit from therapy. Home-based workers in Ramsey County describe themselves as therapists rather than case managers.

An evaluation of home-based services in Ramsey County (Lyle and Nelson 1983) found that families receiving home-based services had a placement rate of 24 percent compared to a rate of 45 percent among a comparable group receiving traditional child protective services. The evaluation used random assignment to home-based services or traditional child protection services for an eighteen-month period. Home-based services used out-of-home placement much less (24 percent versus 45 percent) and were much cheaper, but they involved a great deal of structural change in the team if caseworkers (including the caseload size, teaming, and flexible hours). Home-based workers saw families an average of twenty-nine times compared to twelve times for traditional cases. They had a caseload of between eight and ten families, while traditional caseworkers had fourteen to twenty-two cases. The length of placement differed between the recipients of the two kinds of services: placements in home-based cases lasted an average of 67 days, while placements in traditional cases had an average duration of 119 days. There was no analysis of staff time, although cases were open between forty-three to fifty weeks on average, regardless of whether the families received home-based or traditional services. This time frame is much longer than that provided by many other intensive family preservation services and raises doubts about its degree of intensity as well as its cost-effectiveness.

Nebraska

Like most other family-centered services, the Intensive Services Project in Lincoln and McCook Counties, Nebraska, works to maintain the family through problem resolution (Leeds 1984). Services are home-based and include problem-solving efforts in the family's ecological system. Staff are available twenty-four hours a day, and family resources are maximized. The primary counseling is aimed at helping clients with conflict resolution, assertiveness, mobilizing and developing their resources, developing support systems, dealing with depression and anxiety, and problem solving. Homemaker services, parenting education, and service coordination are also provided.

Staff caseloads range from six to eight families, with a caseworker and a homemaker serving as a team and caseworkers functioning as both therapists and case managers. For cases to be accepted into the Intensive Services Project, the family must have recently become involved in the Child Protective Service system, have at least one child at imminent risk of placement, have a home in which the worker can work, have multiple problems with a new or limited situational problem (as opposed to being a chronic multiproblem family), and be willing to accept intensive services. The Intensive Services Project does not accept families with sexual abuse, chronic psychosis, psychopathic or sociopathic members, or chronic substance abuse. It also does not accept parents who have previously killed a child, parents who have previously had parental rights terminated, or families whose parents were mentally retarded or refused services (Leeds 1984). These restrictions are made because the goal in this program is immediate and short-term gains through treatment, not the long-term supervision of chronic multiproblem families. While this is a valid objective, these restrictions are lengthy and would exclude a majority of abusive and neglecting families.

A study of the Intensive Services Project in Nebraska (Leeds 1984) reported an 86 percent success rate (based on the avoidance of out-of-home placement) among families receiving home-based services in Nebraska. Families received an average of five and a half hours of direct service weekly, and much of this time was spent with the homemaker (two hours, on average), with a little less than two hours spent with the intensive services worker in the home.

New York's Lower East Side Family Union

Another early family preservation program that helped to guide the movement was that provided by the Lower East Side Family Union in New York City (Fanshel, Finch, and Grundy 1992), which was begun in 1972. This program teamed master's-level social workers with social work associates who were neighborhood residents of similar cultural and ethnic background with little formal training. The program's goal was to prevent the foster placement of children whose families were experiencing difficulties. "The Union sees this problem as one that frequently results from inadequate community support in such areas as employment and housing, as well as from inadequate provision and coordination of counseling, homemaking and health care services. Another basic objective, therefore, is to ensure appropriate coordination of such services" (United Nations 1984, 9). The Union contracted with family members and provided concrete services such as homemaking, psychological counseling, and coordination of agency service provision to families to help prevent foster placement.

A study of 160 cases served between 1982 and 1984 found an 87 percent placement prevention rate at case closing (Fanshel, Finch, and Grundy 1992). Among all families served by the program during the period covered by the study, problems with income, housing, and other resource deficits were most common; behavioral problems of children or parents were less frequent. The researchers summarized two key findings from their study: that mothers (or grandmothers) played a key role in family integrity and that a lack of housing was tied to placement risk and risks of other poor outcomes for children and their parents (Fanshel, Finch, and Grundy 1992). The researchers emphasized the important role of family preservation workers as advocates for their families in the community and in the social policy arena.

Northern California

The Emergency Family Care program in San Francisco and Oakland, California, offers intensive family preservation services within an ecological framework. The program emphasizes strengthening the family's social and ecological system and does not follow a conventional family therapy model. It treats parents and their children as partners in the process of strengthening the family. More than many other home-based programs, this one does "whatever it takes" to help families acquire tangible resources, including finding housing and day care for the family if necessary.

The program staff consists of case managers, who have a master's degree in social work, and family care workers, who usually have a bachelor's or master's degree. Each family is assigned a case manager, who supervises the work and workers, and a family care worker, who works most closely with the family. A team meeting is held weekly to allow the case manager and his or her family care workers to discuss all current cases and their status. The case manager and other family care workers offer treatment strategies and are good sources of information about community resources.

Depending on families' presenting problems, workers may help parents learn positive child-rearing skills to replace punitive and abusive patterns. They may also help families acquire adequate housing and apply for appropriate financial aid as well as learn how to budget the income they do have. Family care workers address any problems in the condition of families' buildings or living units and help parents fix broken windows and plumbing; they may also help to persuade landlords to fix heating systems, which are often permanently on or permanently off. Families are taught health care and nutrition practices and are directed to legal assistance if they need it. In these ways their resource deficits, which are assessed when they enter the program, are met with new resources and skills. Treatment focuses on contracts and follows a task-centered model.

Cases are served for about three months, and workers carry two to five cases at a time. Families are eligible for intensive services if they are at risk of child placement. They are not excluded because of mental retardation or substance abuse, as is the case in some other programs.

An evaluation of the Northern California program Emergency Family Care (Berry 1992) found that 96 percent of families studied were still intact at case termination, and 88 percent were still intact twelve months later. Family preservation was most frequent when the family's presenting problem was one of health, mental health, or single parenthood and was much less likely among families experiencing child neglect or parental developmental disability. The largest numbers of families had gains in their discipline skills and general child care skills. Family preservation was associated with family improvement in child care skills and in the cleanliness and physical condition of the household.

Oregon

Oregon has two family-based programs sanctioned by the Children's Services Division of the state: Intensive Family Support and High Impact (Showell, Hartley, and Allen 1987). Intensive Family Support programs are provided to families at imminent risk of placement, while High Impact services are more broadly designed to prevent placement. These programs are based on family systems theory and are aimed at healing relationships within the family. Treatment is expected to be short-term (from 90 to 120 days) and intensive. Families are assigned a team of two cotherapists (Showell, Allen, and Keys 1984).

A study of 261 families in the Intensive Family Support program in 1984 found that 88 percent of the children remained at home during treatment, and 73 percent had not entered any placement besides shelter care (which 7 percent entered) at a twelve month follow-up point (Showell 1985). The success rate for the High Impact program was 87 percent at follow-ups after three to twenty months (Allen 1985). The average cost of treatment was $1,132 per family compared to an average cost of placement of $4,032 per child (Showell 1985).

Utah

Utah's Family Preservation Units have been serving families since 1982 and receive training in the Homebuilders model (Pecora et al. 1985). As in other intensive family preservation projects, family preservation services are provided in the home, and staff are available twenty-four hours a day for up to 90 days. The primary objective is to prevent unnecessary placement. Toward this end, staff try to teach effective coping skills and awareness of community resources.

Families are assigned one worker each, who is usually a master's-level social worker. As in Homebuilders, for a family to receive services, at least one child must be in imminent danger of out-of-home placement. There are differences in implementation of the Homebuilders model in Utah, however: caseloads range from four to six families per worker, and families can be served for a longer period of time.

In an evaluation in 1987 (Pecora et al. 1987), 71 percent of the 120 families served were intact at termination. Cases were open an average of 65 days, compared to 30 days in Homebuilders in Washington and 37 days in Hennepin County, Minnesota. Like the Homebuilders program, the Utah Family Preservation Units reported significant gains in child school adjustment and behavior as well as in parental behavior, attitudes, and knowledge, but these ratings were made by the workers providing the services.

Fraser, Pecora, and Haapala's (1991) evaluation of intensive family preservation services in Utah and Washington found an 89 percent placement prevention rate at termination in Utah, with 53 percent of families still intact twelve months later. Family preservation there was most likely when incremental service goals had been attained, when the physical residence of the family was adequate, when the primary caretaker was female, when the family had not requested child placement at intake, when truancy was not a problem, and when concrete services had been provided.

CONCLUSIONS

Intensive family preservation programs have several distinctive characteristics, as delineated earlier in this chapter. One of those is the intensity of the services they provide, and another is provision of services where the clients live (the home or community), which reflects the philosophy of the settlement houses and other neighborhood-based social work earlier in the twentieth century. The Lower East Side Family Union, for example, provides services through a team that includes a social work associate from the neighborhood who is ethnically and culturally similar to the families being served.

This review has also shown, however, that so-called intensive family preservation programs are often simply home-based programs with little intensive service. For example, the Hennepin County program in Minnesota serves families for an average of 37 days (Pecora et al. 1987). This would seem on the surface to be short-term and intensive, but since the direct contact per day averages less than half an hour, the Hennepin County program is less intensive than other programs. The Homebuilders program reports an average of 1.7 hours per day in direct contact with the family, but other states that say they have implemented the Homebuilders model report daily averages of under one hour (.60 in Iowa, .86 in Michigan).

Home-based services are a basic and helpful element of the range of social services to families. They run the gamut from home-visiting with newborn infants and their families, to general health care services, to other services for which the home is the best site for transferring skills to individuals and families. The label *intensive family preservation services,* however, should be reserved for those services aimed at family preservation that actually are intensive. The ability of a program to sustain intensity of service for a family for many months is questionable. Evaluators need precise and specific measures of service rendered.

Evaluators of family preservation programs advocate for multiple measures of success in addition to the basic outcome of prevention of child placement. The Homebuilders and Utah programs also measure the extent of skills the children and parents learn. The Hennepin County program measures outcome in terms of the number of days available placements were used by study participants. This program also distinguishes between children who are placed in shelter care only, to be returned home in a short time, and children who enter foster care for longer periods.

Evaluations differ in their scope and rigor, but most have found that home-based programs, however designed and practiced, are associated with the avoidance of placement of children and are cheaper than conventional services. However, these evaluations have been weak in their description of the components of home-based services and in long-term follow-up of cases. In these ways family preservation programs have drawn much of their programmatic as well as evaluative methodology from the earlier and less convincing efforts of Head Start and Home Start. As this review has shown, these programs have incorporated elements of these earlier programs into their own methods while targeting more specific problems and goals of treatment.

REFERENCES

Allen, Marcia. (1985). *Report on CSD High Impact Services.* Salem: State of Oregon Children's Services Division.

AuClaire, Philip, and Ira M. Schwartz. (1986). *An evaluation of the effectiveness of intensive home-based services as an alternative to placement for adolescents and their families.* Minneapolis: Hubert H. Humphrey Institute for Public Affairs, University of Minnesota.

Barth, Richard P., and Marianne Berry. (1987). Outcomes of child welfare services under permanency planning. *Social Service Review* 61: 71–90.

Bath, Howard I., Cheryl A. Richey, and David A. Haapala. (1992). Child age and outcome correlates in intensive family preservation services. *Children and Youth Services Review* 14: 389–406.

Behavioral Sciences Institute. (1987a). *Homebuilders cost effectiveness with various client populations, 1974–1986.* Federal Way, WA: Behavioral Sciences Institute.

Behavioral Sciences Institute. (1987b). *Summary of King, Pierce, Snohomish, and Spokane county Homebuilders service, September 1, 1986–August 31, 1987.* Federal Way, WA: Behavioral Sciences Institute.

Berry, Marianne. (1992). An evaluation of family preservation services: Fitting agency services to family needs. *Social Work* 37: 314–21.

Berry, Marianne. (1994). *Keeping families together.* New York: Garland.

Callister, Jerry P., Linda Mitchell, and Grant Tolley. (1986). Profiling family preservation efforts in Utah. *Children Today* 15 (6): 23–25.

Fanshel, David, Stephen J. Finch, and John F. Grundy. (1992). Serving the urban poor: A study of child welfare preventive services. *Child Welfare* 71: 197–211.

Fraser, Mark W., Peter J. Pecora, and David A. Haapala. (1991). *Families in crisis: The impact of intensive family preservation services.* Hawthorne, NY: Aldine de Gruyter.

Fraser, Mark W., Peter J. Pecora, Chirapat Popuang, and David A. Haapala. (1992). Event history analysis: A proportional hazards perspective on modeling outcomes in intensive family preservation services. In David F. Gillespie and Charles Glisson (eds.), *Quantitative methods in social work: State of the art.* New York: Haworth Press.

Friedman, Roger S. (1993, Spring). Homebuilders, family systems and false dichotomies: Reflections on cross-currents in family preservation thinking and steps toward integration. *Prevention Report:* 7–9.

Haapala, David A. (1983). *Perceived helpfulness, attributed critical incident responsibility, and a discrimination of home based family therapy treatment outcomes: Homebuilders model—final report.* Federal Way, WA: Behavioral Sciences Institute.

Hinckley, Edward C. (1984). Homebuilders: The Maine experience. *Children Today* 13 (5): 14–17, 37.

Holliday, Mindy, and Robin Cronin. (1990, May). Families first: A significant step toward family preservation. *Families in Society:* 303–6.

Kinney, Jill, David A. Haapala, and Charlotte Booth. (1991). Getting off to a good start. In Kinney, Jill, David A. Haapala, and Charlotte Booth, *Keeping families together: The Homebuilders model,* 55–70. Hawthorne, NY: Aldine de Gruyter.

Kinney, Jill M., Barbara Madsen, Thomas Fleming, and David A. Haapala. (1977). Homebuilders: Keeping families together. *Journal of Consulting and Clinical Psychology* 45: 667–73.

Leeds, Stephen J. (1984). *Evaluation of Nebraska's intensive services project.* Iowa City: National Resource Center on Family Based Services.

Lyle, Charles G., and J. Nelson. (1983). *Home-based vs. traditional child protection services: A study of the home based services demonstration project in the Ramsey County community human services department.* Oakdale, IA: National Resource Center on Family Based Services.

Magura, Stephen, Barbara S. Moses, and Mary Ann Jones. (1987). *Assessing risk and measuring change in families: The Family Risk Scales.* Washington, DC: Child Welfare League of America.

National Resource Center on Family Based Services. (1994). *Directory of family based services.* Oakdale, IA: National Resource Center on Family Based Services.

Pecora, Peter J., Cathie H. Delewski, Charlotte Booth, David A. Haapala, and Jill Kinney. (1985). Home-based, family centered services: The impact of training on worker attitudes. *Child Welfare* 64: 529–40.

Pecora, Peter J., Mark W. Fraser, David A. Haapala, and Jeffrey A. Bartlomé. (1987). *Defining family preservation services: Three intensive home-based treatment programs.* Salt Lake City: University of Utah Social Research Institute.

Scannapieco, Maria. (1994). Home-based services program: Effectiveness with at risk families. *Children and Youth Services Review* 16: 363–77.

Schuerman, John R., Tina L. Rzepnicki, Julia H. Littell, and Amy Chak. (1993). *Evaluation of the Illinois Family First placement prevention program: Final report.* Chicago: Chapin Hall Center for Children, University of Chicago.

Schuerman, John R., Tina L. Rzepnicki, and Julia H. Littell. (1994). *Putting families first.* Hawthorne, NY: Aldine de Gruyter.

Showell, William H. (1985). *1983–85 biennial report of CSD's Intensive Family Services.* Salem: State of Oregon Children's Services Division.

Showell, William H., Marcia Allen, and Ted Keys. (1984). *The Oregon Intensive Family Services and High Impact family treatment model.* Salem: State of Oregon Children's Services Division.

Showell, William H., Roland Hartley, and Marcia Allen. (1987). *Outcomes of Oregon's family therapy programs: A descriptive study of 999 families.* Salem: State of Oregon Children's Services Division.

Stein, Theodore J. (1985). Projects to prevent out-of-home placement. *Children and Youth Services Review* 7: 109–21.

Theiman, Alice A., and Paula W. Dail. (1992). Family preservation services: Problems of measurement and assessment of risk. *Family Relations* 41: 186–91.

Theiman, Alice A., and Paula W. Dail. (1993, Spring). Iowa's family preservation program: FY 1991 evaluation. *Prevention Report:* 14–15.

Theiman, Alice A., and Jane Gaskill. (1991). Iowa Family Preservation Project: An evaluation. In David Haapala, Vera O. Pina, and Cecilia Sudia (eds.), *Empowering families: Papers from the Fourth Annual Conference on Family-Based Services.* Riverdale, IA: National Resource Center on Family-Based Services.

United Nations. (1984). *The family: Models for providing comprehensive services for family and child welfare.* New York: United Nations Department of International Economic and Social Affairs.

University Associates. (1993). *Evaluation of Michigan's Families First program: Summary report.* Lansing: University Associates.

Chapter 6

ADMINISTRATIVE AND
ORGANIZATIONAL ISSUES
Debora J. Cavazos Dylla

In the early 1990s, funding for family preservation programs was generous. As is typical of developing programs (Rossi and Freeman 1989), however,
sufficient time to implement them has not been a luxury available to most of
their administrators. Outcomes rather than processes have been stressed; programs have been evaluated according to product rather than how the product
was produced. As a result of rapid implementation and emphasis on outcomes,
evaluations of many family preservation programs have revealed poor or mixed
results. The conclusions at which legislators and other decision makers may
thus arrive is that programs are ineffective, poorly conceived, and based on
incorrect assumptions and faulty theoretical foundations.

One of the most important determinants of the success and very existence
of future family preservation programs therefore is valid outcome evaluations
of established and new programs. It is imperative then that family preservation
programs be administratively implemented in comparable ways so that outcome evaluations will be valid and will reveal conclusive findings. Currently
the available evidence from family preservation programs is practically impossible to interpret because the many programs maintain many different program
characteristics (Pecora, Fraser, Nelson, McCroskey, and Meezan 1995). Before
too many variations of family preservation are undertaken, it must be established that basic models work.

Lest family preservation be dismissed as a fad or a bad idea because of the
varied results, clear definitions of family preservation, including how it is to be
administered, must be established. This chapter will present current evidence
of administrative issues that are important to the implementation of family preservation programs. Clearly, there is a great deal of administrative program variety that somehow must be harnessed in order to establish definitive conclusions
about how family preservation programs should operate.

WORKER CHARACTERISTICS

Professional Qualities (Educational and Experiential Requirements)

Many family preservation programs propose that staff need to possess a balanced combination of education, experience, and personal qualities to perform well as family preservation services providers (Butler and Friesen 1988; Kinney, Haapala, and Booth 1991; Knitzer and Cole 1989; Stroul 1988). Yet no consensus regarding the minimum educational and experiential requirements for family preservation workers currently exists (Pecora 1990). Many family preservation programs hire a majority of graduate-level social workers (Pecora 1990), but the effectiveness of these programs with families is difficult to determine with conviction because they also hire workers with master's or bachelor's degrees in fields other than social work, such as counseling, psychology, sociology, and education (Butler and Friesen 1988; Kinney, Haapala, and Booth 1991; Knitzer and Cole 1989; Stroul 1988). In a review of home-based programs, Knitzer and Cole (1989) found that the program with the greatest placement-prevention success rate employed all MSW staff, and the program with the lowest success rate employed no MSW staff. Yet Homebuilders has found no correlation between effectiveness and a worker's educational field or degree (Kinney, Haapala, and Booth 1991). Programs prefer staff who have at least a few years of experience in working with families in areas such as crisis intervention, family therapy, parent training, and case management (Butler and Friesen 1988; Kinney, Haapala, and Booth 1991; Knitzer and Cole 1989; Pecora 1990; Stroul 1988). In addition to professional-level staff, programs also use support staff (for example, family aides, case managers, and volunteers) to work with families. Although this variety in workers may be programmatically necessary, it significantly complicates the process of establishing minimum requirements of workers (Knitzer and Cole 1989; Soule, Massarene, and Abate 1993; Stroul 1988).

Regardless of the types of degrees program workers hold or their level of experience, programs generally prefer to hire workers who have a knowledge base in crisis intervention, family therapy, cognitive behavioral therapy, and case management; who are skilled not only in traditional clinical skills (such as communication, active listening, and relationship building) but also concrete skills (such as household management, household maintenance, and medical routines) (Butler and Friesen 1988; Knitzer and Cole 1989; Stroul 1988); and who possess skills in linking families with community resources and advocating for families (Kinney, Haapala, and Booth 1991). In other words, program administrators prefer workers who are skilled in providing the soft, hard, and enabling services discussed later in chapter 8. Studies examining educational as well as experience level are necessary in beginning to establish a consensus on minimum requirements of workers because, as Pecora (1990) notes, "front-line workers represent one of the organization's most precious resources" (132).

Personal Qualities (Values and Attitudes)

While there is yet little consensus on the desired professional qualities of family preservation workers, programs are relatively consistent in the personal qualities they name as important. In general, these programs want workers who can provide therapeutic as well as case management services in work situations that are demanding, stressful, unstructured, unpredictable, and potentially dangerous (Butler and Friesen 1988; Kinney, Haapala, and Booth 1991; Knitzer and Cole 1989; Stroul 1988). There are external and internal categories of qualities that programs tend to identify as important for workers to possess.

Workers who exhibit external characteristics such as a sense of humor, resourcefulness, cooperativeness, adventurousness, a pleasant and positive attitude, and a warm personality are preferred (Butler and Friesen 1988; Kinney, Haapala, and Booth 1991; Knitzer and Cole 1989; Stroul 1988). Workers are also expected to be team players and to hold values that are consonant with the philosophy of family preservation. Workers who exude internal characteristics such as courage, autonomy, comfort with ambiguity, tolerance for differences, good judgment, common sense, conscientiousness, and pride in their work are also preferred, as are workers who set high standards for themselves.

Workers must also possess emotional strength, which is represented in personal characteristics such as compassion, creativity, sensitivity, consideration, and emotional stability (Butler and Friesen 1988; Kinney, Haapala, and Booth 1991; Knitzer and Cole 1989; Stroul 1988). Above all, workers must be flexible, intelligent, self-confident, dependable, consistent, responsible, and adaptable.

Despite the desirability of all of these characteristics, there are no known ways of identifying them in workers prior to hiring them. It is important to note that the Homebuilders program, which has examined worker characteristics carefully, has found no correlation between worker effectiveness and demographic characteristics such as sex, age, race, marital status, and parenthood status (Kinney, Haapala, and Booth 1991). More studies of this type and studies that examine other characteristics of workers are needed.

Cultural Competence

Much of the literature regarding family preservation work indicates that cultural competence is a necessary ingredient for success in working with family preservation clients (for example, Kinney, Haapala, and Booth 1991; Pellowe 1990; Soule, Massarene, and Abate 1993). However, explanations regarding why cultural competence is important and how it is to be used in practice are clearly lacking. It is essential that cultural information not be used in ways that classify or stereotype families but rather in ways that add to and illuminate work with them. Each family's level of identification with a particular culture and level of acculturation to the majority culture must be considered on an individual basis.

One study, for example, examined racial and cultural issues among workers in a Family First program in Illinois (Pellowe 1990). The study is based on the questionable assumption that race implies culture. (This assumption disregards the facts that different races may function within the same culture and different races may identify with parts of different cultures.) Pellowe (1990) asserts that Family First workers' decisions regarding families are based on their own characteristics, such as race, and that race impacts how clients respond to workers. For example, depending on workers' race, clients perceived workers as authority figures, figures to be feared, or figures with whom they identified. An alternative explanation to these findings that Pellowe does not address is that it may not have been workers' race that clients responded to at all but other characteristics such as their demeanor or age. It is significant that workers reported this information about families; families themselves were not consulted about why they responded to different workers differently. It is difficult at best, then, to conclude that race solely or predominantly determined clients' responses to workers.

Pellowe (1990) points out that Family First often considers workers' race in the treatment process; for example, if an authority figure is needed with a client and a worker believes the client perceives a certain race as authoritative, a worker of that race will be assigned to the case. This appears to be a reasonable practice on the surface as long as it is *determined* and not merely *assumed* that this is what the client perceives. The danger in this type of practice is that Family First uses workers' race as an indicator of specific qualities that people of any color may possess. It is important not to make presumptions or operate under stereotypes in enacting program procedures. Making such assumptions seems far too risky in dealing with families who may have already been victimized by other service systems.

An individual assessment of each family's cultural identification and/ or level of acculturation to American society is necessary. This type of assessment cannot be done on the basis of skin color or name or even the language clients speak but must rather be based on observation of and interaction with the family. For example, it would be wrong to assume that a Hispanic family who speaks both Spanish and English would need a Hispanic worker to be successful. Many Hispanic families continue to speak Spanish with family and friends yet are completely acculturated to American culture and might be offended that a program presumed they needed or wanted a Hispanic worker rather than a worker of a different race or ethnic background. Pellowe (1990) presents the results of a survey of workers' perceptions of clients' cooperativeness with treatment according to the race of both client and worker; higher cooperation was found when clients and workers were of the same race. Again, there are too many other factors that could have influenced client cooperation aside from race, but Pellowe (1990) does not address these. In addition, determinations of cooperation level were made solely on the basis of workers' perceptions; the philosophy undergirding family preservation practice calls for *mutual* ratings of cooperativeness by families *and* workers. Although cultural and racial issues may be examined in determining the success of family preservation programs, the implications of findings such as these tend to perpetuate the division between races and cultures and emphasize harmful stereotypes.

Soule, Massarene, and Abate (1993) present perhaps a more comprehensive picture of the role of racial, ethnic, and cultural factors in working with families. They maintain that regardless of ethnic background, workers typically differ in class and educational level from most clients, even when workers may share similar personal or family histories. This implies that it takes more than identification with workers on the basis of skin color or cultural sameness for clients to be successful. Perhaps more important than these factors is a worker's ability to empathize, to be sensitive and open, to be considerate of each family's situation as unique from others, and to disregard stereotypes in working with families.

It is important not to neglect cultural, racial, or ethnic factors in family preservation work, but it is also important not to allow these factors to be the primary or only determinants in work with families. These are simply factors to be considered in working with families, not factors to determine how to work with families. In a time when separateness and distinction among people is common, it is important that family preservation programs value diversity among people and not perpetuate division among them.

TRAINING OF WORKERS

Benefits and Purposes of Training

Staff training is an organizational support that can serve many purposes. For example, it should enhance the personal and professional development of workers and supervisors by igniting renewed interest, confidence, and hope in workers (Blythe, Tracy, Kotovsky, and Gwatkin 1992). Training, particularly for new staff, should help to establish appropriate staff attitudes and service priorities of family preservation programs (Pecora, Delewski, Booth, Haapala, and Kinney 1985). It should motivate and support staff as well as enhance high work standards (Blythe et al. 1992; Pecora et al. 1985). It should be an important aid to workers and administrators in managing stress and reducing or avoiding burnout (Blythe et al. 1992). Above all, training should help to keep an organization on track in maintaining its original goals, values, and philosophy.

When and How Should Training Be Conducted?

The timing of staff training will vary depending on the size of the program, its growth, and staff turnover (Pecora et al. 1985). At Homebuilders, training is very significant, particularly during a worker's first year (Kinney, Haapala, and Booth 1991). Homebuilders conducts an initial training program when workers are hired and another three-day training session three or four months later; workers then participate in various in-service and outside training programs (Blythe et al. 1992). It is perhaps more economically feasible to conduct training in this manner than to provide extensive training when workers are first hired; if workers do not stay with the job, precious resources may be wasted, and information overload may intimidate and overwhelm them.

A variety of modes of training may be used with family preservation staff, including, for example, lectures, role plays, hypothetical situation exercises, videotapes, and other experiential modes (Kinney, Haapala, and Booth 1991; Stroul 1988). Self-instruction models and tapes may be especially helpful (Blythe et al. 1992). Training should involve a combination of both reading and workshop experience (Kinney, Haapala, and Booth 1991; Stroul 1988).

Training Topics

Stroul (1988) suggests that three areas must be addressed in training staff: (1) the basic philosophies and beliefs of family preservation work; (2) process or technical skills (for example, active listening, modeling, role playing); and (3) therapeutic options (such as behavior modification, rational emotive therapy, mood control techniques, relaxation training, cognitive restructuring). While these areas cover softer skills, they neglect the hard and enabling dimensions of helping. Two additional areas then, that should also be included in training are helping workers provide families' concrete needs, such as household maintenance (for example, budgeting, how to repair broken windows), and advocacy and community-linking skills.

Orientation Topics. Several authors (for example, Blythe et al. 1992; Kinney, Haapala, and Booth 1991) recommend that initial training sessions incorporate historical perspective of how family preservation programs emerged in the human services field, so that the basic philosophy of family preservation is understood in its context. Initial training should also cover administrative procedures and guidelines (Blythe et al. 1992). While the development of a standardized training package may be useful (Blythe et al. 1992), outside training as a source of new perspectives and information is also important for work with families (Kinney, Haapala, and Booth 1991).

Special Topics. Many family preservation authors (for example, Blythe et al. 1992; Kinney, Haapala, and Booth 1991; Stroul 1988) emphasize the necessity of training workers on a variety of topics that are specific to family needs (such as child and domestic abuse, suicide, mental illness, and drug abuse) and also specific to worker competencies (such as diversity and advanced therapeutic skills). Other topics may address systemic issues such as services available in the community, relationship development with other agencies, and client advocacy. Topics and objectives of training should be determined through a needs assessment of workers (Pecora et al. 1985) or at least in part in response to staff requests (Blythe et al. 1992).

On-the-Job Training

Finally, on-the-job training is essential for family preservation work, either by pairing supervisors with new workers (Kinney, Haapala, and Booth 1991; Stroul 1988) or by putting experienced workers with new workers (Blythe et al. 1992). Weekly peer supervision is also a helpful arena in which workers can not only acquire new skills and information but also model good teaching techniques with one another.

Supervision of Workers

The management of family preservation programs and workers should parallel the philosophy of treating families (Henderson 1993; Kinney, Haapala, and Booth 1991; Morton 1989). Essentially, administrators should model the principles that (1) staff behavior is best understood in the context of the larger organization; (2) assessment of organizational problems or situations involves all members who are responsible for action; (3) planning for agency change is based on the collective interpretations of reality and on the goals staff set; and (4) change in an agency involves all its staff (Morton 1989). In essence, if families are helped to understand that their survival is in their hands and that they have a purpose to which workers help them commit in the present, the same philosophy of empowerment and inclusion must be expressed to staff of family preservation programs.

Supervision of workers is a major element of the management of family preservation programs. Following the notion of parallel philosophies, supervision should be intense and should focus on building skills as well as teaching skills in a respectful manner (Blythe et al. 1992; Kinney, Haapala, and Booth 1991). Supervisors should assess, support, and solve problems with workers; help workers verbalize their problems and needs; and aid them in stepping toward solutions (Blythe et al. 1992). Good family preservation supervisors facilitate workers' feelings of ownership of, investment in, and commitment to the program by eliciting their suggestions about procedures and policies, seeking their input on decisions that must be made, and encouraging them to be creative and innovative in dealing with clients as well as in suggesting new paths toward which the program should venture (Henderson 1993). Workers who feel empowered in their work will feel greater ownership in their organization.

Family preservation supervisors should supervise in nontraditional ways. For example, since workers see families beyond normal working hours, supervisors should be available to workers beyond normal working hours (Blythe et al. 1992). Morton (1989) identifies seven essential roles of supervisors in family preservation programs. A supervisor should be (1) an enabler of communication, (2) a mediator of needs and conflict, (3) an integrator of energy, (4) a builder of linkages, (5) a provider of both confrontation and support, (6) a sharer of risks, and (7) a procurer of resources. Inherent in these roles are the elements of informal support and relationship building between worker and supervisor. For example, supervisors may provide workers with concrete assistance, such as helping them with directions and giving them community services information, as well as personal support, such as taking workers out to lunch, arranging birthday celebrations, and acknowledging other events that have personal meaning (Blythe et al. 1992).

A strengths-based view of workers is necessary in all supervisory actions. Supervisors should ask, for example, what a worker needs to be better equipped to deal with families (Blythe et al. 1992). Supervisor interactions with workers may thus be focused on helping them build new skills through exercises such as role playing, brainstorming, group problem solving, and constructive feedback. Supervisors should help workers learn from both successes and failures through the consistent exhibition of high levels of acknowledgment, consideration, reinforcement, and encouragement (Stroul 1988).

Good supervision will help reduce worker burnout (Stroul 1988). Specifically, supervisors are most effective in meeting worker needs and preventing burnout when workers are exposed to both individual and group supervision on a regular basis; when techniques such as a buddy system (pairing workers) are used, or workers at least have access to backup, consultation, and support from supervisory and other staff; and when workers have regular opportunities to share information, ideas, problems, and support through meetings, staff breakfasts, or special staff events. Homebuilders' administrators and supervisors meet with new staff to discuss the mission and philosophy of the program as well as to explain policies and procedures and to demonstrate the kind of support and concern management maintains for workers (Kinney, Haapala, and Booth 1991).

Paralleling low caseloads for workers, supervisors should be responsible for a relatively small number of workers. Homebuilders' supervisors, for example, generally supervise six or fewer counselors (Kinney, Haapala, and Booth 1991). Group or team case consultation is provided once or twice a week, and individual consultation (from both supervisors and other team members) is provided as needed and requested by workers. Emergency consultation after normal working hours is also available to workers, as workers are available to families after normal working hours. Regular weekly meetings are necessary to add some certainty in the crisis-ridden work with clients (Blythe et al. 1992). Meetings oriented toward program issues and needs are also occasionally needed.

Though it is not the norm in traditional administration in human services organizations, peer supervision is essential to family preservation (Blythe et al. 1992). It may be spontaneous or planned between workers. To facilitate peer supervision, supervisors should strive to identify individual worker strengths from which other workers may benefit. It is important to remember that supervisors also need support. They should seek a network of other family preservation supervisors, through consulting with personnel from other programs, perhaps, and through attending outside training programs and conferences. With the explosion of computer interactive technology, family preservation supervisors can also communicate with others across the country through existing communications programs.

ORGANIZATIONAL MANAGEMENT

In-Office versus In-Home Service Provision

The issue of where family preservation services are to be provided to families is an important one. In a review of several family preservation programs, Nelson, Landsman, and Deutelbaum (1990) and Nelson and Landsman (1992) contend that in-home services are most appropriate for families with multiple concrete and therapeutic needs, while families who have limited, situational problems are served best by in-office services. The authors surmise that in-home services focus more on material needs and teaching skills, problems that are more typical of hard-to-reach families (such as families experiencing neglect, physical abuse, and youth status offense problems). In-office services, on the other hand, focus more on therapy and may be best suited for families with greater resources and higher motivation. An office setting can be used to establish structure in working with family problems, such as delinquency and sexual abuse, in which "family hierarchy and boundaries are most at issue" (Nelson and Landsman 1992, 147), and in cases where the worker's safety is a concern.

In-Office Services. Showell and White (1990) argue that in-home and in-office services can be equally successful with family preservation clients. These authors maintain that assessment information can be obtained wherever a family is congregated because assessment focuses primarily on the family's belief system; beliefs are internal to family members and therefore can be assessed as easily in the office as in the home. Showell and White (1990) maintain that in-office work is more convenient for the worker, less costly, and less time-consuming. They also contend that although clients may be anxious about coming to an office, this anxiety helps to facilitate change.

These arguments may be bona fide for certain therapeutic situations and certain family problems. However, they are not consonant with the philosophy of family preservation; rationales such as those outlined above seem to be justification for providing traditional services while proclaiming them to be consistent with the philosophical and values base of family preservation.

Finally, studies of in-office services are inconclusive because of methodological issues. For example, a study of 1,752 families in Oregon's Intensive Family Services program (Showell and White 1990) revealed no significant differences in reported treatment outcomes between families seen primarily in the office and families seen primarily in the home. This information appears to be compelling until closer inspection reveals otherwise. First, the data used to determine treatment outcomes were workers' perceptions of clinical success; it is difficult to imagine that perceptions of success would not be influenced by workers' preference for an in-home or in-office setting. Second, these perceptions were obtained *after* services had been completed, and information collected after the fact may be tainted because memories can distort reality. Other measures of treatment success (for example, clients' perceptions of success) could have been researched to make these findings more convincing. A third and perhaps more important factor clouding the validity of these findings is that the Oregon program requires workers to maintain a 75 percent success rate (measured by avoidance of placement) during service provision; this alone makes interpretation of any findings difficult and potentially moot. Further explanation of the benefits of in-office services for family preservation is necessary as current findings are not convincing.

In-Home Services. Literature regarding in-home family preservation services is derived predominantly from the Homebuilders program. Technically, supporters of in-home services advocate for services provided in the client's "natural environment," which typically involves the home but may also include the client's neighborhood, the schools, or the client's place of employment (Hawkins and Catalano 1990; Kinney, Haapala, and Booth 1991; Kinney, Haapala, Booth, and Leavitt 1990). Practitioners of this mode of service provision maintain that in-home services facilitate accurate assessment not only of family belief systems but also of behavior, risk factors, interactions, child management, and conflict (Hawkins and Catalano 1990). Clients tend to have greater trust and respect for workers, and workers tend to achieve greater credibility, because clients know that workers really understand their situation and their circumstances (Kinney, Haapala, and Booth 1991; Kinney et al. 1990).

Advocates maintain that in-home (or more accurately, in-environment) services remove many of the barriers of engagement and retention of clients. Problems that may be eased or eliminated when service providers go to families rather than the reverse include arranging for transportation; finding the energy and resources to get family members organized for office visits; and possible embarrassment or negative feelings about previous social services (Hawkins and Catalano 1990; Kinney, Haapala, and Booth 1991; Kinney et al. 1990). In-environment service provision allows for "teachable moments" in which greater skills acquisition, generalization of skills, and transfer of learning are likely to occur; when clients can practice new skills with supervision and receive immediate corrective feedback and praise, they are more likely to retain those skills and internalize them (Hawkins and Catalano 1990; Kinney, Haapala, and Booth 1991; Kinney et al. 1990). Further, "clients are more likely to experiment with new options when they feel comfortable" (Kinney, Haapala, and Booth 1991,

26). There is also a greater likelihood that all family members will participate when services are provided on clients' own turf. Perhaps most important, in-home services are more convenient for families, and families may feel less embarrassment about asking for help with their problems when they are in their own environment; the willingness and openness that workers convey to families by going to them cannot be matched by even the best of in-office services.

Research findings on in-home services only begin to illuminate their benefits. Homebuilders, because of their firm belief in the theoretical justification for in-home services, has not experimented with in-office services to any measurable extent. Yet their high rates of placement prevention add to the credibility of in-home service provision. A compelling study of family preservation services with families of children fourteen and under found that when workers spent over half of their time in a family's home, there were *no* placements of children at both service termination and one year later; however, among cases in which over half of workers' time was spent in the office, the placement rate was 28 percent (Berry 1992, 1994). Although the theoretical basis for in-home services appears very convincing, greater quality research is needed to support or refute both types of services.

Teams versus Single Workers

Teams. Another important issue in family preservation programs is whether services should be provided by teams of workers or single workers. Many family preservation programs use a team approach to provide services to families. Either each team member performs a different function (for example, one provides therapy and another provides concrete services) or all members of the team jointly provide all services (Soule, Massarene, and Abate 1993; Stroul 1988). The advantages of using a team approach include the following: (1) teams assure shared responsibility, mutual support, and assistance in working with especially difficult clients; (2) service continuity and emergency coverage are enhanced; (3) objectivity, expertise, and service variety are expanded; (4) team members may assume complementary roles with families (challenging versus nurturing); (5) there is greater flexibility in therapeutic roles; (6) some exercises are more effective with two workers; (7) families can observe two adults acting appropriately, collaboratively, cooperatively, and responsibly; (8) teams diffuse the potential for family dependency on one worker; (9) the possibility of reducing service time is enhanced; and (10) the safety of workers is enhanced (Kinney, Haapala, and Booth 1991; Soule, Massarene, and Abate 1993; Stroul 1988).

Some programs use teams composed of two professionals or one professional and one support worker (lay or paraprofessional). One of the advantages of using support staff is that "support workers are more likely to share common backgrounds with families, and are thus more able to develop rapport with families who will not use professional services or who have negative histories with such services" (Soule, Massarene, and Abate 1993, 41). Family support workers can often engage family members and create a bond of understanding and support because of common life experiences. Support workers may also help professional staff overcome distance between themselves and clients that is due to educational, professional, or class differences. Although this practice appears logical, it needs further exploration and research.

Disadvantages of using a team approach may include the following: (1) the intimacy of the worker-family relationship might be reduced when it is shared between two workers; (2) greater professional distance between workers and families may result; (3) the potential for conflict and competition between team members may surface; (4) logistical problems may arise (for example, coordinating schedules and responsibilities); (5) difficulty in separating therapy issues from other types of services could result; and (6) teams tend to be more costly (Stroul 1988).

Single Workers. Homebuilders is probably the most ardent supporter of single workers in family preservation programs. From the Homebuilders perspective, the preference for a single worker has to do with the design of the entire program; all elements of the model are interdependent. If programs have low caseloads and a short time frame (four to six weeks) of service provision, it is more difficult and costly and requires too much coordination to practice teamwork with individual families (Kinney, Haapala, and Booth 1991). If a program moves away from low caseloads and toward longer treatment, teams become more appealing and attractive. Proponents of the Homebuilders model do not necessarily object to team composition of workers; they are aware of its obvious advantages. However, if low caseloads and brief service time are maintained, teams cost twice as much as single providers.

The potential advantages of single workers include the following: (1) there is a greater potential for integration and synthesis of family problems and issues; (2) the motivation of one worker could tend to be greater than that of two; (3) a single worker must act in the same manner to all family members in order to facilitate good communication; (4) one worker has total responsibility for all family members, which avoids the potential problem of workers' allying with certain members or subsystems of families; (5) one worker is less invasive to families; (6) it is generally easier for one worker to engage with families and for families to accept one professional; (7) there is a greater potential for building rapport between worker and family members with workers who provide both concrete and therapeutic services, which results in increased effectiveness of both kinds of intervention; (8) one worker is more cost-effective in short-term intensive interventions; (9) engagement and trust are easier to establish with only one worker; (10) one worker takes less time for planning, debriefing, and recordkeeping; (11) valuable information is not lost in the translation or transfer to another worker; (12) there is a greater opportunity for spontaneous interventions; (13) there are no negative coworker relationship issues such as control or hard feelings; 14) the line of accountability is not diluted; and 15) the sense of accomplishment or lack thereof is clearer (Kinney, Haapala, and Booth 1991; Soule, Massarene, and Abate 1993).

The greatest evidence of whether single or team workers are better is only experientially and theoretically sound; sufficient empirical evidence that one is better or more effective does not currently exist. This may be the wrong question, however; perhaps the right question to be asked is, "For which families, and/or for what types of placement issues is one or the other model more appropriate?" (Soule, Massarene, and Abate 1993, 41). The most important element in choosing single workers or teams is to assure that services are tailored to each family and flexible to meet each family's needs. Often one worker may be sufficient for a family, while at other times more than one worker may be necessary. There is no single recipe that will work for each family, thus the plan must be individually tailored for each.

Public versus Private Auspices

Another unanswered question regarding family preservation programs is whether services should be provided by private agencies, public institutions, or some combination of the two. As is the case with many other areas of family preservation, because the field is truly in its infancy, the evidence on this issue is minimal, and results are mixed and difficult to interpret conclusively. For example, in a study of four public and three private family preservation providers in four states, Nelson and Allen (1989) found that private agencies tended to serve more challenging families, but there were few differences between private and public agencies in how services were provided. Across the board, therapeutic services were provided most frequently, and few supportive services were provided by either private or public agencies. Public agencies tended to provide greater case management, and, when offered, supportive services were provided to families from both within and outside of the agency. Private agencies tended to help families in coordinating community services rather than providing them directly more often than public agencies did; supportive services were generally provided by community agencies other than the private agencies. The findings of this study, however, are somewhat problematic because the clients served by public and private agencies are not comparable.

In another study of eleven private and public agencies, Nelson and Landsman (1992) found that private agencies tended to serve more difficult families (for example, poorer families with problems of greater severity) than public agencies did. The cost of private agencies was also found to be less than that of public agencies. Private providers tended to have greater flexibility, more service time with families, more time in families' homes, and lower caseloads than public agencies. Private agencies spent less time on administrative paperwork and more time consulting with other workers. However, private agencies were dependent on public agencies for referrals and had to follow strict reporting requirements to keep the public agencies informed of actions taken with families. It is important to note that private agency providers reported that their cases failed most often because of inappropriate case goals established solely by the public agency providers.

In a comprehensive examination of the private Illinois Family First program, which contracts with the state Department of Children and Family Services (DCFS), Howard and Johnson (1990) found that problems between the two agencies stemmed predominantly from a difference in philosophy, with the private agency maintaining a family orientation and the public agency having a child orientation. This difference in philosophy resulted in a lack of trust between providers, which led to a decreased number of referrals and/or referrals of lower-risk cases from the public agency to the private agency. DCFS subsequently became more vigilant in scrutinizing the private agency through such means as holding more meetings and requiring excessive documentation.

Howard and Johnson (1990) observed that the presence of a liaison between DCFS and Family First seemed to ease the misunderstandings between agencies and to enhance trust somewhat. Thus collaboration between public and private workers appears to be crucial to the public-private relationship. For example, practices such as joint first visits between public and private workers as well as increased consultation between the two workers may be necessary. This study showed that when joint visits occurred, families appeared to benefit.

The Howard and Johnson (1990) study raises a number of issues in need of resolution, particularly in light of the funds coming to public agencies from the 1993 Family Preservation and Family Support Act. For example, how much information about the family should be shared between the public agency and the private agency? How should cases be closed (that is, jointly or separately)?

Unfortunately, there is no clear consensus on which kind of agency is better equipped to provide services or how procedures should be established when public agencies contract with private agencies. Further exploration of these relationships is undeniably necessary.

Pecora, Kinney, Mitchell, and Tolley (1990) suggest that the question today is not whether to contract but rather which services are most effectively and most appropriately contracted to private agencies. It seems that all options are potentially viable. However, there must be philosophical congruency in all programs that provide family preservation services. As long as all providers of family preservation are philosophically consistent with the values of family preservation, service provision should be acceptable from any provider.

An Organizational Model of Management for Family Preservation

Whittaker (1991) contends that family preservation programs should function within organizational models of management that affirm not only practice but also administration and research; in essence, "we cannot practice family empowerment in an organizational structure that is paternalistic, nonsupportive, uncommunicative, sexist" (299). Historically, human service fields such as social work embraced a human relations model of administration that was centered around worker satisfaction (Grasso 1993). However, because this model has not proven to be empirically sound, human services have moved more toward a classical, bureaucratic model in which control of the worker and productivity are stressed (Grasso 1993). Many (for example, Austin 1989; Lewis, Lewis, and Souflée 1991; Patti 1983; Weiner 1990), however, have suggested that social work in particular but other fields as well do not use exclusively either a classical or a human relations model of operation but rather elements of both. Rino Patti (1983) predicted that human services would move toward an organizational model of management that is specific to social welfare and working with human behavior, human behavior change, and the environment.

Family preservation programs and specifically their administrators have the opportunity to lead the way in defining and designating elements of this new model. Just as the concept and values of family preservation represent a move back toward a more traditional paradigm of social work practice that encompasses an ecological perspective, social action, and community involvement, the administrations of these programs have the opportunity to define a model of management that is appropriate and specific for these types of services.

The Homebuilders Model of Management. The Homebuilders model provides a number of indicators that may begin to define this new organizational management model. The administration of Homebuilders encourages mission-oriented research, exhibits entrepreneurial leadership, and models social action because its primary goals are to produce empirically-based practice, foster an entrepreneurial management style, and advocate for the purpose of changing public policy (Fraser and Leavitt 1990). Rather than viewing workers as producers of products (as the bureaucratic model does) or as satisfied professionals (as they are seen in the human relations model), the administration of Homebuilders views them as both personal scientists and social change agents simultaneously. There are four guiding principles that Homebuilders follows in enabling staff to be personal scientists and social change agents.

Administrative Principles. First, workers are encouraged to identify and exploit opportunities, for example, that will enhance program resources (entrepreneurial spirit and social action) (Fraser and Leavitt 1990). For example, staff are encouraged to actively seek agencies that are willing to be involved in the work of helping families by serving as referral avenues for help. Staff are encouraged to pursue political goals as well as clinical ones by advocating for social change and public policies that support families. Second, program staff are continuously reminded (for example, through training) of the value of the ecological view of families and are expected to be committed to the family preservation model. Administrators model this commitment by interacting with the social and political environment of the community in which the agency operates.

Third, Homebuilders services have been developed with great specificity, and any revisions, deletions, or additions to the practice model are carefully conceptualized and implemented (Fraser and Leavitt 1990). Administrators and staff share a common values base as well as common perceptions about families. Finally, data are collected for the purposes of advancing both the clinical and social action missions of Homebuilders. These principles are the guiding forces in the program's success; they are comprehensive and complex and require a commitment to the overall mission of helping families in need.

Administrative Practices. In specific terms, Kinney, Haapala, and Booth (1991) suggest four administrative practices that promote the principles listed above. First, workers' jobs are made as easy as possible because workers deal with very difficult clients; administration attempts to foster the ability of both clients and staff to maximize control over their own destinies. For example, staff have a voice in decisions that affect them; flex time is practiced, and there are no rigid in-office time requirements; staff are rewarded with compensatory time and generous vacation and holiday time. Mistakes are not punished because they are viewed as learning experiences. The administration tries to create an atmosphere that is "pleasant, positive, and even fun" (163).

Gurnack and Schoech (1981) raise the issue of incentive systems in human service organizations, explaining that incentives used to motivate employees in social service agencies are unlike those used in business organizations. For example, the business world uses systems based on productivity, output, quotas, and customer satisfaction, whereas human service organizations cannot even define consistently what productivity, output, quota, or client satisfaction should be, much less set levels to which employees should strive in order to be rewarded for attainment. Incentive systems are one of the main difficulties for human services providers; unlike business products, which can be quantified, human services products are often qualitative and excessively difficult to define numerically. Thus the incentive systems of social service agencies must be totally different from those of business and perhaps nonnumerical. The Homebuilders model provides a helpful precedent for human service agencies to follow in developing incentive systems for staff by focusing not on numbers for motivation but on the problems they work with and the goals they strive to attain in family preservation work.

A second administrative practice, then, addresses this need for appropriate incentives. Homebuilders maximizes communication, connectedness, and teamwork from a strengths-based perspective through such activities as yearly all-staff retreats, miniteam retreats, annual awards ceremonies at which all employees receive an honor of some type, and acknowledgment of special events in employees' lives (for example, birthdays and anniversaries) (Kinney, Haapala, and Booth 1991). Administrative staff take clinical staff to lunch, post "good works" notices on a bulletin board for all staff to view, and create T-shirts with the organization's name on them to distribute to staff. Staff are allowed to bring babies to work as long as normal operations are not interrupted. Homebuilders has even developed a "Paperwork Anonymous" group for staff who are negligent about getting paperwork done. These incentives are appropriate in human service organizations.

A third administrative practice in which Homebuilders engages in the involvement of staff in decision-making activities of the organization. As Kinney, Haapala, and Booth (1991) note, "time spent in reaching consensus diminishes time needed for effective implementation of decisions" (166). Administrators guide workers in the beliefs that there are very few perfect decisions; that issues are dilemmas, not problems; that revised decisions are not bad decisions but rather the best possible decisions at the time they were made. The

Homebuilders administration attempts to reach consensus among staff on agency decisions, though it balances this openness by retaining ultimate decision-making power. This type of participatory management is rooted in the belief that "involving staff with organizational issues increases the likelihood that the best ideas will surface and bad choices will be minimized" (166).

Finally, administrators support and validate staff by rewarding good work and by recognizing each staff person's uniqueness. In essence, Homebuilders uses the same principles with staff that are used with clients in a positive, strengths-based environment. Kinney, Haapala, and Booth (1991) summarize this perspective thus: "We focus on eliminating barriers to our work with families, clarifying goals, expectations, and values, encouraging communication, maximizing involvement in decisions, and providing support and recognition. These factors minimize staff turnover and keep the organization running smoothly" (168).

It is important to recognize that Homebuilders manages workers in ways that defy common practice. To many, this management style may appear disorganized and chaotic. However, because workers deal with families in crisis, clients who are unpredictable, and situations that are continuously potentially explosive, management recognizes the importance of remaining flexible, positive, empowering, and supportive. Homebuilders staff are managed in ways that are not necessarily difficult or particularly sophisticated but that require a great deal of trust and faith in workers and in the agency's mission. It is much easier and much safer to administer organizations from a control, or bureaucratic, perspective, and it takes more time to listen to staff ideas for new policies than to dictate policy. But perhaps it is more effective and more appropriate to listen, to empower, to support, to use the same methods with staff that staff are expected to use with clients. Perhaps some of these principles and practices are the foundation of the new organizational model of management for human service organizations that Patti predicted in 1983.

INTERORGANIZATIONAL RELATIONS

While internal organizational management is a major element in the formula of success for family preservation programs, external organizational relationships are another important element. Family preservation programs have the opportunity to facilitate changes not only in how the business of social welfare is accomplished but also in how people in need are viewed and treated. First, as a philosophy, family preservation has upgraded the status of case management and the case manager (Allen 1990). A major part of family preservation services involves attending to families' concrete and supportive needs and linking families to community agencies and services (Kinney, Haapala, and Booth 1991); this is case management in its truest form. The philosophy of family preservation places case management on an equal footing with therapeutic interventions.

The most important factor, however, in *maintaining* case management as an equal partner in services to families is how well communities and community agencies collectively support family preservation efforts. The long-term success of families who have received family preservation services will rely in large part on the many other human service programs in a family's community. Because family preservation services are intended to be short-term and oriented to crisis resolution, some of a family's problems will not be resolved at service termination. Thus part of the family preservation worker's task is to connect families to agencies and services in the community that can help them on an ongoing basis or in times of future need. These community agencies and services must first exist and, second, be willing to serve families. Family preservation as a practice has the opportunity to lead the way in helping communities become empowered and begin to adopt a firm position in "coalition politics"—that is, the politics of collaboration and coordination among family service providers not only at local levels but also at state and federal levels (Whittaker 1991).

Practical ways family preservation workers can begin to achieve a system of coalition politics and community empowerment are through, for example, (1) promoting and participating in periodic education and orientation sessions on the philosophy, purposes, and goals of family preservation programs and the need for community support; (2) leading or holding joint training programs with other agencies in which organizational collaboration is emphasized; (3) creating common screening and referral and other forms that can be used by many agencies; and (4) continuously networking and exchanging information with other agencies (Blythe et al. 1992; Pecora et al. 1995).

Unless community agencies and indeed communities as a whole operate under or at least support the concepts of strengths, empowerment, and doing "whatever it takes," family preservation will not be perennially effective. It is essential that family preservation workers continually educate and orient other service providers about the philosophy of family preservation and family support. Taking the lead in facilitating and fostering multidisciplinary and interdisciplinary action teams and building relationships worker by worker, agency by agency, are steps in the right direction toward community empowerment and coalition politics.

An important point that must not be overlooked in any discussion of family preservation is that family preservation programs must be one part of the continuum of services available to families in need. As Pecora et al. (1995) note, "Evaluation studies appear to suggest that we cannot expect single services to produce dramatic changes in complex social problems" (114). Family preservation is one piece of the puzzle, not the whole; it is not appropriate for all families or for all problems that families experience. Family preservation can be the facilitator of community collaboration, but it should never be viewed as the only answer or as a replacement for existing or potential community services. Its long-term success hinges on a community's maintaining a full range of family support services.

CONCLUSION

This chapter has examined a number of administrative issues that family preservation programs currently face, including characteristics of workers and their training and supervision, as well as organizational management and interorganizational relations. There are many unanswered questions and many areas in need of more descriptive, exploratory, qualitative, and empirical research.

REFERENCES

Allen, Marcia. (1990, Spring). Why are we talking about case management again? *Prevention Report:* 1–2.

Austin, David M. (1989). The human service executive. In Yeheskel Hasenfeld (ed.), *Administrative leadership in the social services: The next challenge,* 13–36. New York: Haworth Press.

Berry, Marianne. (1992). An evaluation of family preservation services: Fitting agency services to family needs. *Social Work* 37: 314–21.

Berry, Marianne. (1994). *Keeping families together.* New York: Garland.

Blythe, Betty J., Elizabeth M. Tracy, Avis Kotovsky, and Selma Gwatkin. (1992, October). Organizational supports to sustain intensive family preservation programs. *Families in Society:* 463–70.

Butler, T. E., and B. J. Friesen. (1988). *Respite care: A monograph.* Portland, OR: Families as Allies Project, Portland State University.

Fraser, Mark, and Shelley Leavitt. (1990). Creating social change:

"Mission-oriented" research and entrepreneurship. In James K. Whittaker, Jill Kinney, Elizabeth M. Tracy, and Charlotte Booth (eds.), *Reaching high-risk families: Intensive family preservation in human services,* 165–73. Hawthorne, NY: Aldine de Gruyter.

Grasso, Anthony, J. (1993). Developmental social administration. *Administration in Social Work* 17: 17–19.

Gurnack, Anne, and Dick Schoech. (1981). Incentive systems for mental health organizations. *Administration in Mental Health* 9: 79–90.

Hawkins, J. David, and Richard F. Catalano. (1990). Intensive family preservation services: Broadening the vision for prevention. In James K. Whittaker, Jill Kinney, Elizabeth M. Tracy, and Charlotte Booth (eds.), *Reaching high-risk families: Intensive family preservation in human services,* 179–90. Hawthorne, NY: Aldine de Gruyter.

Henderson, Kent. (1993). *An outline of systems change in Idaho Division of Family and Children's Services.* Ft. Lauderdale, Florida: National Empowering Families Conference, November 10, 1993.

Howard, Jeanne, and Penny Johnson. (1990). *Considering partnership: DCFS and private provider relationships in family preservation.* Chicago: Chapin Hall Center for Children, University of Chicago.

Kinney, Jill, David Haapala, Charlotte Booth, and Shelley Leavitt. (1990). The Homebuilders model. In James K. Whittaker, Jill Kinney, Elizabeth M. Tracy, and Charlotte Booth (eds.), *Reaching high-risk families: Intensive family preservation in human services,* 31–64. Hawthorne, NY: Aldine de Gruyter.

Kinney, Jill, David Haapala, and Charlotte Booth. (1991). *Keeping families together: The Homebuilders model.* Hawthorne, NY: Aldine de Gruyter.

Knitzer, Jane, and Elizabeth S. Cole. (1989). *Family preservation services: The program challenge for child welfare and child mental health agencies.* New York: Changing Services for Children Project, Bank Street College of Education.

Lewis, Judith A., Michael D. Lewis, and Federico Souflée, Jr. (1991). *Managing human service programs.* 2d ed. Pacific Grove, CA: Brooks/Cole.

Morton, Thomas D. (1989). *Redefining supervisory/management roles and systems to support family centered practice.* Atlanta, Georgia: Child Welfare Institute.

Nelson, Kristine E., and Marcia Allen. (1989). *Public-private provision of family-based services: Research findings.* Iowa City: National Resource Center on Family Based Services.

Nelson, Kristine E., and Miriam J. Landsman. (1992). *Alternative models of family preservation: Family-based services in context.* Springfield, IL: Charles C. Thomas.

Nelson, Kristine E., Miriam J. Landsman, and Wendy Deutelbaum. (1990). Three models of family-centered placement prevention services. *Child Welfare* 69: 3–21.

Patti, Rino. (1983). *Social welfare administration: Managing social programs in a developmental context.* Englewood Cliffs, NJ: Prentice-Hall.

Pecora, Peter J. (1990). Designing and managing family preservation services: Implications for human services administration curricula. In James K. Whittaker, Jill Kinney, Elizabeth M. Tracy, and Charlotte Booth (eds.), *Reaching high-risk families: Intensive family preservation in human services,* 127–43. Hawthorne, NY: Aldine de Gruyter.

Pecora, Peter J., Cathie Hanes Delewski, Charlotte Booth, David Haapala, and Jill Kinney. (1985). Home-based, family-centered services: The impact of training on worker attitudes. *Child Welfare* 64: 529–40.

Pecora, Peter J., Mark W. Fraser, Kristine Nelson, Jacquelyn McCrosky, and William Meezan. (1995). *Evaluating family-based services.* Hawthorne, NY: Aldine de Gruyter.

Pecora, Peter J., Jill M. Kinney, Linda Mitchell, and Grant Tolley. (1990). Selecting an agency auspice for family preservation services. *Social Service Review* 64: 289–307.

Pellowe, Diane. (1990). *Race and culture in Family First.* Chicago: Chapin Hall Center for Children, University of Chicago.

Rossi, Peter H., and Howard E. Freeman. (1989). *Evaluation: A systemic approach.* 4th ed. Newbury Park, CA: Sage.

Showell, William, and Jim White. (1990, Spring). In-home and in-office intensive family services. *Prevention Report:* 6, 10.

Soule, Charles R., Kaarina Massarene, and Kathleen Abate. (1993). Clinician-support worker teams in family preservation: Are two heads better than one? In E. Susan Morton and R. Kevin Grigsby (eds.), *Advancing family preservation practice,* 39–55. Newbury Park, CA: Sage.

Stroul, Beth A. (1988). *CASSP Technical Assistance Manual.* Washington, DC: CASSP Technical Assistance Center, Georgetown University Child Development Center.

Weiner, Myron E. (1990). *Human services management: Analysis and applications.* 2d ed. Belmont, CA: Wadsworth.

Whittaker, James K. (1991, May). The leadership challenge in family-based services: Policy, practice, and research. *Families in Society:* 294–300.

Chapter 7

Determining "Risk" and Targeting Appropriate Cases

Intensive family preservation programs have a primary goal of reducing the risk of imminent child placement. Risk assessment is not yet a science, and child placement into foster care can be a result of many forces both from within the family and from within the service system. As a result, defining the requisites of placement prevention can be complicated. This chapter will discuss the current state of knowledge on the assessment of risk of placement and risk of continued mistreatment and will offer suggestions to make risk assessment more relevant to family preservation practice models.

THE ROLE OF RISK IN THE PRESERVATION OF FAMILIES

Intensive family preservation programs are aimed at families at risk of placement of one or more children because of abuse or neglect. This risk of placement is usually a result of family difficulties or dysfunction. Intensive family preservation services work to remove or reduce the problems that may lead to placement, whatever those may be for a particular family. Therefore, in targeting services to appropriate families, practitioners and policy makers must be aware of the empirically sound family and environmental characteristics correlated with abuse and neglect in addition to the correlates of placement of children into foster care, which are sometimes different.

This tenuous balance between preventing unnecessary removal while reducing the risk of abuse or neglect is most directly addressed by assessing the risks present in a family and its environment. A focus purely on the prevention of further abuse would result in the removal of children in all risky situations, regardless of the level of risk. As discussed in previous chapters, such indiscriminate placement of children ignores the role of families in children's development and the potential effects of placement, which are equally negative. Therefore, the assessment of risk factors should result in a determination of the *level* of risk present in the family, with less risky families receiving less intensive services and less intrusion into family life.

Although the goal of services is to preserve the family, the safety of the child(ren) is still the paramount concern. The primary question is, Do programs that aim to prevent the imminent danger of placement succeed also in removing the risk of further abuse? If they do not, and abuse subsequently occurs, then the value of family preservation is questioned.

For this and other reasons, assessment of risk should be an ongoing process, beginning with a thorough and comprehensive assessment at the investigation stage and continuing throughout the provision of services with follow-up assessments six months or one year later. Contrary to the assertion by some that the discovery and assessment of risk during an investigation of an allegation of abuse or neglect are antithetical to establishing a helping relationship with a family (Pelton 1991), a sensitive and thorough discussion of risk factors with family members (incorporating a discussion of family strengths as well) can help to set the stage for a productive and realistic treatment relationship (DeJong and Miller 1995; Sandau-Beckler and Salcido 1992).

It is also necessary to ask the question, At risk of what? Definitions of "at-risk" families remain vague. Every family preservation program uses the term, but with varying meanings. The description of families at risk has ranged from "families who are poor and headed by a single parent and families of adolescents" (Landsman 1985, 1) to families with members "judged as having high potential for removal to another living situation" (Kinney, Madsen, Fleming, and Haapala 1977, 670–71). In some contexts, "at-risk" is not defined at all (Blythe, Salley, and Jayaratne 1994; Ruger and Wooten 1982). Ambiguity thus clouds the understanding of programs designed to reach families at risk.

Risk assessment is, or should be, focused on the prediction of future recurrence of child maltreatment (Johnson 1994). The distinction of systematic risk assessment is that it is future-oriented (Doueck, English, DePanfilis, and Moote 1993) and thus helps caseworkers make judgments based not on past behavior or the severity of maltreatment but on a clear assessment of the potential for continued harm to the child. For example, if the perpetrator of the abuse is removed from the home or if other situational factors preclude the likelihood of further abuse, preventive or preservative services are not warranted, regardless of the severity of an injury.

While severity of past abuse is an important consideration, it must be evaluated in the overall context of a range of risk factors in order to check the tendency to rescue children or respond overprotectively to traumatic indicators of harm. However, "a recent survey of states [Berkowitz, 1991] found that, despite the experimentation with or adoption of risk-assessment models in 42 states, most states still offered services to families based on the severity of mistreatment" (Doueck, Levine, and Bronson 1993, 450).

As discussed in a previous chapter, child welfare services are not intended to serve as a form of child rescue or as retribution for abusive or neglectful parents for past behavior. Systematic and objective assessments can help to diminish the likelihood that investigators, caseworkers, and other professionals will use child removal as punishment of abusive or neglectful parents or as an excessively protective response.

RISK ASSESSMENT AND DECISION MAKING

Risk assessment is an integral element of decision making in all child welfare services, not just those aimed at family preservation. In general, risk assessment serves two practical and important purposes: to target services to appropriate cases (and screen out "low risk" cases or divert them to other, less intensive treatment) and to aid in decision making and case planning of individual treatment based on specific risks. By assessing the types and severity of risk factors present, the child welfare worker can decide whether a child is in immediate risk of abuse, whether he or she should be removed from the home in the imminent future, what "safety plan" will initially help to reduce risk, and what services or other resources will help to protect the child from continued abuse (Pecora 1991a).

In many cases, a risk assessment system is a checklist or inventory of characteristics of the child, caretaker, environment, and abuse, which are rated by the child welfare caseworker during the initial stages of investigation of suspected maltreatment or the initiation of services. Many such systems are in use around the country, such as the Washington Risk Factor Matrix (Miller, Williams, English, and Olmstead 1987), the Illinois CANTS17B (Martinez 1989), the Child Welfare League of America's Child Well-Being Scales and Family Risk Scales (Magura, Moses, and Jones 1987), and the ACTION for Child Protection Child at Risk Scales (Doueck, Levine, and Bronson 1993; Holder and Corey 1986). Child welfare caseworkers and investigators systematically assess each characteristic identified on the checklist, with guidance as to how to rate and weigh each of the indicators in making a summary determination of risk.

McDonald and Marks (1991) reviewed eight risk assessment instruments and identified eighty-eight variables across all eight instruments, each of which contained different combinations of variables. They itemized these variables as pertaining to one of the following categories: "characteristics of the child; the primary caretaker; environment; maltreatment; the perpetrator's access to the child; the family; and parent-child interaction" (113). This array of indicators is indicative of the relevance of an ecological approach to risk assessment and services to preserve families.

Such relevance is also bolstered by the most recent research on predicting child maltreatment or the potential for it. A large study of abuse prediction and prevention in Philadelphia (McCurdy 1995) found the following factors to be highly correlated with the potential for child abuse: financial difficulties, social isolation, substandard or temporary housing, and a parent's history of physical discipline. Another large study of risk assessment, this one in Canada (Reid, Sigurdson, Christianson-Wood, and Wright 1995), found similar results; the key predictors of child abuse were a history of maltreatment, belief in physical discipline, and "complicating factors" (45) such as substance abuse, mental illness, intellectual incapacity, predisposition to violence, and social isolation. Clearly, a thorough assessment of risk must go beyond parental motivations or behavior and consider social and environmental stressors and resources.

Many of the empirically-based correlates of child maltreatment and child removal are reviewed in chapter 3 and can be fitted into the seven categories offered by McDonald and Marks (1991), given above. A decade of empirical research into formal risk assessment and the prediction of child maltreatment, however, has not found consistent results (McDonald and Marks 1991; Pecora 1991). Thus the application of risk assessment in family preservation has its benefits and limitations.

Benefits of Risk Assessment

Peter Pecora (1991b) identifies several characteristics of a careful and systematic assessment of risk factors present in a family. First, a good system identifies for caseworkers the most critical and relevant factors on which to gather information during investigation and the initial stages of case planning. Such a systematic approach also helps to structure decision making, reduce the likelihood of worker bias, and encourage careful documentation.

Another key benefit Pecora identifies as characteristic of a systematic and empirically-based checklist is reduced emphasis on the severity of maltreatment. Given that as many children may die from child neglect as from child abuse (Pecora, Whittaker, and Maluccio 1992), the severity of a physical injury such as a broken bone can mislead a caseworker into believing the likelihood of continued abuse is greater when the incident may be an isolated altercation, as compared to chronic, albeit more minor, abuse that does not produce traumatic bruises or other indicators of harm. Pecora gives an example of this, which was developed by Eric Oleson of ACTION for Child Protection:

> Consider the case where Mark, an 11–year-old boy, receives a concussion and head lacerations because he fell accidentally into a coffee table when his father pushed him during a heated argument over his first curfew violation. The family usually functions in a healthy fashion, and the father is aware that his concern for his son was translated inappropriately into an angry incident that had tragic results. This case would be considered low or moderate risk by most child welfare staff.
>
> Contrast Mark's case with the situation of a 19–year-old parent who lives with her 1–year-old infant in a one-bedroom mobile home 10 miles outside of a small town. The child, Susan, has been spanked over eight times a day but there are no bruises on her buttocks. However, Susan has colic, and her mother feels trapped in the house while her husband is traveling for business for weeks at a time. She expresses a great deal of frustration and anger with her situation and Susan's fussy behavior, but does not recognize any solutions. Which child's injuries are more severe? Which child is more at risk of future mistreatment? (Pecora 1991b, 79–80)

With more refinements, risk assessment systems will also help workers assess risk on a continuing basis to determine whether service provision is indeed leading to a reduction in the salient risk factors that were present at the beginning of the case.

Finally, several risk assessment checklists reflect a strengths perspective by including, along with indicators of resource and skill deficits, information on the presence of positive or ameliorative resources and skills on which the family and caseworker can draw to reduce risk and improve family functioning (see figure 4 in chapter 3). "Faced with the task of explaining when and why an adult puts a child at risk, it should be balanced with knowledge about factors that predict when an adult will nurture and protect a child" (Curtis, Schneider, and Calica 1995, 70–71). Such a perspective also helps to frame assessment and practice in a more culturally competent approach (Ronnau and Marlow 1993) by identifying client-defined resources. In this way, these risk assessment systems are coming into concurrence with family preservation practice models (DeJong and Miller 1995).

Limitations of Risk Assessment

The extent to which systematic assessments of risk are made is unknown, but recent evidence is less than promising. In a review of 129 cases of children in foster care in Baltimore (Slaght 1993), in which data on risk factors were gathered from case records as well as interviews with caseworkers, the researcher concluded that "most workers seemed to be more concerned with finding an alternative living arrangement for the child and getting him out of foster care than with documenting or investigating risk factors or remediating family problems" (148).

McDonald and Marks (1991) raise concerns as well about the accuracy of ratings made on standardized risk assessment instruments. For example, the parents' capacity for child care is conceptualized variously as parenting skills and knowledge, competency in applying knowledge, parents' feelings, parents' history of maltreatment, parents' view of the child, their beliefs about the family, and quality of parental affect toward child. The reviewers find that "the variation in the ways parental capacity for child care is defined, and subsequently measured across instruments, is representative of [the subjective and broad definitions of] the variables with the exception of the more objective variables such as age, number of children in the family, and services provided" (115–16).

Beyond vagaries in the definition of variables, McDonald and Marks (1991) also note a surprising lack of empirical validity for many of the identified variables: "Of the 88 variables identified in the eight risk-assessment instruments reviewed, 39, or less than half, have been examined in the empirical literature" (117).

This lack of empirical bases may partly account for the mixed findings regarding the predictive validity of risk assessment tools (Wald and Woolverton 1990). For example, Thieman and Dail (1992) found no relationship between level of risk, using the CWLA Family Risk Scales, and actual child placement following family preservation services to 995 families. This led the researchers to question the utility of this tool. Similarly, a large study of the implementation of the Child at Risk Field in New York (Doueck, Levine, and Bronson 1993) found a high false positive rate, from which the researchers concluded that "the [CARF] Final Risk Rating should not be used as a predictor unless and until there is further supportive research on its predictive validity" (464).

Doueck, Bronson, and Levine (1992) assert that establishing the validity of current risk assessment tools is made more difficult, if not impossible, by the inconsistent implementation of risk assessment models. These researchers have found large inconsistencies in the implementation of the Child at Risk Field (Doueck, Levine, and Bronson 1993). For example, "some workers, particularly the more experienced, reported that they tended to match [CARF] ratings to their impressions rather than allowing the CARF ratings to guide their decision making" (Nohejl, Doueck, and Levine 1992, 194).

This reliance on gut reactions, practice wisdom, or chance is evident in other studies of risk assessment as well. Berry (1991) found a risk assessment tool completed at intake to be more accurate at predicting actual placement outcomes after families received family preservation services than at predicting the determination of imminent risk of placement at intake (its stated purpose) for 367 families in a program in California. This author, like Doueck and colleagues (Doueck, Bronson, and Levine 1992; Nohejl, Doueck, and Levine 1992), postulated that caseworkers were relying on gut reactions or practice wisdom and overriding or ignoring the instruments.

Clearly, the faithful implementation of risk assessment models is a critical area of concern in determining the role of risk assessment in family preservation. As mentioned in a previous chapter, family preservation work is built upon empirically tested practice to reduce risks that have been shown to be associated with child maltreatment. Until risk assessment instruments have been further refined and more consistently applied, their applicability to family preservation practice will thus be limited.

Risk Assessment as a Guide to Targeting Services

A careful delineation of risk factors helps a child protective services caseworker to target (1) appropriate families for services and (2) appropriate services to families. These two goals are separate but interdependent; a family may be "risky" because of characteristics internal to the family and its members or because it lacks helpful resources or effective services (Curtis, Schneider, and Calica 1995).

Targeting Appropriate Families. Intensive family preservation services are usually reserved for families at imminent risk of child placement. Families in crisis that are appropriate for intensive services are those families who can be helped in the short term by concrete resources and basic skill building in parenting and family interaction. In a review of effective abuse prevention programs, Cohn and Daro (1987) summarized,

Those clients who received educational or skill development classes, such as household management, health care and vocational skills development, were 16 percent less likely than the clients who did not receive this kind of services to demonstrate a continued propensity for future maltreatment. . . . Successful intervention with maltreating families requires a comprehensive package which addresses both the interpersonal and concrete needs of all family members. (437)

Intensive family preservation services may not be appropriate, however, for families beset by chronic child neglect, substance abuse, and/or developmental disabilities (Berry 1993; Quinn and Berry 1995; Yuan and Struckman-Johnson 1991). Several recent outcome evaluations (Bath, Richey, and Haapala 1992; Berry 1993; Yuan and Struckman-Johnson 1991) have found that short-term services are less than sufficient in ameliorating problems of a more chronic and multiplicitous nature.

Research for more than a decade has established the difficulty of working successfully with families beset by chronic neglect (Cohn and Daro 1987; Polansky, Chalmers, Williams, and Buttenweiser 1981). "The difficulty of forming and sustaining parents' groups for dealing with the neglectful has been . . . consistently underestimated. . . . These are not people to be invited, by letter, to a series of twelve sessions of parent education in a local church basement" (Polansky et al. 1981, 218).

At the same time, program planners and practitioners must be careful not to select families based on their presenting problems or specific types of risk. The intensity of service and focus of this type of intervention may be more effective in engaging and effecting change with all types of families regardless of risk (Kinney, Haapala, and Booth 1991). This hypothesis remains to be confirmed, however (Dore 1993; Fraser, Pecora, Popuang, and Haapala 1992).

Additionally, specifically targeting family preservation services to families in crisis (precipitated by abuse or chronic neglect) is in part an attempt to make services more meaningful for families and in part a response to criticisms that have been leveled at general home-based family support programs, which have been faulted for poor selection of families for intervention and other research design flaws (Ayoub and Jacewitz 1982; Halpern 1984, 1986; O'Keefe 1973; Simeonsson, Cooper, and Scheiner 1982). If family preservation programs can be evaluated with rigor and shown to be effective with a high-risk population, their place in the continuum of child welfare services will be less controversial and more compelling (Nelson 1990). For these and other reasons, it is premature to withhold family preser-

136

vation services from families experiencing chronic neglect.

Targeting Appropriate Services. A careful and thorough assessment of the risk factors present in a given family will naturally lead to a discussion of the specific objectives, goals, and necessary services to ameliorate or eliminate these risks. Some, but not all, families will need help with parenting skills. Others will need assistance with concrete needs. Still others may need training in the health care of a child. Not all families will need a referral to counseling or to parent training. A systematic assessment of risk should indicate whether these conventionally offered services are unnecessary for a given family.

Many family preservation programs are case-management oriented. In such programs, families are linked with community and social supports (Allen 1990). This presumes, of course, that such supports exist and are accessible and that the short-term and intensive services to a family have emphasized the continuing use of supports after formal family preservation services have been terminated. It also presumes that the assessment of risk has focused not only on internal family characteristics but also on environmental dangers, risks, and resources. Until communities embrace a more preventive and supportive orientation and begin to value families, and until risk assessments are sufficiently comprehensive in scope and more universal in implementation, these presumptions will remain presumptions rather than actualities.

RECOMMENDATIONS

Family preservation services are directed at families at imminent risk of dissolution because of the continued or recurrent abuse or neglect of the child(ren). These are "high-risk" cases deserving of such an intensive and focused model of service with the goal of reducing risk to the point that families can remain safely together. (The more general risk of "rotten outcomes" [Schorr 1988, 1] for children and families is not the focus of family preservation services but is the worthy emphasis of broader family support services.) A thorough assessment of risk should help practitioners select appropriate high-risk families for service and track progress toward the reduction of those risks to safe or acceptable levels.

Many improvements in the assessment of risk are necessary before its role in the accurate treatment and preservation of families can be confirmed, including (1) further testing and establishment of the faithful implementation of models of risk assessment, (2) relating decision making and service planning to assessments, and (3) conducting assessment as an ongoing process. It is recommended that risk assessment tools and instruments be modified to reflect a strengths perspective and be periodically reassessed throughout the life of a case (including follow-up or booster sessions).

Tools currently meeting these criteria include those developed by researchers at the University of North Carolina (Kirk and Reed 1995). A battery of instruments has been developed by these researchers for a statewide evaluation of family preservation services. Included in this package of assessment and data collection forms is one for an assessment of family conditions at intake and assessment again at case closure. Each condition is measured on a five-point scale by the caseworker. Domains include the environment, social support, caregiver(s), and child(ren). Items are assessed as stressors or strengths to a family's overall condition, although it is unknown to what extent families contribute to the assessment of these items. Research and utilization findings will attest to the accuracy of these tools.

REFERENCES

Allen, Marcia. (1990, Spring). Why are we talking about case management again? *Prevention Report:* 1–2.

Ayoub, Catherine, and Marion M. Jacewitz. (1982). Families at risk of poor parenting: A descriptive study of sixty at-risk families in a model prevention program. *Child Abuse and Neglect* 6: 413–22.

Bath, Howard I., Cheryl Richey, and David A. Haapala. (1992). Child age and outcome correlates in intensive family preservation services. *Children and Youth Services Review* 14: 389–416.

Berkowitz, S. (1991). *Key findings from the state survey component of the study of high risk child abuse and neglect groups.* Rockville, MD: Westat.

Berry, Marianne. (1991). The assessment of imminence of risk of placement: Lessons from a family preservation program. *Children and Youth Services Review* 13: 239–56.

Berry, Marianne. (1993). The relative effectiveness of family preservation services with neglectful families. In E. Susan Morton and R. Kevin Grigsby (eds.), *Advancing family preservation practice,* 70–98. Newbury Park, CA: Sage.

Blythe, Betty J., Mary P. Salley, and Srinika Jayaratne. (1994). A review of intensive family preservation services research. *Social Work Research* 18: 213–24.

Cohn, Anne Harris, and Deborah Daro. (1987). Is treatment too late: What ten years of evaluative research tell us. *Child Abuse and Neglect* 11: 433–42.

Curtis, Patrick A., Mary W. Schneider, and Richard H. Calica. (1995). *Capella Project: Potential impact on public child welfare policy and practices.* Eighth National Roundtable on CPS Risk Assessment: Summary of Highlights. Washington, DC: American Public Welfare Association.

DeJong, Peter, and Scott Miller. (1995). How to interview for client strengths. *Social Work* 40: 729–36.

Dore, Martha Morrison. (1993, November). Family preservation and poor families: When "homebuilding" is not enough. *Families in Society:* 545–56.

Doueck, Howard J., Denise E. Bronson, and Murray Levine. (1992). Evaluating risk assessment implementation in child protection: Issues for consideration. *Child Abuse and Neglect* 16: 637–46.

Doueck, Howard J., Diana J. English, Diane DePanfilis, and Gerald T. Moote. (1993). Decision making in child protective services: A comparison of selected risk-assessment systems. *Child Welfare* 72: 441–52.

Doueck, Howard J., Murray Levine, and Denise E. Bronson. (1993). Risk assessment in child protective services: An evaluation of the Child at Risk Field system. *Journal of Interpersonal Violence* 8: 446–67.

Fraser, Mark W., Peter J. Pecora, Chirapat Popuang, and David A. Haapala. (1992). Event history analysis: A proportional hazards perspective on modeling outcomes in intensive family preservation services. In David F. Gillespie and Charles Glisson (eds.), *Quantitative methods in social work: State of the art.* New York: Haworth Press.

Halpern, Robert. (1984). Lack of effects for home-based early intervention? Some possible explanations. *American Journal of Orthopsychiatry* 54: 33–42.

Halpern, Robert. (1986). Home-based early intervention: Dimensions of current practice. *Child Welfare* 65: 387–97.

Holder, Wayne, and Michael Corey. (1986). *Child protective services risk management: A decision-making handbook.* Charlotte, NC: ACTION for Child Protection.

Johnson, Will. (1994). *Effects of numbers of in-person visits on rates of child maltreatment recurrence.* Paper presented to the Second Annual

Roundtable on Outcome Measures in Child Welfare Services. San Antonio, March 30–April 1, 1994.

Kinney, Jill M., David A. Haapala, and Charlotte Booth. (1991). *The Homebuilders model.* Hawthorne, NY: Aldine de Gruyter.

Kinney, Jill M., Barbara Madsen, Thomas Fleming, and David A. Haapala. (1977). Homebuilders: Keeping families together. *Journal of Consulting and Clinical Psychology* 45: 667–73.

Kirk, Raymond, and Kellie Reed. (1995). *Evaluation of family preservation services: The next generation.* Ninth Annual National Association for Family Based Services Empowering Families Conference. Chicago, December 7, 1995.

Landsman, Miriam J. (1985). *Evaluation of fourteen child placement prevention projects in Wisconsin, 1983–1985.* Iowa City: National Resource Center on Family Based Services.

Magura, Stephen, Beth Silverman Moses, and Mary Ann Jones. (1987). *Assessing risk and measuring change in families: The Family Risk Scales.* Washington, DC: Child Welfare League of America.

Martinez, L. (1989). *The family assessment worksheet in the Illinois Department of Children and Family Services.* Third National Roundtable on CPS Risk Assessment, San Francisco.

McCurdy, Karen. (1995). Risk assessment in child abuse prevention programs. *Social Work Research* 19: 77–87.

McDonald, Thomas, and Jill Marks. (1991). A review of risk factors assessed in child protective services. *Social Service Review* 65: 112–32.

Miller, Janet, Katherine Williams, Diana English, and Judy Olmstead. (1987). *Risk assessment in child protection: A review of the literature.* Olympia, WA: Department of Social and Health Services.

Nelson, Douglas. (1990). Recognizing and realizing the potential of "family preservation." In James K. Whittaker, Jill Kinney, Elizabeth M. Tracy, and Charlotte Booth (eds.), *Reaching high-risk families: Intensive family preservation in human services,* 13–30. Hawthorne, NY: Aldine de Gruyter.

Nohejl, Cheryl A., Howard J. Doueck, and Murray Levine. (1992). Risk assessment implementation and legal liability in CPS practice. *Law and Policy* 14: 185–208.

O'Keefe, R. A. (1973). Home Start: Partnership with parents. *Children Today* 2 (1): 12–16.

Pecora, Peter J. (1991a). Using risk assessment technology and other screening methods for determining the need for child placement in family-based

140

services. In David Haapala, Vera O. Pina, and Cecelia Sudia (eds.), *Empowering families: Papers from the fourth annual conference on family-based services.* Riverdale, IA: National Association for Family-Based Services.

Pecora, Peter J. (1991b). Investigating allegations of child maltreatment: The strengths and limitations of current risk assessment systems. *Children and Youth Services Review* 15: 73–92.

Pecora, Peter J., James K. Whittaker, and Anthony N. Maluccio. (1992). *The child welfare challenge: Policy, practice and research.* Hawthorne, NY: Aldine de Gruyter.

Pelton, Leroy H. (1991). Beyond permanency planning: Restructuring the public child welfare system. *Social Work* 36: 337–43.

Polansky, Norman A., Mary Ann Chalmers, David P. Williams, and Elizabeth W. Buttenweiser. (1981). *Damaged parents: An anatomy of child neglect.* Chicago: University of Chicago Press.

Quinn, Peggy, and Marianne Berry. (1995). *Family preservation services to families with physical and developmental disabilities.* University of Texas at Arlington.

Reid, Grant, Eric Sigurdson, Jan Christianson-Wood, and Alexandra Wright. (1995). *Basic issues concerning the assessment of risk in child welfare work.* Winnipeg: University of Manitoba.

Ronnau, John P., and Christine Marlow. (1993, November). Family preservation, poverty, and the value of diversity. *Families in Society:* 538–44.

Ruger, June B., and Wooten, Roberta H. (1982). A developmental approach to helping families at risk. *Social Casework* 63: 3–14.

Sandau-Beckler, Patricia, and Richard Salcido. (1992). *Infusing family preservation values into child protection practice.* Las Cruces: Family Preservation Institute, New Mexico State University.

Schorr, Lizbeth B. (1988). *Within our reach: Breaking the cycle of disadvantage.* New York: Doubleday.

Simeonsson, Rune, D. Cooper, and A. Scheiner. (1982). A review and analysis of the effectiveness of early intervention programs. *Pediatrics* 69 (5): 635–41.

Slaght, Evelyn F. (1993). Reexamining risk factors in foster care. *Children and Youth Services Review* 15: 143–54.

Thieman, Alice A., and Paula W. Dail. (1992). Family preservation services: Problems of measurement and assessment of risk. *Family Relations* 41: 186–91.

Wald, Michael S., and Maria Woolverton. (1990). Risk assessment: The emperor's new clothes? *Child Welfare* 69: 483–511.

Yuan, Ying-Ying, and David L. Struckman-Johnson. (1991). Placement outcomes for neglected children with prior placements in family preservation programs. In Kathleen Wells and David E. Biegel (eds.), *Family preservation services: Research and evaluation,* 92–118. Newbury Park, CA: Sage.

Chapter 8

THE RELATIVE EFFICACY OF
HARD AND SOFT SERVICES

Because intensive family preservation services are intended to be responsive to the needs of a family related to its placement risk, the specific services provided should therefore vary from family to family. As discussed earlier, the family preservation model is based on the proposition that there should be a range of flexible services to strengthen the family and reduce the risk of placement and/or continued abuse. This calls for the family preservation worker to access a myriad of resources and services, both "hard," or concrete (such as material goods and financial assistance), and "soft," or clinical (such as counseling and parent training), depending on the particular strengths, risk factors, and needs present in a family.

SERVICE PROVISION

The components provided by intensive family preservation services have been categorized as hard and soft services, but they actually comprise a continuum ranging from the softer services, such as counseling and family assessment, to enabling services devoted to building social supports (both informal and formal), to the harder services of household maintenance help and provision of furniture, car repairs, a telephone, or other basic needs (Fraser, Pecora, and Lewis 1991). Thus the enabling services bridging the gap between hard and soft services facilitate access to both the harder and softer services and appear to be an essential feature of intensive family preservation services.

Soft Services

Family preservation caseworkers strive to engage the family and instill hope early in the intervention (Kinney, Haapala, and Booth 1991). Workers provide emotional understanding and support by listening to families and helping them define their problem(s) and set their own goals for treatment. Because of the short duration of services, most family preservation programs do not emphasize the truly soft services of psychological individual or family counseling. Rather, Whittaker, Schinke, and Gilchrist (1986) focus on the teaching of specific life skills. This form of soft services is especially applicable in short-term interventions, in which the less tangible emotional support from agency workers is available only for a finite period, usually two to three months. The skill building that occurs will continue to support and reinforce positive family interaction in the long run, after formal services have ended.

Treatment based on an ecological model focuses on modeling life skills, such as parenting skills, and teaching and practicing with family members the positive and constructive communication and negotiation skills that will contribute to a more positive and less abusive family environment. Workers assess parenting and communication skills, help parents and children identify nonpunitive methods of interacting, and model and practice positive interaction. These skills not only apply to parent and child interaction but also help families interact more productively with landlords, doctors, teachers, social workers, neighbors, relatives, and other individuals who contribute to the support or stress in their social environments. Such a training or teaching model is also practiced in supervisory and peer relationships in the family preservation model.

Enabling Services

Establishing (or reestablishing) linkages to informal supports is also productive, particularly because family preservation services are of such short duration. Reconciling parents with extended family members or helping them establish friendships in the community can set in place a continuing support system. Because social isolation of parents is a key correlate of child abuse and neglect, such relationships can be a resource as important as health care skills or high self-esteem.

Some friendships are more a strain than a resource, however. Since many isolated mothers may indeed be stressed more than helped by interchanges with relatives and friends (Tracy 1990; Van Meter, Haynes, and Kropp 1987; Wahler and Dumas 1984), enabling social support in a more formal sense may be appropriate for multistressed families. Formal social support could include assistance from the housing bureau, day care centers, schools, and hospitals. It could also include food stamps, weekly support groups, continuing education, and other such services. Enabling work with families focuses on helping them negotiate access to the supportive services offered by agencies and institutions.

Hard Services

The ecological family preservation model recognizes the importance of providing concrete resources such as housing, adequate furniture, and food to families at risk. Provision of concrete resources is important for three reasons. First, families who improve their communication skills and increase the self-esteem of their members will continue to be stressed by their physical environment if they cannot provide for the basic needs of their children, such as safe housing, food, and medical care. A systems perspective recognizes the importance of these physical and environmental resources to family well-being and the fact that they can reduce the accumulation of stressors toward a crisis situation.

Second, Kinney, Haapala, and Booth (1991) at Homebuilders have noted that the provision of concrete resources helps to establish rapport between the caseworker and the family by showing the family that the program understands its concrete needs and applying a direct and real solution early in the intervention. Surveys of practitioners in other programs have noted the same result (Littell, Howard, Rzepnicki, Budde, Pellowe, Schuerman, and Johnson 1992). Intensive family preservation caseworkers often help families fix broken windows, shop for food, obtain furniture, access car repairs, and do other tasks of household maintenance and family care. These hard services improve the impoverished circumstances of families and the physical environment, and they also provide an opportunity to model the repair, shopping, or negotiation skills involved so that families can learn to do them on their own.

Third, research on child placement decisions indicates that child welfare caseworkers are influenced by the physical environment and economic impoverishment of the family when deciding whether to place children in foster care (Lindsey 1991; Pelton 1989; Stehno 1982). Any program that hopes to decrease the likelihood of child removal, both while the family is in treatment and following case closure, must work to improve the physical aspects of the household and the economic stability of the family.

EXAMINATIONS OF SERVICE COMPONENTS IN FAMILY PRESERVATION PROGRAMS

In evaluations of a variety of intensive family preservation programs, most report their placement prevention rate as the primary criterion of success. Only a few evaluations have addressed other effects on the reduction of risks, such as child behavior or family functioning (Berry 1992; Fraser, Pecora, and Haapala 1991).

Even fewer studies have evaluated service provision in intensive family preservation services in detail. It is precisely the provision of service that is of utmost importance to an understanding of the effectiveness of family preservation services, because "without an appreciation of how services are provided and thus of how a program is implemented, all information about the outcomes of an intervention becomes ephemeral, tied to a particular program or service setting, and not amenable to generalization" (Staff and Fein 1994, 195).

An overview of the Homebuilders program in Washington (Kinney, Haapala, and Booth 1991) showed that of 86 families served, 56 percent had been provided transportation, but decreasing proportions were provided other concrete services such as help finding employment (21 percent), opportunities for recreational activities (19 percent), help in getting transportation (17 percent), help with housework (17 percent), and financial assistance (16 percent). No information is given, however, on the correlation of specific services to family improvements.

Leonard Feldman's 1991 evaluation of the Homebuilders model in New Jersey classified services in seven categories, using the Client Clinical Services Checklist and the Concrete Services Rating Sheet (Kinney, Haapala, and Booth 1991). Feldman found that the most common services concerned teaching child management skills (these were used by 54 percent of families), providing basic clinical services such as relationship building and building hope (54 percent), teaching emotion management (49 percent), and advocating for the client (45 percent). Less common were coaching in interpersonal skills (36 percent) and other services such as money management, time management, and increasing informal support (21 percent). Concrete services (defined as providing or helping clients get transportation, food, clothing, housing, and so on) were used by only 9 percent of the families in that program.

Correlating Services to Family Outcomes

Two published studies to date (Berry 1992; Fraser, Pecora, and Haapala 1991) have examined the correlation of hard and soft services with case outcomes, namely placement prevention, risk reduction, and treatment goal attainment. Neither of these studies incorporated a control group or comparison group into the study design, so research findings cannot establish whether families would have made these gains without the program but only whether gains are associated with particular services received.

146

Homebuilders

Fraser, Pecora, and Haapala (1991), including Robert Lewis (Fraser, Pecora, and Lewis 1991, Lewis 1991) conducted a detailed evaluation of the Homebuilders program with 453 families and found that only one concrete service, the provision of transportation, was used by more than half of the families served, while thirty-three clinical, or soft, services were as commonly provided, centering around development of the treatment relationship, improving parenting effectiveness, modifying problem behaviors, teaching an understanding of child development, building self-esteem, and consulting with other services. Almost half of the clinical services provided were educational in nature. Lewis postulated that the variation in provision of services to families indicated a sensitivity to the needs of individual families.

Using the Concrete Services Checklist (Fraser, Pecora, and Haapala 1991), Lewis (1991a) found that about three-fourths of all families studied in Washington and Utah received some form of concrete services, with provision of transportation and recreational activities at the top of the list. Also common were helping clients get a job, doing housework with them, arranging recreational activities, and helping them secure financial assistance. In those cases receiving concrete services, the services accounted for an average of 25 percent of service time. Lewis (1991b) describes how concrete services have two primary functions: to improve families' conditions and to help workers build relationships with families. In this second function, concrete services assist in engaging families in softer services by demonstrating the caseworker's understanding of the concrete circumstances they face and their basic needs for safety, financial and material resources, and human comforts. In the Homebuilders evaluation, Lewis (1991b) found that one concrete service, "giving financial assistance," was associated with "establishing trust between therapists and families" (230).

In bivariate analyses, Fraser, Pecora, and Lewis (1991) reported that the overall amount of time spent providing concrete services was significantly associated with reduced risk of placement. On the other hand, only one area of clinical services (teaching time and money management) was associated with program success, in addition to the specific activities of listening to the client, encouraging the client, providing literature, and teaching money management.

In a multivariate analysis, concrete services remained critically important.

Service success also was significantly correlated with the use of concrete services. Controlling for the behavior of the children and their parents plus goal achievement, families that received an enabling concrete service had a

32.8 percent lower risk of placement. Concrete services appear to be a critical ingredient in providing effective treatment. . . . More successful therapists appear to have trained family members to seek and obtain tangible help from community agencies. (Fraser, Pecora, and Lewis 1991, 215)

Similarly, the one characteristic of families at termination that predicted subsequent child removal, holding service and demographic and social characteristics of clients constant, was the presence of serious environmental and structural problems in the household.

It should be noted, however, that while concrete service provision was a statistically significant predictor of success in this sample using discriminant analysis, this variable lost its predictive ability in a more rigorous analysis using event history analysis (Fraser, Pecora, Popuang, and Haapala 1992). Clearly, more research remains to be done.

Northern California

Berry's (1994) evaluation of a program in Northern California examined 327 cases served from 1985 to 1987. Records were examined in late 1988 to allow a sufficient period of time after treatment for families to demonstrate their stability or instability. This evaluation found a preservation rate of 86 percent overall and 88 percent a year after treatment. The families for whom treatment was successful, or who remained intact, were those with many resources on which to build, such as an older and more cooperative mother. Families who had more money coming in every month, including Aid to Families with Dependent Children, were more likely to remain together, as were families who were self-referred to the program. The problems that the program was best able to alleviate were poor economic conditions, parental handicaps or illness, and parental emotional disturbance. Problems that centered around resource deficits, such as parent handicaps or illness or economic conditions, saw the most improvement, which is not surprising considering that this program focused on helping families build personal resources and make connections with community resources.

The families who were most likely to have a child removed were those with a history of adjudicated child neglect. These families had many accompanying stressors and few resources on which to build. Neglecting families were likely to have a parent or child with a developmental disability, a history of child removals, more children in the home, a younger mother, and parental substance abuse problems. Neglect families had a placement rate of 24 percent.

In accord with an ecological framework, family care workers kept detailed reports of the number and focus of their interactions with the families as well as with other agencies and individuals enlisted to help. Family assessment notes were on a multitude of standardized forms that were used at case opening and repeated at closing and one-month, six-month, and one-year follow-ups.

Service Provision. In their detailed and standardized logs of the service time they spent with each family, workers noted times in minutes. The service model emphasizes teaching parenting skills and appropriate discipline as well as anything else the family needs help in, such as budgeting, housekeeping and home safety, health care, and nutrition and food preparation. Caseworkers also provided very concrete services such as help with finding housing, day care, employment, financial aid, legal help, medical care, and transportation. This was all noted in the service log. For example, a worker might spend one hour in the grocery store teaching the family how to select economical and nutritious food, spend another hour in the home helping to prepare the dinner, then stay another hour to model parenting skills and positive family interaction skills. Each of these hours would be entered into a service log specifying the site, length, and focus of the service. This evaluation took a subset of 116 cases with this detailed service log data.

The services provided to families most, in terms of time, included assessment (a mean of 6.75 hours), parent education (3.3 hours), supplemental parenting (3 hours), and teaching family care (2.2 hours). Families also received on average at least an hour of counseling, household maintenance, transportation, and referral services. The most commonly provided services were assessment, case planning, referral, and parent education.

One of the most intriguing findings of this study was that no children were removed in cases in which more than 50 percent of service time had been spent in the home. When more than 50 percent of service time had been spent in the agency, the placement rate was 28 percent, double that for the entire sample. Even though this is an in-home program, only about a third of the time, on average, was spent in the home; a third was spent in the agency (not on the phone); and another third was spent on the phone or in other locales. The agency time can be accounted for partially by weekly team meetings and supervisory meetings held in the office. Also, much of the focus of the program is on building social supports and helping families to acquire resources, and many workers chose to make personal contacts and phone calls related to these goals in the office. This evaluation showed that when such contacts and calls were made from the home instead, this increased the service time in the home and helped to model the contact-making skills to the family.

Beyond these basic agency-versus-home comparisons, the associations between more specific services and outcomes become more difficult to ascertain, mostly because services are tailored to families' needs. In-home services are supposed to be whatever it takes to strengthen the family and help keep it together. And, indeed, there were significant correlations between many types of services and various presenting problems of families in the program. For example, workers spent large amounts of time teaching developmentally disabled parents how to budget. Clients with family interaction problems received lots of time in respite care, counseling, parent education, and help with housing. Handicapped or ill parents received respite care and transportation. Families in which a parent was newly absent received respite, counseling, transportation, crisis intervention, and supplemental parenting.

Despite the fact that services varied across families, the concrete and enabling services were indeed associated with better outcomes for families in general. Families were most likely to remain intact when services had included modeling effective parenting skills, teaching family care (like cooking and health care), and securing food and medical help. Families who received these services made the greatest gains in skills and were the most likely to remain intact after leaving the program. The softer or more clinical services, such as counseling and assessment, were not associated with better outcomes even though they were provided in greater (though not significantly so) amounts to families who subsequently had a child placed.

Concrete and enabling services contributed most to parents' gains in parenting skills and betterment of the physical conditions of the household. The skills in which parents showed most gains were discipline, general child care, and acquiring household resources. The more concrete skill gains tended to last longer, particularly concerning child care and parenting, as indicated by assessments at one-month, six-month, and one-year follow-up visits. In fact, these skills tended to continue to show improvement after services had ended (except among families in which a child was placed, in which cases skills tended to continue to deteriorate until the placement).

Enabling Services. Family care workers tapped a variety of other agencies and individuals to provide services to clients. Most of these collateral contacts involved formal agencies, particularly the Department of Social Services and private social service agencies. Other agencies commonly used were hospitals and public health agencies.

One interesting finding brought up issues of social support for families in the program. Families were asked at intake if they had relatives nearby who would be able to help. Those parents who said they had relatives able to help were significantly more likely to have their children placed into foster care later. Perhaps the relatives became the foster home when a child was removed. Possibly they were more of a drain than a resource to families, or maybe they were the ones who later reported the families for abuse or neglect. The study could not answer this question, but this finding begs to be looked at in further research in light of two increasing bodies of research examining the nature of kinship foster care (Berrick, Needell, and Barth 1995; Dubowitz, Feigelman, and Zuravin 1993) and the influence of negative social networks (VanMeter, Haynes, and Kropp 1987).

The Association of Services with Clients' Gains. The services that were least effective—that is, the services that were provided most to families who subsequently had a child placed—were assessment, counseling, crisis intervention, and legal help. Since this program is not family-therapy oriented, it may be that the family preservation workers were simply not very good at counseling and crisis intervention. An alternative explanation, and one that is supported by other research (Fraser, Pecora, and Haapala 1991), is that families who require an inordinate amount of crisis intervention and counseling are very difficult to help in a short period of time.

Multivariate Analysis. The question remains whether it is the problem or the service that makes a difference in outcome. The amount of time workers spent in the home contributed to skill gains for parents regardless of the level of risk for the family. In a multivariate analysis examining the contribution of family characteristics, presenting problems, and services, the biggest correlate of family preservation was determined to be the amount of service time spent *in the home with the family,* over and above any problems, the total amount of time spent with the family, the stressors facing the family, or the level of risk with which the family entered the program.

FITTING SERVICES TO FAMILY NEEDS

Do family preservation programs actually tailor services to fit family needs? Few evaluations have attempted to answer this question. In the evaluation of intensive family preservation services in Northern California (Berry 1994), the amount of time that a worker spent in the home was shown to relate to the environmental needs of the family in that workers spent more time in the homes that needed improvements in safety, cleanliness, and comfort of the environment at case opening. Total case time as well as home time and agency time were positively correlated with the poor physical condition of the building and the living unit at case opening. Workers also spent more time in the agency on cases in which the building and living units were in worse physical shape. However, there was a positive correlation between the number of household resources a family had and the amount of time the worker spent. Workers spent more time (in total and in the agency) when there were resources in the home such as separate bedrooms for parents and children, books, magazines, a television, a clock, and a calendar.

There were no associations between the total time, time spent in the home, or time spent in the agency with a client's initial levels of general child care skills or specific skills regarding discipline, health care, or encouragement of development. Thus the initial assessment of the client's skills in providing child care did not affect how much time the worker eventually spent with the family.

It is difficult to identify the key determinants of how much time a worker was to spend with a family because initial ratings of client skills and environmental conditions were strongly interrelated. For example, among the group of families with service log data, the orderliness, cleanliness, and comfort of the household were all significantly correlated at levels from .33 to .86. In addition, these household conditions were all significantly correlated with the level of household resources available to the family. Child care skills (both in general and specifically regarding discipline, health, and development) were all significantly intercorrelated at levels from .70 to .80 as well as correlated with household resource availability (.20 to .25).

Similarly, problems with the condition of the building or the living unit were negatively correlated with many of the environmental assessments and child care skills. The number and strength of all of these correlations indicate the interrelatedness of these skills areas. They may also be an indication of workers' inability to discriminate between areas when rating a parent and the household at intake.

CONCLUSION

These two studies of two different programs have both found concrete and enabling services to be more highly correlated than the soft services with families' making gains while receiving services and with their remaining together after services have ceased. As to why this is so, the authors of the program evaluations postulate that the provision of concrete and enabling services demonstrates to families that such services are not "beneath" the worker. The ready provision of concrete resources or assistance that can address an immediate need early in the relationship demonstrates to the family that the worker is there to help, not just to talk. Solving these early crises or needs helps to engage the family, which is of critical importance in short-term interventions and interventions with involuntary clients (Fraser, Pecora, and Haapala 1991; Rooney 1993; Schuerman, Rzepnicki, and Littell 1994).

The agencies in these evaluations stress that they hire family preservation workers who believe in the importance and effectiveness of concrete services. While most of the training in the programs is on the softer services, such as counseling, assessment, crisis intervention, and special problems like substance abuse, and workers do not receive much formal training in budgeting, house-cleaning, and other hard services, they are hired partly because they are willing to help families with such concrete needs. Workers teach each other things like how to cut window glass, how to shop on a limited budget, and how to negotiate with landlords.

Regarding the softer services, the evaluators of the Homebuilders program (Fraser, Pecora, and Haapala 1991) found that clinical services ranged from psychotherapeutic techniques to cognitive behavioral techniques and that almost half of all clinical services were educational in nature. The evaluation of the Northern California program (Berry 1994) found that the educational techniques, in which family preservation workers modeled and taught parenting and household maintenance skills, were associated with the greater gains for families and a greater likelihood of their remaining together after services ended. These preliminary evaluations suggest that when a program is short-term in nature, service time appears to be best spent in the home setting, modeling and practicing those skills that are most likely to reduce the risk of placement and continued mistreatment of children, and these skills appear to involve health care and discipline of children.

There are many staff and training elements that probably contribute to the association of the more concrete services with positive outcomes in family preservation programs. First, both programs hire staff who have life experience and/or job experience with household management, child care, child development, budgeting, and general positive functioning in the world. Workers are also hired for diversity of expertise and experience.

In addition, training in more concrete skills is usually emphasized in team meetings and supervision. The Northern California program has team meetings weekly or twice weekly in which workers share with each other the kinds of approaches and skills they use with their families. This is particularly helpful because it relates to specific current problems. Staff also provide informal one-on-one help and training to each other in concrete tasks such as bathing infants, replacing window glass, and negotiating with landlords. Finally, the agency subscribes to two parenting magazines that provide parenting tips for staff and are photocopied and shared with clients.

These findings have important implications for other child welfare services. They show that any work that can be done in the home should be done in the home, from working with families to making phone calls to doing paperwork. Workers can model a variety of skills in arranging for resources for families that will continue to serve families after treatment has ended. On the surface, it may seem unfair to a family to set up an office in the home. But tasks that concern the family and that the family can learn to handle by watching the worker do so (for example, finding a bed for a child or persuading the landlord to fix the heating system) are best done in the home with the family rather than from the office.

The evaluations also show that the most concrete types of services were most likely to be associated with preservation and with parents' gains in skills. While a great deal of counseling was provided to most families, it was teaching family care skills and parenting skills and securing medical help that helped to keep families together and led to improvements in parents' skills in child care, discipline, health care, and the general encouragement of child development.

Thus skills that strengthen families and decrease the risk of placement are easy to impart to workers during training and easy for workers to teach to families in need. Training workers how to teach parenting and housekeeping skills can have an efficient, effective, and enduring impact on families.

REFERENCES

Berrick, Jill D., Barbara Needell, and Richard P. Barth. (1995). *Kinship care in California.* Berkeley: Family Welfare Research Group.

Berry, Marianne. (1992). Evaluation of a family preservation program: Fitting agency services to family needs. *Social Work* 37: 314–21.

Berry, Marianne. (1994). *Keeping families together.* New York: Garland.

Children's Home Society of California. (1980). *Case record tracking forms.* Oakland, CA: Children's Home Society of California.

Dubowitz, H., Stan Feigelman, and Susan Zuravin. (1993). A profile of kinship care. *Child Welfare* 72: 153–70.

Feldman, Leonard H. (1991). Evaluating the impact of intensive family preservation services in New Jersey. In Kathleen Wells and David E. Biegel (eds.), *Family preservation services: Research and evaluation,* 47–71. Newbury Park, CA: Sage.

Fraser, Mark W., Peter J. Pecora, and Robert E. Lewis. (1991). The correlates of treatment success and failure for intensive family preservation services.

In Mark W. Fraser, Peter J. Pecora and David A. Haapala (eds.), *Families in crisis: The impact of intensive family preservation services,* 181–224. Hawthorne, NY: Aldine de Gruyter.

Fraser, Mark W., Peter J. Pecora, Chirapat Popuang, and David A. Haapala. (1992). Event history analysis: A proportional hazards perspective on modeling outcomes in intensive family preservation services. In David F. Gillespie and Charles Glisson (eds.), *Quantitative methods in social work: State of the art.* New York: Haworth.

Kinney, Jill, David A. Haapala, and Charlotte Booth. (1991). *Keeping families together: The Homebuilders model.* Hawthorne, NY: Aldine de Gruyter.

Lewis, Robert E. (1991a). What are the characteristics of intensive family preservation services? In Mark W. Fraser, Peter J. Pecora, and David A. Haapala (eds.), *Families in crisis: The impact of intensive family preservation services* (93–107). Hawthorne, NY: Aldine de Gruyter.

Lewis, Robert E. (1991b). What elements of service relate to treatment goal achievement? In Mark W. Fraser, Peter J. Pecora, and David A. Haapala (eds.), *Families in crisis: The impact of intensive family preservation services* (225–71). Hawthorne, NY: Aldine de Gruyter.

Lindsey, Duncan (1991). Factors affecting the foster care placement decision: An analysis of national survey data. *American Journal of Orthopsychiatry* 61 (2): 272–83.

Littell, Julia H., Jeanne Howard, Tina L. Rzepnicki, Stephen Budde, Diane Pellowe, John R. Schuerman, and Penny Johnson. (1992). *Intervention with families in the Illinois family preservation program.* Chicago: Chapin Hall Center for Children, University of Chicago.

Pelton, Leroy. (1989). *For reasons of poverty: An evaluation of child welfare policy.* New York: Praeger.

Rooney, Ronald H. (1993). *Strategies for work with involuntary clients.* New York: Columbia University Press.

Schuerman, John R., Tina L. Rzepnicki, and Julia H. Littell. (1994). *Putting families first.* Hawthorne, NY: Aldine de Gruyter.

Staff, Ilene, and Edith Fein. (1994). Inside the black box: An exploration of service delivery in a family reunification program. *Child Welfare* 73: 195–211.

Stehno, Sandra M. (1982). Differential treatment of minority children in service systems. *Social Work* 27: 39–45.

Tracy, Elizabeth M. (1990). Identifying social support resources of at-risk families. *Social Work* 35 (3): 252–58.

VanMeter, Mary Jane S., O. Maurice Haynes, and Joseph P. Kropp. (1987). The negative social network: When friends are foes. *Child Welfare* 66 (1): 69–75.

Wahler, Robert G., and Jean E. Dumas. (1984). Changing the observational coding styles of insular and noninsular mothers: A step toward maintenance of parent training effects. In Richard F. Dangel and Richard A. Polster (eds.), *Parent training: Foundations of research and practice,* 379–416. New York: Guilford.

Whittaker, James K., Stephen P. Schinke, and Lewayne D. Gilchrist. (1986). The ecological paradigm in child, youth, and family services: Implications for policy and practice. *Social Service Review* 60: 483–503.

Part IV

Emerging Research, Practice, and Policy Issues

Chapter 9

COMBINING RESEARCH AND PRACTICE TOOLS

Marianne Berry and Debora J. Cavazos Dylla

There are many unanswered questions about family preservation as a practice model. For example, it is unknown whether family preservation actually prevents placement better or more frequently than other types of services (Besharov and Baehler 1992; Wells and Biegel 1990). It is unknown with which family problems or populations of children and families family preservation is most appropriate (Wells and Biegel 1990). It is not known which service elements or what amounts of certain service elements work best with particular types of families (Wells and Biegel 1990). For example, are families served more effectively by one worker or two? By services in the home or in the office? By short-term or long-term service provision? The endurance of the consequences of family preservation services is another area for exploration (Wells and Biegel 1990). Further, many different types of evaluations are needed before we can begin to answer some of these questions.

EVALUATION AND RESEARCH AS
A DEVELOPMENTAL PROCESS

Evaluation and research must be viewed from a developmental or evolutional perspective. The evaluation of social service programs and the research of specific variables that exist within programs yield two distinct types of information that are both useful and important for the social services arena. From a developmental perspective, both evaluation and research activities build on, learn from, and evolve from the other; that is, evaluation may produce findings that invoke new views regarding research, and research may produce results that shed new meaning on evaluation. A developmental perspective allows for the occurrence of cyclical processes in which evaluation leads to research that in turn leads to more evaluation and again more research. A developmental perspective views evaluation and research as moving through stages: at certain times in a program's existence, evaluation may be more important than research; at other times, research may be more important than evaluation; sometimes both are equally important. A developmental perspective allows evaluation and research to be viewed as a process with a definite beginning, followed by interaction and intermingling of the two, followed by a clearer picture of each.

A developmental perspective recognizes the differing expectations of evaluation and research. For the agency, evaluation should ideally provide information that will help it improve its operations; research, on the other hand, should provide information that will further a particular theoretical and/or knowledge base. Decision makers of programs need both types of information during the life cycle of their programs, but at different times evaluation information is more important than research information and vice versa. The seeming error that has been committed in evaluations not only of family preservation programs but of many social services programs is that the developmental nature of these two activities has been disregarded. If the general purpose of evaluation is to improve practice and determine whether current operations are effective, evaluations that are more process-oriented should be conducted before more research and outcome-oriented evaluations are completed. A program must discover what it is doing, whether specific activities are conducted consistently, and whether it is doing what it was designed to do before any analysis of dependent and independent variables is attempted. Once a program is relatively certain of performing not only consistent but also quality operations, an evaluation of whether these operations affect clients in the theoretically expected manner is appropriate, but not before this time.

This is rarely the path that is taken, however. Many program administrators and agency personnel have often discovered that the findings from evaluations conducted by very competent researchers contain little useful information about agency functioning and client outcomes (Chambers, Wedel, and Rodwell 1992; Gordon 1991; Harrison 1994; Patton 1987; Rossi 1992; Sherman and Reid 1994; Videka-Sherman and Reid 1990; Wells and Biegel 1990). This is due to differences in the expectations of evaluation and research. Program administrators, policy makers, and decision makers need information that can be readily applied to program operations to improve practice and help agencies better address the needs of clients. Researchers want information from evaluations that will contribute to a theory and thus to the knowledge base of a specific area. In this light, it is not surprising that evaluation results are so seldom used.

In the family preservation field, certainly, evaluation results have not been used to a significant extent. The intensive family preservation service models of treatment are so individualized that a general purpose research design is not sufficient to capture meaningful information about the specific services provided or the specific outcomes participants experience. Many times evaluations are fruitless when they are done by general evaluators who have too little understanding of the program being evaluated and who use an all-purpose evaluation procedure with general questions to evaluate a complex and highly individualized family preservation program. The resulting information is typically meaningless and leaves workers and clients feeling misunderstood (Rossi 1992; Videka-Sherman and Reid 1990).

A developmental perspective recognizes that evaluation and research in one field, such as family preservation, should build on what is already known in another field, such as child abuse. Therefore it is imperative that family preservation practice not reinvent the wheel but build on what is already known in other fields about issues such as the correlates of child maltreatment, the environment of family stress, and effective ways of working with families and systems (see chapter 3).

In a developmental approach to evaluation and research, family preservation evaluators should be chosen carefully for their knowledge of family preservation. As noted earlier, many evaluation efforts have failed in various ways because evaluators have misunderstood the complexity of family preservation programs (Fraser 1990). They should understand the inclusiveness and comprehensiveness of the family preservation philosophy and reflect these qualities in their evaluation design.

Many efforts have also failed because workers have not understood the value of evaluation (Posavac and Carey 1989; Rossi and Freeman 1993; Royse 1992). In a developmental approach, program administrators allow practitioners to assume the role of practitioner-evaluator. In the Homebuilders model, workers are considered to be personal scientists who engage in both practice and research simultaneously (Blythe 1990). This is not only efficient in terms of the cost of expert evaluators but also appropriate because workers are in the best position to understand the complexity of family preservation services. Thus the need for good evaluation and research training for workers is crucial.

Somehow the evaluation world must begin to bridge the two distinct but equally important expectations of evaluation and research. Viewing them developmentally as parts of a continuum— on which one step precedes the other, one part learns from the other, and one part builds on what the other produces— is one possible bridge. But however appealing this perspective may be, the general public, the mass media, politicians, and legislatures are far less tolerant of a developmental perspective and much more demanding of immediate results. This creates a situation in which it is nearly impossible to complete evaluations competently before research studies have been initiated. This is no small problem, and there seems to be no way around it except to keep trying to convince stakeholders of the developmental nature of evaluation and research in the social service arena and to begin to produce more studies that have developmentally appropriate integrity.

Process Evaluations

Although some family preservation programs have existed for a fair length of time and are well established (for example, Homebuilders), the majority of family preservation programs are new and in the beginning stages of development. Thus it may be more important for them to complete evaluations of service delivery processes and program implementation than to evaluate on the basis of outcomes (Staff and Fein 1994; Wells and Biegel 1992). Wells (1994) notes that "without investigations of how programs function, our understanding of how to improve them will be limited significantly" (480). Typically, process evaluations describe the types and quantities of program activities (Tripodi, Fellin, and Epstein 1978), and their purpose is to determine whether the implementation of a program followed its design as well as whether the program is serving its target population (Posavac and Carey 1989; Rossi and Freeman 1993).

In process evaluations, program elements of family preservation services must be clearly defined. Although some authors (for example, Wells 1994) contend that the definition of family preservation services (that is, short-term services that last four to twelve weeks, include eight to ten hours per week of face-to-face contact with families, offer twenty-four-hour service availability, and are home-based) is clear, programs that in effect do very different things and provide variations of services (services that last longer than twelve weeks and office-based services [see, among others, Showell and White 1990]) refer to themselves as family preservation services and subsequently are compared to each other. This comparison yields varying results (see chapter 5). If there is a clear definition of family preservation services, it appears to be a well-kept secret to many service providers. Competent and thorough process evaluations should produce information that will clarify and standardize this definition.

A particularly important goal of process evaluations is to provide enough evidence and information to enable the replication of successful programs (Wells and Biegel 1992); without process evaluations, this has very little chance of occurring. Currently "no one knows what actions and interventions are included in the programs whose outcomes are being compared" (Staff and Fein 1994, 209). Process evaluations with complete information about how program effects are produced must be given equal priority so that programs may be replicated and fairly compared to one another (Staff and Fein 1994). The determination of "what the workers in the program did with and for their clients" (Staff and Fein 1994, 197) is essential for the replication of programs (Besharov and Baehler 1992). As Staff and Fein (1994) contend, "Without an appreciation of how services are provided and thus of how a program is implemented, all information about the outcomes of an intervention becomes ephemeral, tied to a particular program or service setting, and not amenable to generalization" (195).

A second area that needs attention in process evaluations is the delineation of program elements (Wells and Biegel 1990). Thus far, family preservation programs have not been described well in the family preservation literature (Staff and Fein 1994; Wells and Biegel 1990). Program descriptions that are available have lacked information on important service elements such as theoretical rationales; technology or interventions used; training, educational, and experience level of staff; and associations and linkages with community agencies (Wells and Biegel 1990). Program integrity and stability over time should also be examined (Wells and Biegel 1990). The collection of data on program activities is methodologically difficult and time-consuming, and it requires creativity on the part of the evaluator that is not necessary for more standard, quantitative outcome evaluations. Nevertheless, efforts must be made to describe the complexities and details of the service delivery process. Otherwise, evaluations and comparisons of programs are likely to generate faulty findings (Fraser 1990).

The ecological context of which family preservation services are a part must also be assessed (Wells and Biegel 1992). There should be evaluations of how community family service systems respond to and support family preservation programs as part of the continuum of services for families and as bona fide services in their own right.

Outcome Evaluations

Both the general public and human service decision makers demand that programs produce effective outcomes in the delivery of services to clients. This demand for outcomes is present especially in the early stages of a program's existence (Staff and Fein 1994). But however justified this requirement of accountability may be, programs must be in place long enough to be clearly defined and clearly established before valid outcome results can be obtained (Besharov and Baehler 1992; Rossi 1992; Tripodi, Fellin, and Epstein 1978).

Many new programs experience a number of modifications in service activities, particularly in the first year (Tripodi, Fellin, and Epstein 1978); evaluations of program outcomes during such development are thus premature. Programs must be ready for outcome evaluations (Fraser 1990); an assessment of a program's readiness to be evaluated would be beneficial (Chambers, Wedel, and Rodwell 1992). Programs need sufficient time to "work out the bugs" in design before outcome evaluations will be meaningful (Tripodi, Fellin, and Epstein 1978). This in no way implies that evaluations cannot be conducted during this time; it does mean, however, that they should address issues other than outcome—for example, process.

Outcome evaluations are typically conducted to determine whether services and service providers are effective in meeting families' needs—that is, to determine whether clients are receiving the intended benefits of a program (Posavac and Carey 1989) and whether intended outcomes and beneficial unintended consequences emerge from service efforts (Tripodi, Fellin, and Epstein 1978). Outcome studies are needed to generalize findings regarding family preservation services of particular types of models to other family preservation services of the same models (Besharov and Baehler 1992; Staff and Fein 1994; Wells and Biegel 1992).

One of the primary premises in being able to generalize findings is that services are provided to appropriately identified families (Besharov and Baehler 1992; Tracy 1991; Wells and Biegel 1992). However, there is no consensus on target populations for family preservation programs (Scannapieco 1994; Tracy 1991; Wells and Biegel 1990, 1992). At the present time, most programs state that services are provided to families at imminent risk of a child being removed from the family, yet the definition of "imminent risk" is not clear or universal (Berry 1992; Besharov and Baehler 1992; Fraser, Pecora, Popuang, and Haapala 1992; Tracy 1991; Wells and Biegel 1990). There is great diversity in the definition of what constitutes placement once services have been initiated as well (Fraser et al. 1992; Pecora, Fraser, and Haapala 1991). These issues must be defined unambiguously and explicitly so that the results of outcome studies are meaningful, particularly when control or comparison groups are used in evaluation designs.

Many of the outcome studies in family preservation (and other fields as well) also produce unclear findings on program effectiveness (Berry 1992; Feldman 1991; Kinney, Haapala, and Booth 1991; Nelson, Landsman, and

Deutelbaum 1990; Pecora, Fraser, and Haapala 1991; Schwartz, AuClaire, and Harris 1991; Showell, Hartley, and Allen 1987; Showell 1985; Wells and Biegel 1990). Like the process evaluations, outcome studies are often inconclusive because programs are compared to each other without full examination of whether they are comparable.

Outcome studies of individual programs that are successful as well as those that are not successful will further the knowledge base regarding theoretical conceptualizations and the types of problems, types of families, and types of communities for which family preservation programs are most beneficial and most appropriate. Outcome studies that are competently conducted aid in garnering support for family preservation programs and/or guide the paths that should be taken in altering, improving, or eliminating existing programs.

Cost Evaluations

Evaluations establishing cost and benefit factors, or program efficiency indices, are also needed (Grubb 1976; Tripodi, Fellin, and Epstein 1978; Wells and Biegel 1992). The political processes in social welfare programs require that service efforts be not only socially responsible but also fiscally accountable.

The cost of family preservation programs must be evaluated in better ways than have been employed thus far. Traditionally, the cost of the most expensive placement has been compared to the cost of family preservation services (Kinney, Haapala, and Booth 1991; Schuerman, Rzepnicki, and Littell 1994; Wells and Biegel 1990). If programs could be absolutely sure that all families receiving family preservation services would have experienced a placement without these services, this type of cost comparison would be valid. However, there are many problems with this comparison because conclusive evidence that all family preservation service recipients would have experienced a placement without intervention does not exist (Schuerman, Rzepnicki, and Littell 1994; Wells and Biegel 1990).

For instance, Schuerman and colleagues (1994) at the University of Chicago studied the Illinois state family preservation program and found that while the family preservation group had a low placement rate, the comparison group also had a low placement rate; both groups defined their families as at imminent risk of placement. Although the majority of the children involved were judged to be at imminent risk of placement, placement was not the outcome for the majority of children, regardless of which service they received. A cost comparison was not completed in this study, but if it had been, it would have been erroneous because there was no way to know whether or not all of these children were truly at imminent risk of placement, and results suggest that not all of them were.

Cost analyses have also neglected to include the cost of follow-up services for family preservation clients (Wells and Biegel 1990). For example, the cost of delayed placement (a child placed, say, a year after receiving family preservation services) has not been established (Wells and Biegel 1990). As with both process and outcome evaluations of family preservation practice, the evaluation of its costs, benefits, and effects can be analyzed in creative, perhaps nontraditional, ways. For example, analysis could be conducted on the costs and benefits over the long term. Also, the true cost of a family preservation service package should include the costs of referral services and other linkages made to community agencies. Computing only those costs of the family preservation agency neglects the larger costs of the surrounding and supporting community services in which the program is embedded.

WHAT IS EVALUATED?

One of the most pressing concerns in family preservation evaluation and research is what should be evaluated to determine effectiveness and success. The first issue in determining what to evaluate is definitional; that is, success and effectiveness need to be clearly defined and universally accepted by family preservation providers.

In many programs, the primary measure of program success has been the prevention of child placement (for example, Feldman 1991; Kinney, Haapala, and Booth 1991; Nelson, Landsman, and Deutelbaum 1990; Pecora, Fraser, and Haapala 1991; Schwartz, AuClaire, and Harris 1991; Showell, Hartley, and Allen 1987; Showell 1985). This may be an erroneous outcome indicator for family preservation programs, however (Rossi 1992). Although there is no doubt that the goal of family preservation is to preserve the family, family preservation is about much more than the prevention of placement. Further, there are many system determinants besides program effects that may result in a child's removal, such as the availability of a foster home on a particular weekend or the amount of funding available for placement. In addition, sometimes child placement is a good outcome (Besharov and Baehler 1992; Scannapieco 1993; Wells and Biegel 1992; Wells 1994). It may be appropriate because it increases child safety, or it may be the best decision for a parent to make (Besharov and Baehler 1992). Examining only child placement does not reveal much about what happened to the family or child during the receipt of family preservation services—what gains they made, what specific risks might have been reduced, and other changes or improvements to the household or family. Besharov and Baehler (1992) note that "the ultimate evaluation question is not whether foster care [or other] placements rise or fall, but, rather, whether the program protects the welfare of children and whether, in the process, unnecessary placements are reduced" (17).

Researchers, legislators, and the general public place far too much emphasis on the "big" or crude indicators of success such as placement prevention, absence of child death, or reduction of abuse; these are administrative criteria, not measurements of the condition of children and families (Besharov and Baehler 1992). In addition, crude measures focus too much concern on reducing the negative forces in families' lives. It is important to track these indicators, of course, but the result is that too little attention is paid, in both evaluation and practice, to increasing the positive forces such as greater resources and skills. If a program evaluates only the occurrence of child placement and cannot document that it has enhanced skills and/or resources, then it is much more likely not to perform services that enhance skills and/or resources and thus more likely to see cases reopened six months or a year later.

APPROPRIATE EVALUATION ELEMENTS

Client Characteristics

There are essential elements other than child placement that may be evaluated (Scannapieco 1993; Wells and Biegel 1992). Multiple measures of these other elements should become standard operating procedure in family preservation evaluations (Besharov and Baehler 1992; Fraser 1990). They include, for example, client characteristics such as demographic information and presenting problems and strengths of families (Fraser 1990; Scannapieco 1994; Wells and Biegel 1990, 1992). To date, the family preservation literature has been incomplete and inconsistent in reporting this information. Further, the information is generally considered descriptive and therefore in the realm of process evaluation data; thus, with the dearth of process evaluations, it is not surprising that such information has been neglected. However, it cannot be ignored; it is an essential piece of the entire family preservation evaluation puzzle. Without knowing who the recipients of family preservation services are, it is meaningless and invalid to compare programs under the assumption that all programs serve the same types of clients (Wells and Biegel 1990).

Program Goals

Program components are also in need of evaluation. Primary among these components are program goals and objectives. The goals of family preservation are typically reflected in crude indicators such as the prevention of unnecessary placements and the reduction of child maltreatment. While these are important, they are the only indicators of a program's success; as noted earlier, they do not reveal much about how family members and family situations are directly affected, and one may be left wondering at what cost these goals were achieved. For example, if placement was prevented, was it because the service was effective or because there were no public funds available for placement? Goals such as these can be measured, but they should also be accompanied by specific program objectives (Bovaird and Mallinson 1988) to show more precisely the impact of family preservation services.

Attainment of Program Objectives

Besharov and Baehler (1992) explain that family preservation program effectiveness should be based on child and family functioning—that is, whether the well-being of children and families has been enhanced by program service provision. Relatively few family preservation studies of family functioning currently exist, and there are methodological problems with many of those that have been done (Scannapieco 1993; Wells and Biegel 1990). For example, the determination of family functioning is often reported only from the worker's perspective, and the evaluation of prefunctioning and postfunctioning have often both been established post hoc (see, for example, Scannapieco 1993; Showell and White 1990). Further, sample sizes tend to be very small (Scannapieco 1993). Standardized measures and client perceptions of improvements in family functioning have typically not been used.

Evaluations must attend to the individualized nature of family goals and objectives (Wells 1994). Because family preservation by nature involves principles such as self-determination and the view of clients as colleagues in the helping process, families establish their own treatment goals. It is therefore important to determine whether families believe that they have achieved those goals in their partnership with family preservation services. Family preservation programs strive to relieve family crises (Wells 1994) and to teach families skills that will enable them to stay together (Wells 1994; Wells and Biegel 1990); it is paramount to discover whether or not families believe these objectives have been accomplished. Family preservation services are client-centered; thus evaluations must also be client-centered (Scannapieco 1993). Family-defined goals and objectives should encompass four specific family preservation program objectives: (1) gains in concrete and supportive resources, (2) increases in knowledge and skills, (3) reductions in risk factors, and (4) improvements in family relationships.

Concrete and Supportive Resources. First, assessments should determine the presence and extent of various concrete and material resources in the household, including, for example, financial resources, housing, food, a telephone, adequate furniture and space for each family member, and a car or access to transportation. For process measures, both the types of concrete services provided as well as the amount (for example, duration of services, hours per week of services) should be measured (Fraser 1990). Social support resources should also be assessed, including such things as the availability and assistance of relatives, friends, and neighbors and access to community services, legal aid, child care, respite care, educational services, health services, and recreational opportunities. Both the kinds of social support and the sources of social support should be documented and assessed (Cooke, Rossmann, McCubbin, and Patterson 1988; Tracy 1990).

Knowledge and Skills. In addition to concrete and social support resources, studies must measure the knowledge and skills family members acquire to help them avoid mistreating each other in the future. These may include things that will bolster family cohesiveness and adaptability, such as parenting skills; knowledge of child development and appropriate developmental expectations of children; effective ways of communicating and of controlling anger; means of nurturing, supervising, and protecting young children; new abilities in household maintenance, budgeting, and general coping; knowledge of nutrition; health care skills; job skills; literacy; and the ability to mobilize community resources. Again, in terms of process, it is important to measure both the types of services used to help clients gain such knowledge and skills as well as the amount of service time provided (for example, hours of in-home contact) (Fraser 1990).

Reductions in Risk Factors. Third, a thorough assessment of risk factors is necessary to address issues such as safety, abusive and/or violent behavior in families, drug use, the physical condition of the household, and the degree of social isolation of the family. Thus far, these areas have not been sufficiently addressed in the literature (Wells and Biegel 1990). Risk factors that have been found to correlate with a greater likelihood of child placement, such as parental mental health problems, previous placement of a child, low family income, and age of at-risk child, should also be assessed (Wells 1994). Widely used risk assessment tools, such as those discussed in chapter 5, and the conclusions of caseworkers about the imminence of placement risk may be the best determinants of risk factors. As with concrete and support services and knowledge and skills gains, the types and number of risk factors as well as their severity should be examined (Wells 1994).

Family Relationship Factors. Family relationship factors such as caring, love, affection, nurturance, attachment, and hope could also be assessed; these are the elements that will likely determine a family's success in staying together over the long term. Yet the inclusion of these variables should be consistent with the theory upon which the program is based (Fraser 1990). Although they are difficult to operationalize and thus to measure, this difficulty of operationalization suggests that perhaps these factors should be assessed by family members according to their own definitions. Because factors such as love are perception-oriented and individualized, family-defined and family-assessed evaluations may be the only appropriate measurements available for evaluating these concepts. Family preservation has the opportunity to take a risk and perhaps be a leader in beginning to assess these crucial elements in family relationships.

HOW IS EVALUATION DONE?

Like other fields in human services and social welfare, family preservation strives to document its credibility through evaluation and research, among other means. Yet studies of family preservation programs have produced information that is difficult to interpret and almost impossible to generalize to other programs (see, for example, Feldman 1991; Nelson, Landsman, and Deutelbaum 1990; Showell, Hartley, and Allen 1987; Wells and Biegel 1990). Perhaps one of the reasons the studies are inconclusive is that evaluators have relied almost completely on quantitative methodology. Because the provision of services is not "business as usual" in family preservation programs, evaluations of its practice must move away from a fixed, traditional, "one size fits all" approach to demonstrate its true benefits.

An important corollary to the principle that evaluation and research are a developmental process is that evaluators should not jump the gun in trying to evaluate programs—that is, try to do more than current knowledge or tools will allow them to do. They must begin to understand the developmental nature of evaluation and research in general and specifically to realize that designing experiments and evaluations and gathering quantitative data are not the only valid ways of knowing or understanding efforts to aid people in need. The human services world's nearly complete reliance on experimental, quantitative evaluative methods neglects the fact that these methods provide decision makers with only part of the information they need to make decisions. Qualitative methods may provide the other part of the information they require, and evaluators should begin to use these more frequently either independently or in conjunction with quantitative methods. In brief, evaluators need to start broadening their evaluation resources and embracing additional ways of evaluating human service efforts.

Evaluators should also carefully select designs, data collection procedures, and measures that are pertinent to the questions being asked. They should begin to differentiate between evaluation questions and research questions and to choose methods that appropriately answer the questions they use. Because of the focus on scientific and quantitative ways of knowing, there is currently a serious push for research rigor, which often outweighs researchers' cautions about the validity of measures and designs (see, for example, Brawley and Martinez-Brawley 1988; Fraser 1990). Researchers may sometimes choose designs and standardized measures knowing that they will be altered and/or compromised in ways that may invalidate or at least weaken the evaluation findings. Evaluators may know that specific measures, while standardized, may not capture exactly what is occurring as a result of a specific intervention. Because of problems such as these, evaluators and researchers must begin to broaden the list of designs and measures available from which to choose, to include not only scientific and standardized methods but also qualitative methods in order to answer either the evaluation questions, the research questions, or some combination of both.

EVALUATION METHODS

Qualitative Research

In its purest form, the qualitative research perspective emphasizes that there are multiple realities that are individualistic and subjective. These realities can only be understood, not measured or controlled; what is true for one person, time, or place is likely not to be true of other persons, times, or places. The researcher's presence and values always play an interactive role with those being observed (Chambers, Wedel, and Rodwell 1992; Gordon 1991; Harrison 1994; Loneck 1994; Patton 1990; Rodwell and Woody 1994; Sherman and Reid 1994). The ultimate goals of qualitative research are holism, depth, description, and interpretation that generates understanding that can improve practice (Chambers, Wedel, and Rodwell 1992; Gordon 1991; Patton 1990). Qualitative research values the specificity of persons, places, and times that leads to general patterns; as Chambers, Wedel, and Rodwell (1992) note, "Qualitative analysis is guided not by hypotheses but by questions, issues, and a search for patterns" (300).

Qualitative research designs are flexible and may change over the course of the evaluation period. The design is allowed to emerge, unfold, and develop as the study progresses rather than being firmly established before the evaluation begins; research questions, data collection procedures, and subjects are thus allowed to change as the evaluation proceeds (Chambers, Wedel, and Rodwell 1992). In essence, as situations change, the design adapts to that change; this overcomes one of the major problems in quantitative research, which is that a situation may change, but the design cannot be altered without compromising the results of the evaluation (Chambers, Wedel, and Rodwell 1992). Samples are chosen according to specific purposes rather than for generalization; purposive sampling allows researchers to sample (1) extreme or deviant cases, (2) typical cases, (3) a variety of clients or problems, (4) critical cases (for example, the most difficult to serve clients or the most costly cases), or (5) politically important cases (Patton 1987).

Qualitative research uses the evaluator, the worker, the client, and others as primary data gathering instruments (Besharov and Baehler 1992; Chambers, Wedel, and Rodwell 1992; Fraser 1990). It is conducted under the assumption of tacit knowledge, the belief that "it is not possible to describe or explain everything that one knows in language form; some things must be experienced to be understood" (Chambers, Wedel, and Rodwell 1992, 297). Researchers are thus required to understand the situation under examination, to become a part of it, to get to know staff and clients on a personal level (Patton 1990). Rather than striving for internal and external validity, reliability, and objectivity, qualitative researchers strive to achieve credibility, authenticity, dependability, confirmability, and transferability of methods to other contexts (Chambers, Wedel, and Rodwell 1992).

Data collection and data analysis occur cyclically rather than sequentially (as with quantitative research) (Sherman and Reid 1994). Data are gathered on multiple aspects of a situation that will produce a complete and comprehensive picture of the whole situation. Qualitative data collection identifies the presence or absence of something; events and activities are described in words rather than numbers (Sherman and Reid 1994). Data collection methods rely on looking, listening, speaking, and reading; thus interviewing, observing, recording, and analyzing verbal and nonverbal communication and documents are typical data collection procedures (Chambers, Wedel, and Rodwell 1992).

Findings from qualitative research are interpreted in terms of the specific issues addressed in the evaluation rather than in lawlike generalizations or nomothetic interpretations (Chambers, Wedel, and Rodwell 1992). They are held to the standard of substantive and relevant significance rather than statistical significance. Findings are tentatively applied, and they are viewed within a social, historical, and temporal context. The evaluator negotiates the meanings and interpretations of the findings with the program stakeholders because "it is their construction of reality that the inquirer is seeking to accurately reconstruct" (Chambers, Wedel, and Rodwell 1992, 303).

Qualitative evaluation and research promise decision makers practical case decision-making utility and findings that will help them make program improvements. Thus qualitative research is more appropriate for process evaluations, in which the issues of implementation and process are more pertinent to decision makers. Qualitative research can capture the complexity, holism, and context of programs serving people in need, and it can produce the depth and detail of information that quantitative research cannot. But despite these apparent benefits, there are no known qualitative studies of family preservation programs in the literature at this time (Wells and Biegel 1992).

Quantitative Research

Quantitative research in its purest form emphasizes that there is one reality that will lead to a body of knowledge comprised of generalizable laws of truth across person, place, and time. This type of research can be conducted more objectively than qualitative with less influence from the researcher's presence or values. Reality can be broken down into parts that can be measured, controlled, held constant, and predicted (Chambers, Wedel, and Rodwell 1992; Gordon 1991; Harrison 1994; Loneck 1994; Patton 1990; Rodwell and Woody 1994; Sherman and Reid 1994).

The ultimate goal of quantitative research is the generalizability of findings to other persons, times, and settings. Researchers strive to discover evidence that will contribute to (and validate or invalidate) a theoretical base of knowledge. In research, statements are desired that exactly specify the linkages between variables and rule out alternative explanations of these relationships. Precise measurement of variables and phenomena that can be quantified are the norm. Quantitative research designs are thus typically experimental or quasi-experimental studies, with data collection occurring before and after intervention. The use of large samples randomly selected and/or assigned and the use of a control or comparison group are ordinarily desired. Evaluators are viewed as impartial, value-free, objective, expert observers of actions taking place. Data are collected customarily by the evaluators through standardized measures, structured interviews, structured questionnaires, and covert observation. Evaluators perform statistical analyses and determine findings to be statistically significant according to prescribed levels of probability. They interpret findings and present them to program personnel (see, for example, Gordon 1991; Patton 1987, 1990).

Several quantitative evaluations of family preservation programs have been completed at this point, but most are plagued by a number of design limitations such as the lack of a control or comparison group, insufficient sample sizes, and the application of improper statistical analyses (Rossi 1992; Wells and Biegel 1990). Family functioning has not been examined systematically, nor have multiple measures been used (Wells and Biegel 1990). Effect size differences (that is, substantive differences expected rather than statistical differences desired) between control and treatment groups have not been clarified (Wells and Biegel 1992). More important, programs evaluated have typically not been fully operational or stable at the time outcome evaluations have been conducted (Rossi 1992), nor have data collection procedures (for example, who collected what kind of data, at what time, and under which conditions) been described well (Wells and Biegel 1990).

The questions that have been explored thus far have also been rather simplistic; for evaluations to reveal information of clinical, substantive significance, the questions should reflect the complexity of the services provided in family preservation programs (Wells and Biegel 1990). Wells and Biegel contend that "some relationships among client characteristics, programs' characteristics, and outcomes of programs are not linear . . . [rather] these characteristics and outcomes are mutually interactive; some have both positive and negative consequences for how clients experience treatment, how programs are implemented, and the consequences of programs" (19). Thus the causal assumption of a linear, unidirectional relationship between independent and dependent variables may be flawed for family preservation practice. This assumption is another indicator of evaluators' attending only to issues that are amenable to current methods and neglecting issues that workers and clients consider important.

There are both qualitative and quantitative ways to address this problem. For example, more studies could embrace a developmental perspective of evaluation and research. Process evaluations could be conducted more frequently, and programs could be allowed to become stable and capable of being evaluated in quantifiable terms. More sophisticated quantitative analysis methods could be employed to test nonlinear or interactive relationships between variables. More pilot studies should be conducted, and methodology should be more conscientiously described. Not only should study implications and limitations be discussed, but also ways of overcoming limitations should be recommended (Wells and Biegel 1990).

Qualitative versus Quantitative Research Methods

Quantitative methods can aid in the establishment of causal relationships and generalizability, while qualitative methods can shed light on the individualization of clients, their situations, program practices, and agency operations. Quantitative methods depend on control, constancy, and validation to establish generalizable outcomes. While validation is a useful outcome for social service programs, understanding that leads to the improvement of practice is equally important and generally more amenable to qualitative methods. The realities of changing clients, changing environments, and changing interventions and treatments often prevent the successful implementation of quantitative research methods. Thus these methods are perhaps more appropriate for programs that are more stable and experiencing less change. While variability of client factors is important for research, stability of program operations is important for evaluation.

Ultimately, the choice of whether to use quantitative or qualitative methods should be based on the questions that are being asked rather than preference of one over the other (Wells and Biegel 1990). Some questions will be naturally amenable to quantitative research, while other questions will be more appropriate for qualitative research. The necessity of having multiple designs in one evaluation seems clear. In the end, perhaps a new paradigm in family preservation evaluation will emerge, prescribing that programs be assessed in "the broadest possible context" (Wells and Biegel 1990, 20), including both quantitative and qualitative methods (Besharov and Baehler 1992; Fraser 1990; Wells and Biegel 1992).

EVALUATION TOOLS

The tools used in evaluation are an additional factor in evaluating family preservation programs. Multiple tools can be used to gather multiple measurements of each variable, event, or activity to maximize the power of evaluation findings (Fraser 1990). Both quantitative and qualitative measures can be useful for these purposes, perhaps most optimally when combined (Patton 1990).

Qualitative Tools

Qualitative data collection tools, as noted previously, rely on looking, listening, speaking, and reading; thus verbal and nonverbal communication and documents are assessed through such means as interviewing, observing, and recording (Chambers, Wedel, and Rodwell 1992). There are four main types of procedures for collecting qualitative data: (1) interviews, (2) observation, (3) document analysis, and (4) unobtrusive measures (Chambers, Wedel, and Rodwell 1992; Patton 1990). These procedures can be used in a variety of creative ways with a multitude of program stakeholders (for example, clients, workers, administrators, community citizens, field experts) and any documents associated with the program or community. Several evaluation authors provide detailed information on creative ways to administer qualitative data collection procedures; see, for example, Chambers, Wedel, and Rodwell (1992); Patton (1987, 1990); and Royse (1992).

As noted previously, there are no known qualitative studies of family preservation services in the literature at this time (Wells and Biegel 1992). Information is lacking, as Wells and Biegel (1992) note, on "how programs develop, how intensive family preservation service workers perceive their jobs, or even how families experience treatment" (26). It is hoped that future evaluation studies will begin to use these tools more frequently and to answer some of the pertinent questions presently needing attention.

Quantitative Tools

The means of acquiring quantitative data are not necessarily different from the means for qualitative data. For example, though quantitative studies use interviewing, observation, and document analysis, the tools methods are typically structured, and the data they produce are quantifiable. Experimental and quasi-experimental designs employed in current family preservation studies have not been particularly rigorous or consistent in terms of the tools they use. Wells and Biegel (1992) reviewed several family preservation studies and found that in general, they described data collection procedures poorly or not at all, and they often failed to address the reliability of the measures used.

It is important for evaluators to choose measures that not only capture essential evaluation information but also are useful to family preservation practice and workers' decision making. The choice of any standardized (or unique) instrument should be consistent with the treatment focus and approach of the program. As illustrated by the review of existing family preservation programs (in chapter 5), many of them target specific populations such as families with adolescents or families experiencing problems with communication. In these cases, a comprehensive package of measures would be of little help to a program that did not address other family needs such as concrete resources or community supports. The best selection of instruments would include those that assist and guide workers in assessment and case planning with families in those areas of import to family preservation and family safety.

Additionally, standardized measures should be employed in conjunction with other types of measures. Both future family preservation practice and evaluation should first decide which of the many standardized measures available are pertinent to family preservation programs. Then they must begin to use these measures consistently if quantitative tools are to be helpful in answering questions about family preservation practice.

In a review of a small sample of recently conducted experimental and quasi-experimental design studies, six of seven used interviewing tools, none used observation tools, six used document analysis, and five used standardized measures. It is important to note that there was very little across-study consistency in the actual measures that were used, and there was little consistency in the subject of the measures. For example, six studies interviewed workers (Berry 1992; Feldman 1991; Pecora, Fraser, and Haapala 1991; Schwartz, AuClaire, and Harris 1991; Showell, Hartley, and Allen 1987; Yuan and Struckman-Johnson 1991), and only two interviewed clients (Feldman 1991; Pecora, Fraser, and Haapala 1991). Of the five studies that used standardized measures, only three used the same instrument, the Child Well-Being Scales developed by Magura and Moses (1986) (Feldman 1991; Nelson 1991; Yuan and Struckman-Johnson 1991). Even though additional standardized forms were used in some of the studies, none were used in common across studies.

There are numerous standardized measures available that family preservation programs may use in evaluation. These fall into four basic categories: (1) family functioning measures, (2) child functioning measures, (3) parent functioning measures, and (4) social support or community measures. Measures that may be appropriate for family preservation are shown in the table below; most of these have been recently reviewed and critiqued by Pecora and his colleagues (1995). In general, and if possible, designs should include these four types simultaneously in family preservation program evaluations (Pecora, Fraser, Nelson, McCroskey, and Meezan 1995).

STANDARDIZED MEASURES FOR USE IN
FAMILY PRESERVATION PROGRAMS AND EVALUATIONS

Family Functioning Family Adaptability Cohesion Evaluation Scales (FACES IV)
Self-Report Family Inventory
Family Environment Scale
McMaster Family Assessment Device
Index Family Relations
Child Well-Being Scales
Family Systems Change Scale
Family Assessment Form
Family Risk Scales*

Child Functioning Bayley Scales of Infant Development
Denver Developmental Screening Test
Peabody Picture Vocabulary Test (Revised)
Bzoch-League Receptive-Expressive Emergent Language Scale
Standard Progressive Matrices
System of Multicultural Pluralistic Assessment*
Adaptive Behavior Social Inventory
Child Behavior Checklist
Youth Self-Report
Vineland Adaptive Behavior Scales
Conners Parent Symptom Questionnaire and Teachers Rating Scales
Family Relations Test
Children's Depression Inventory
Coopersmith Self-Esteem Inventories
Personality Inventory for Children
State-Trait Anxiety Inventory for Children
Home Observation for Measurement of the Environment
Urban Childhood Level of Living Scale

Parent Functioning Adult-Adolescent Parenting Inventory
Child Abuse Potential Inventory
Parental Disposition Subscale of the Child Well-Being Scales
Level of Living Scale*
Parenting Stress Index
Parental Locus of Control Scale
Parental Acceptance-Rejection Questionnaire
Child at Risk Field*

Social Support/
Community Family Relationship Index
Social Network Map
Inventory Milardo Social Support
Family Support Scale
Inventory of Social Support
Personal Network Matrix
Life Event Scale**
Interpersonal Support Evaluation List**

Note: Measures reviewed by Howing, Kohn, Gaudin, Kurtz and Wodarski (1992) are indicated by a single asterisk (*). Those reviewed by Feldman (1991) are indicated by two asterisks (**). All others are reviewed by Pecora, Fraser, Nelson, McCroskey, and Meezan (1995).

Though there are a number of standardized measures, many experts believe that there are problems with many of them. Besharov and Baehler (1992) contend that there is an absence of appropriate child- and family-oriented outcome measures for family preservation practice. Wells (1994) questions whether existing standardized measures are adequate to address the complexity of individual families. She notes that typical measures are too general, do not consider contextual issues, and are not sensitive to low income and/or poorly educated families. Many measures are based on middle-class standards that may be inappropriate for family preservation clients, and they do not address "the basic elements of the child's health, safety and physical development" (Besharov and Baehler 1992, 10). Further, too often these measures rely on only one person's perceptions (typically the worker's) (Wells 1994).

In light of these problems, Cooke et al. (1988) call for the creation of standardized measures that are more sensitive to individual experiences and provide a longitudinal or life cycle approach. However justified this request may be, the development of standardized measures that are individualized and developmental in nature may be a long time in coming. On the other hand, qualitative nonstandardized measures that capture these factors may adequately meet the need until such individualized and developmental measures are created.

WHEN IS EVALUATION CONDUCTED?

The issue of when evaluations are conducted seems to be less complex than other areas of family preservation program evaluation. There is fairly clear consensus regarding the importance of collecting baseline assessment information (that is, preintervention data), treatment interval data (data collected during treatment), treatment completion or termination data (postintervention data), and follow-up data (longitudinal data) (for example, Posavac and Carey 1989; Rossi and Freeman 1993; Royse 1992).

Process evaluations should generally be conducted on a continuous basis for programs interested in improvement over time (Royse 1992). If resources are not available for continuous process monitoring, then process evaluations should be conducted at least during the time a program is being established (for example, usually the first year) (Royse 1992). Outcome evaluations, on the other hand, should generally be conducted on an ongoing basis once a program's policies and procedures are firmly established (Rossi and Freeman 1993). Typically, outcome evaluations are most appropriate when goals and objectives of the program are stable and after a process evaluation has been completed (Rossi and Freeman 1993).

As to when to evaluate specific client outcomes, program objectives should be set with the family and evaluated at the first contact with a family as well as during service provision at regular intervals, at the completion of services, and at designated follow-up periods. For example, the need for concrete and support services can be rather easily assessed in the early stages of contact with a family. The resulting service plan or treatment contract should be based on the strengths and deficits discovered in the assessment. Treatment contracts can be created to cover services and learning opportunities that will enable a family to acquire necessary resources to remedy the resource deficits identified in assessment. Continuous monitoring of progress during treatment will show whether these resources are being acquired and to what degree. Determinations at the end of service provision as well as at follow-up periods will reveal whether gains have been maintained over time. The same time periods are relevant for the assessment regarding knowledge and skills levels, risk factors, family relationship factors, and family-defined treatment goals and objectives.

Longitudinal data must be collected in greater frequency than it is now to determine whether program gains are maintained over time (Besharov and Baehler 1992; Wells and Biegel 1992). Essential to the collection of this type of follow-up data are realistic determinants of what families are expected to gain and how they are supposed to change as a result of family preservation services. For example, it must be determined whether family preservation is intended to prevent out-of-home placement of a family member forever or only for a specified period.

WHERE IS EVALUATION COMPLETED?

An issue that has not received as much attention as other matters of evaluation is where the actual data collection is completed. Perhaps part of this neglect stems from the fact that the place is determined by the evaluation design and measures. Evaluations will typically be conducted in an agency's offices; but depending on the measures used, parts of evaluations will likely be conducted in family homes and community settings as well.

WHO CONDUCTS THE EVALUATION?

Finally, the issue of who executes the evaluation is still up for debate. Traditionally, human service evaluations are completed by outside evaluators or, in agencies that have the luxury, by evaluation staff employed by the agency (see, for example, Rossi and Freeman 1993; Royse 1992; Sichel 1982; Tripodi, Fellin, and Epstein 1978). However, family preservation programs generally will not have the resources either to hire staff just to conduct research or to hire experts to come in to evaluate their programs. Alternatives must therefore be defined.

The developmental approach to practice and research, referred to earlier in this chapter, provides the opportunity for persons other than expert evaluators to aid in the evaluation process. For example, workers are generally in the best position to collect information (by observation, for instance), to disseminate forms for clients to complete, or to provide accurate perceptions of what is occurring with a family. It is important to augment workers' perceptions with collateral and client perceptions as well.

In general, there has been a seeming aversion to collecting information based on client perceptions in the human services field. Client-based data are typically seen as biased, not scientific, and not credible (Rapp and Poertner 1988; Royse 1992). However, family preservation is so tied to the client that it begs for information from the client. Royse (1992) recommends using a reliable scale that has been used in other studies; using the same measure repeatedly and developing baseline data with that measure; using a combination of open-ended and closed-ended questions on measures; and generating information from both new and former clients. It is important that information collected from clients focus not only on client satisfaction with services (for example, ease of access to services) but also on client perceptions regarding the course of treatment (for example, whether a client's situation is improved or not).

CONCLUSION

Relevant research and evaluation of family preservation programs are dependent on a true reflection of the families and services in these programs. Similarly, provision of quality services is dependent on a competent assessment of a family. Therefore the inclusion of sound measurement tools should aid caseworkers in the clear assessment of families rather than simply add to their paperwork burden. This requires deliberate and careful investigation, selection, and/or creation of measurement tools based on the characteristics of the population served, the foci of services, and program goals and objectives. Just as programs tailor services to families, the methods used to evaluate programs must incorporate the flexibility to adapt to individual family needs and goals, most naturally through a combination of qualitative and quantitative measures and the inclusion of client feedback.

REFERENCES

Berry, Marianne. (1992). An evaluation of family preservation services: Fitting agency services to family needs. *Social Work* 37: 314–21.

Besharov, Douglas J., and Karen Baehler. (1992). Demonstration and evaluation strategies. *Children and Youth Services Review* 14: 1–18.

Blythe, Betty J. (1990). Applying practice research methods in intensive family preservation services. In James K. Whittaker, Jill Kinney, Elizabeth M. Tracy, and Charlotte Booth (eds.), *Reaching high-risk families: Intensive family preservation in human services,* 147–63. Hawthorne, NY: Aldine de Gruyter.

Bovaird, Tony, and Ian Mallinson. (1988). Setting objectives and measuring achievement in social care. *British Journal of Social Work* 18: 309–24.

Brawley, Edward A., and Emilia E. Martinez-Brawley. (1988). Social programme evaluation in the USA: Trends and issues. *British Journal of Social Work* 18: 391–413.

Chambers, Donald E., Kenneth R. Wedel, and Mary K. Rodwell. (1992). *Evaluating social programs.* Boston: Allyn and Bacon.

Cooke, Betty D., Marilyn M. Rossmann, Hamilton I. McCubbin, and Joan M. Patterson. (1988). Examining the definition and assessment of social support: A resource for individuals and families. *Family Relations* 37: 211–16.

Feldman, Leonard H. (1991). Evaluating the impact of intensive family preservation services in New Jersey. In Kathleen Wells and David E. Biegel (eds.), *Family preservation services: Research and evaluation,* 47–71. Newbury Park, CA: Sage.

Fraser, Mark W. (1990). *Assessing the effectiveness of family preservation programs: Implications for agency-based research.* Paper presented at the Family Preservation Institute for Social Work University Educators, August 9–11, 1990, National Association for Family-Based Services, Kansas City, MO.

Fraser, Mark W., Peter J. Pecora, Chirapat Popuang, and David A. Haapala. (1992). Event history analysis: A proportional hazards perspective on modeling outcomes in intensive family preservation services. In David F. Gillespie and Charles Glisson (eds.), *Quantitative methods in social work: State of the art.* New York: Haworth Press.

Gordon, K. H. (1991). Improving practice through illuminative evaluation. *Social Service Review* 65: 365–78.

182

Grubb, C. T. (1976). *Program evaluation and local administration.* Chapel Hill: Institute for Social Service Planning, School of Social Work, University of North Carolina.

Harrison, W. D. (1994). The inevitability of integrated methods. In Edmund Sherman and William J. Reid (eds.), *Qualitative research in social work,* 409–22. New York: Columbia University Press.

Hartman, Ann. (1994). Setting the theme: Many ways of knowing. In Edmund Sherman and William J. Reid (eds.), *Qualitative research in social work,* 459–63. New York: Columbia University Press.

Howing, Phyllis T., Sheldon Kohn, James M. Gaudin, Jr., P. David Kurtz, and John S. Wodarski. (1992). Current research issues in child welfare. *Social Work Research and Abstracts* 28: 5–12.

Kinney, Jill, David Haapala, and Charlotte Booth. (1991). *Keeping families together: The Homebuilders model.* Hawthorne, NY: Aldine de Gruyter.

Loneck, B. (1994). Commentary: Practitioner-researcher perspective on the integration of qualitative and quantitative research methods. In Edmund Sherman and William J. Reid (eds.), *Qualitative research in social work,* 445–51. New York: Columbia University Press.

Maugura, Stephen and Barbara S. Moses (1986). *Outcome measures for child welfare services: Theory and applications.* Washington, D.C.: Child Welfare League of America.

Nelson, Kristine E. (1991). Populations and outcomes in five family preservation programs. In Kathleen Wells and David E. Biegel (eds.), *Family preservation services: Research and evaluation,* 72–91. Newbury Park, CA: Sage.

Nelson, Kristine E., Miriam J. Landsman, and Wendy Deutelbaum. (1990). Three models of family-centered placement prevention services. *Child Welfare* 69: 3–21.

Patton, M. Q. (1987). *How to use qualitative methods in evaluation.* Newbury Park, CA: Sage.

Patton, M. Q. (1990). *Qualitative evaluation and research methods.* 2d ed. Newbury Park, CA: Sage.

Pecora, Peter J., Mark W. Fraser, and David A. Haapala. (1991). Client outcomes and issues for program design. In Kathleen Wells and David E. Biegel (eds.), *Family preservation services: Research and evaluation,* 3–32. Newbury Park, CA: Sage.

Pecora, Peter J., Mark W. Fraser, Kristine E. Nelson, Jacqueline McCroskey, and William Meezan. (1995). Hawthorne, NY: Aldine de Gruyter.

Posavac, E. J., and R. G. Carey. (1989). *Program evaluation: Methods and case studies.* Englewood Cliffs, NJ: Prentice-Hall.

Rapp, Charles A., and John Poertner. (1988). Moving clients center stage through the use of client outcomes. In *Managing for service effectiveness,* 23–38. New York: Haworth Press.

Reichardt, C. S., and T. D. Cook. (1979). Beyond qualitative versus quantitative methods. In T. D. Cook and C. S. Reichardt (eds.), *Qualitative and quantitative methods in evaluation research.* Beverly Hills: Sage.

Rodwell, Mary K., and D. Woody III. (1994). Constructivist evaluation: The policy/practice context. In Edmund Sherman and William J. Reid (eds.), *Qualitative research in social work,* 315–27. New York: Columbia University Press.

Rossi, Peter H. (1992). Assessing family preservation programs. *Children and Youth Services Review* 14: 77–97.

Rossi, Peter H., and Howard E. Freeman. (1993). *Evaluation: A systematic approach.* 5th ed. Newbury Park, CA: Sage.

Royse, David. (1992). *Program evaluation: An introduction.* Chicago: Nelson-Hall.

Scannapieco, Maria. (1993). The importance of family functioning to prevention of placement: A study of family preservation services. *Child and Adolescent Social Work Journal* 10 (6): 509–20.

Scannapieco, Maria. (1994). Home-based services program: Effectiveness with at risk families. *Children and Youth Services Review* 16 (5/6): 363–78.

Schuerman, John R., Tina L. Rzepnicki, and Julia H. Littell. (1994). *Putting families first: An experiment in family preservation.* Hawthorne, NY: Aldine de Gruyter.

Schwartz, Ira M., Philip AuClaire, and Linda J. Harris. (1991). Family preservation services as an alternative to the out-of-home placement of adolescents: The Hennepin County experience. In Kathleen Wells and David E. Biegel (eds.), *Family preservation services: Research and evaluation,* 33–46. Newbury Park, CA: Sage.

Sherman, Edmund, and William J. Reid. (1994). Introduction: Coming of age in social work—the emergence of qualitative research. In Edmund Sherman and William J. Reid (eds.), *Qualitative research in social work,* 1–15. New York: Columbia University Press.

Showell, William H. (1985). *1983–85 biennial report of CSD's Intensive Family Services.* Salem: State of Oregon Children's Services Division.

Showell, William H., Roland Hartley, and Marcia Allen. (1987) *Outcomes of Oregon's family therapy programs: A descriptive study of 999 families.* Salem: State of Oregon Children's Services Division.

Showell, William, and Jim White. (1990, Spring). In-home and in-office intensive family services. *Prevention Report:* 6, 10.

Sichel, J. (1982). *Program evaluation guidelines: A research handbook for agency personnel.* New York: Human Sciences Press.

Staff, Ilene, and Edith Fein. (1994). Inside the black box: An exploration of service delivery in a family reunification program. *Child Welfare* 73 (3): 195–211.

Tracy, Elizabeth M. (1990). Identifying social support resources of at-risk families. *Social Work* 35: 252–58.

Tracy, Elizabeth M. (1991). Defining the target population for family preservation services. In Kathleen Wells and David E. Biegel (eds.), *Family preservation services: Research and evaluation,* 138–58. Newbury Park, CA: Sage.

Tripodi, Tony, P. Fellin, and I. Epstein. (1978). *Differential social program evaluation.* Itasca, IL: F. E. Peacock.

Videka-Sherman, Lynn, and William J. Reid. (1990). Introduction: A time to take stock. In Lynn Videka-Sherman and William J. Reid (eds.), *Advances in clinical social work research,* xi–xiii. Silver Spring, MD: NASW Press.

Wells, Kathleen. (1994). A reorientation to knowledge development in family preservation services: A proposal. *Child Welfare* 73 (5): 475–88.

Wells, Kathleen, and David E. Biegel. (1990). *Intensive family preservation services: A research agenda for the 1990s.* Final Report presented at the Intensive Family Preservation Services Research Conference, September 25–26, 1989, Cleveland.

Wells, Kathleen, and David E. Biegel. (1992). Intensive family preservation services research: Current status and future agenda. *Social Work Research and Abstracts* 28 (1): 21–27.

Yuan, Ying-Ying T., and David L. Struckman-Johnson. (1991). Placement outcomes for neglected children with prior placements in family preservation programs. In Kathleen Wells and David E. Biegel (eds.), *Family preservation services: Research and evaluation,* 92–118. Newbury Park, CA: Sage.

Chapter 10

FUTURE DIRECTIONS FOR FAMILY PRESERVATION

Intensive family preservation services are grounded in a philosophy of flexibility and fitting services to families and communities (rather than a practice of prescribing one remedy or set of remedies for all families and all communities). Fidelity to this philosophy requires innovative and flexible structuring of services, which cannot be done within old administrative and programmatic structures. Intensive family preservation services cannot be the innovative new program "in a box," removed from or added to traditional child welfare services; they cannot be viewed as a new type of categorical service.

EMBEDDING INTENSIVE FAMILY PRESERVATION IN AN ARRAY OF SERVICES

Intensive family preservation services are not so flexible that they eschew defining program characteristics and components. As delineated in chapter 4, they reflect a strengths perspective, are home- and community-based, are family-centered, are provided to families in crisis, and are typically short-term and intensive.

These program characteristics, particularly those emphasizing the provision of intensive and short-term services to families in crisis, presume the existence of other preventive services and longer-term treatment and placement services for troubled or risky families who have not reached a crisis level. These characteristics presume that services exist to serve families for a longer period of time than intensive family preservation services or to serve out-of-home needs (Lloyd and Sallee 1994). This necessitates the conceptualization and implementation of intensive family preservation services into an array of services ranging from preventive educational and family support services to a range of treatment and placement options for those families who need them.

Barriers to Services Integration

Inadequate Resources and Increasing Need. It is common for new programs to be seen as the answer to all problems. The difficulty of broadly implementing intensive family preservation services as well as preventive and family support services is compounded by the increasing level of need in many communities over the past decade and the more severe needs among many families related to substance abuse, poverty, and chronic child neglect. As noted earlier, the reports of child abuse increase in number every year, as do state rates of child poverty and other indicators of family stress (Children's Defense Fund 1990).

As the need for services and effective treatment has increased over the past decade, funding for social services has not grown. The strain on resources is most evident in the low salaries and lenient employment requirements in many public child welfare agencies, the high caseloads of child welfare caseworkers, and the resulting high turnover rates among public child welfare staff in many states (Pecora, Whittaker, and Maluccio 1992). Strained budgets also do not allow for the "flexible funding" component of many family preservation programs, wherein a pool of cash funds is available to meet the many and diverse needs of families that do not fit into predefined categorical areas of funding.

Poor Coordination among Agencies. The provision of short-term and intensive community-based services presumes the presence of other community supports to which caseworkers can link families to put in place ongoing supports for longer-term improvements and future needs. This necessitates a wide range of available supports for families, both formal and informal, from counseling, housing, and financial assistance to churches and neighborhood groups.

Because resources are inadequate and needs are great, the presence of these services is crucial. But their presence is not enough. It is also necessary that they be coordinated and that communication exist among their providers. The long history of categorical programs in states and local communities has in many areas resulted in "turf" issues regarding responsibility for families and the provision of services as well as what are sometimes called "silo" problems (Sallee 1994), which means, for example, that mental health agencies are responsible only for the family's mental health needs, schools are responsible only for education, and juvenile justice agencies are responsible only when a teenager gets into trouble.

187

Supports for Services Integration

As mentioned earlier, family preservation must be part of a continuum of services for families, paying particular attention to poverty and providing alternatives for families with chronic problems. One innovative community-based approach borrowed from Britain is the "patch" approach, which is being piloted in Pennsylvania and Iowa (Adams and Krauth 1994).

> The term "patch" refers to a limited geographical area which is served by a locally-based team of human service workers. . . . The patch team, usually employees of public social services departments and sometimes of housing or health authorities, supports and builds on the resources of informal networks of kin and neighbors, and joins with the efforts of voluntary and statutory agencies, churches, schools, and neighborhood organizations, to solve both individual and community problems. (2)

The patch project has operated for two years in Iowa (Adams and Krauth 1994). In describing its evolution, Adams and Krauth note that the patch team "came to see the worker-consumer relation as only one part of a system that includes family members, neighbors, informal groups, church, voluntary organizations, school, and other health and human service providers" (3). They continue:

> Just as the settlement workers did earlier this century, the team also set out to learn from patch residents—whether or not they were service users at the time—about their perceptions of the needs and resources of the neighborhood and how the team could collaborate with them. They used the technique of "exchange meetings" learned from British patch trainers. Pairs of teammates began to meet with small groups of parents, neighbors, and others, such as residents at the homeless shelter and teens participating in a community support group, to exchange information about the perceptions, resources, and concerns of local people and team members. (4)

If intensive family preservation services are to be as successful as possible, certain elements related to this patch approach must be in place across community and state agencies, such as communication, cooperation, coordination and community cohesion, all incorporating this systemic understanding of families in their communities.

188

TREATMENT FIDELITY

Much of the evaluative and research literature critiqued in this book has identified treatment fidelity as a critical issue in the current implementation of intensive family preservation services. The faithful implementation of program models is always a concern, particularly in the beginning stages of program evolution. Anxiety about implementation is heightened by the federal mandate of the Family Preservation and Family Support Act, which is leading fairly rapidly to the broad implementation of intensive family preservation services nationwide.

Barriers to Faithful Implementation of Models

Poor Delineation of Program Models. Howard Doueck and colleagues (Doueck, Bronson, and Levine 1992), in their review and analyses of current risk assessment processes, emphasize the possibility of a "Type III error"—drawing conclusions from the evaluation of a program that has been poorly implemented. Type III errors may be common in the development of family preservation programs that are based on early evaluations, given the lack of attention to process in these early evaluations. When programs have been found to be successful in preventing a large proportion of imminent placements, replication has been frequent; but often this replication has had to proceed without a careful delineation of program structure or service components because these have not been well described.

When services are defined only as doing "whatever it takes" to keep families together, it is difficult to know whether worker activities are faithful to an original model. Vaguely defined goals and objectives for programs, workers, and families and poorly described program components lead to programs being all things to all administrators, with little accountability for actual gains with families or communities.

Lack of Training. Tied to this fuzzy description of intensive family preservation service models, a lack of training and knowledge in the values base and structure of intensive family preservation services results in these services often being laid on top of conventional services or instituted as add-on program units in child welfare agencies. Implementation is often undertaken with little understanding of the corresponding changes in values and practices inherent in the family preservation model, such as viewing clients as colleagues rather than coercively, defining families in terms of strengths rather than diagnoses or problems, and building or linking into community networks, which often requires political or advocacy work.

189

Lack of understanding of the values base of family preservation service models often results in conflicting values among workers, administrators, and communities. If workers are coming from a "rescue" mentality or a punitive and coercive mindset, the intensive hours in the home will only be ones of conflict and impasse. Value conflicts between worker and program structure can also impede treatment. There is often a lack of consistency between workers' jobs and the administrative structure in which they operate. If workers are expected to provide flexible services, they need to be flexibly supervised and supported; if workers provide services in families' homes after hours and on weekends, they will not put in many service hours in the office between 9 a.m. and 5 p.m.

Supports of the Faithful Implementation of Models

Training and Continuous Supports for Workers. It is imperative when implementing a new program that all the individuals involved, particularly those delivering the services, receive adequate grounding in the values, theoretical, and practice bases of the program. Well-trained and experienced front-line workers are an agency's most precious asset (Pecora 1990). To bolster this resource, child welfare agencies in many states have joined with universities and schools of social work to provide family-centered curricula to students and child protective services employees, with approximately nine universities offering a specialization in family preservation services (Lloyd and Sallee 1994).

Because the values base of family preservation is so integral to its implementation, intensive or longer-term training, rather than one-day workshops, is the most effective means of achieving or helping workers achieve proficiency in this new approach to families. "These are not simple innovations," notes Smale (1994). "If you're casting around for an innovation that's simple, easy to use, doesn't challenge the status quo . . . community-centered practice is not it. Certain parts are easier than others. Although as any manager could tell you, it is far from easy to get staff repositioned; yet this component of the innovation is simple compared to the required change in attitude whereby 'clients' are deemed resources rather than bundles of deficits. That is a complex change" (10).

Internalizing Values throughout the Organization. Not only workers need training in family preservation values and service structures. Administrators and policy makers need to understand the goals, service components, and other structural elements of the program. They must also understand the benefits of strengthening families rather than focusing purely on the ramifications of preserving risky families. "The statement, 'we train everybody,' has become ritual refrain for agencies involved in system-wide family preservation efforts. . . . Much resistance is dispelled simply by sharing the facts about what family preservation is, how it will be implemented, and how protection of children will not be compromised" (Lloyd and Sallee 1994, 5).

Flexibility while Maintaining Fidelity. The values and service components that frame family preservation services are fairly well defined (see chapter 4). Beyond this basic framework, services are intended to be flexibly tailored to the individual strengths and needs of the family, moving away from the practice of providing contracted parenting education classes to every parent or self-esteem counseling to every neglectful mother and toward services that are specific, relevant, and individualized.

A thorough assessment of a family's strengths and needs should lead naturally and logically to a concrete and well-defined service plan or contract that is formed in partnership between a family and its family preservation worker. This plan will usually entail the provision or acquisition of a mix of concrete and softer services, with the bulk of services directly provided by the caseworker rather than through referral to contracted providers. This moves away from the "mystical reliance" of social workers on mental health and other providers evidenced in reviews of child welfare case records (Stein, Gambrill, and Wiltse 1978, 14) and toward better communication and coordination among service providers.

Basing case decisions on such a thorough assessment of strengths and needs is predicated on a sound technology for assessing strengths and risks (see chapter 7) and, again, effective training in this technology and its theoretical and empirical base. Family preservation practice and risk assessment must thus continue apace, each informing the other, as improvements and refinements are established in each field. Neither practice, however, should be adopted wholesale without a cautious respect for the interrelatedness of the two or the shortcomings of either.

PROCESS AND OUTCOME EVALUATIONS

The components of family preservation practice will continue to emerge and evolve as research technology improves and as the strengths and risks of families continue to shift and grow. As this review has illustrated, the evaluative methods used to develop the knowledge base supporting and refining family preservation services are slowly becoming more complete and more rigorous, although to a varying degree in different locales. This is appropriate, given that different programs are in varying stages of development and that the empirical bases of knowledge are more complete in some areas than in others (as discussed in chapter 3).

Barriers to Relevant and Productive Research and Evaluation

Measurement Issues. Most programs are evaluated for the purpose of illuminating certain program outcomes and are evaluated in their starting-up stage, with changes in staff and program clouding the results. Many programs have not distinguished between families who are reunified and those who have never been separated, and most have not examined the long-term outcomes regarding cases that close and then reopen at a later date. In addition, programs differ in their measure of outcome.

Approaching practice and services from a strengths-based perspective rather than a diagnosis perspective increases the difficulty of measurement and evaluation. Measurement tools that are framed in terms of psychopathology, problem diagnosis, and maladaptation are much more common than are those documenting the strengths and resources of families or individuals. Similarly, tools that focus on the individual rather than on interactions between family members or the relationships between families and their communities are much simpler to conceptualize and construct.

Accountability Issues. Defining family strengths and needs in terms of systemic relationships and community wellness dilutes the ability of both administrators and evaluators to pinpoint areas of specific accountability among all those serving the family. This is a critical problem among programs that contract out many of the services that are provided to their families. For example, with parenting education, programs can easily document that parents were referred to a class and can even measure how many such classes a particular parent attended. But more concrete and behavioral measures of how a parent improved in terms of knowledge and attitudes or how those improvements resulted in actual behavior changes in the home with the child are quite rare in this field (Berry 1988). Until the accountability problem is resolved by using more instrumental and behavioral measures tying service provision to actual gains, programs will keep operating in the dark as to what is effective in preserving families and protecting children.

Pressure to Succeed. Finally, family preservation programs are by philosophy open systems, incorporating input from all systems levels and responding flexibly to this input. The philosophy of flexibility and modifying in response to new information is being instituted under great pressure by legislators and administrators to help cut foster care costs (by preventing placement) relatively quickly. This pressure can result in creaming of clients with easily solved problems, inappropriate targeting of services to nonrisky families, and other such problems.

Research Innovations to Support Relevant and Productive Research and Evaluation

There are many research initiatives in place under the Family Preservation and Family Support Act that focus on determining imminent risk, defining program success in a multitude of ways, developing more rigorous research designs, achieving better delineation and testing of service components, and using more standardized measures across studies.

Most professionals agree that family preservation services and other home-based approaches are but one element of an effective child welfare system. It is to their detriment that few studies of home-based services adequately describe the differential contribution of their separate components. It is important to assess not only whether a program worked but how and why it worked (Zigler and Weiss 1985). This more specific and discriminating type of assessment will "help the policy community learn how to deal more wisely with social problems" (Weiss 1981, 400).

Because of the deficit in the existing empirical base for family preservation services, the next goal for evaluations of these services is to determine the most effective elements of service, the clients best suited for this type of service, and the best delivery system for these services. Reaching this objective will involve both small-scale and system-wide evaluations, using the most specific and behavioral measures possible and the most rigorous methods of analysis appropriate to correlate service provision to the gains observed in the family and community.

CONCLUSION

While controlled studies of the effectiveness of these programs have found mixed rates of placement prevention, many researchers and scholars in the field agree that family preservation is an appropriate service model for many families, particularly those in acute—not chronic—crisis and when used discriminantly as one element in an array of child welfare services.

A landmark review of social services to children, youth, and families in the United States (Kamerman and Kahn 1989) found that decentralizing responsibility for social programs down to the state level over the past decade and reducing funding for these programs have resulted, obviously, in very different approaches from state to state to the problems of child abuse and neglect, but that the overarching stressors facing families are common in all locales.

Social services are essential for helping troubled children, youth, and families. At their best, these services rescue, sustain, help, rehabilitate, and even enrich development. Nonetheless, only the naive or the irresponsible would blame major social problems on social service failures *or* claim that social services reform will eliminate poverty or social pathology. Social service reform is urgent *but* it cannot be successful unless the society attends to much else as well. (306–7)

The implementation and evaluation of family preservation programs across the country must take place within a larger focus on community wellness and the additional family support programs outlined in the Family Preservation and Family Support Act—programs that surround and support intensive family preservation programs. Similarly, this focus must extend to holistic needs of children and their families that go beyond the issues of protection and parenting and attend to the employment, equity, housing, and health needs of all families.

REFERENCES

Adams, Paul, and Karin Krauth. (1994, Fall). Community-centered practice to strengthen families and neighborhoods: The patch approach. *Prevention Report:* 2–5.

Berry, Marianne. (1988). A review of parent training programs in child welfare. *Social Service Review* 62: 302–23.

Children's Defense Fund. (1990). *S.O.S. America: A children's defense budget.* Washington, DC: Children's Defense Fund.

Doueck, Howard J., Denise E. Bronson, and Murray Levine. (1992). Evaluating risk assessment implementation in child protection: Issues for consideration. *Child Abuse and Neglect* 16: 637–46.

Kamerman, Sheila B., and Alfred J. Kahn. (1989). *Social services for children, youth and families in the United States.* Hartford, CT: Annie E. Casey Foundation.

Lloyd, June C., and Alvin L. Sallee. (1994). The challenge and potential of family preservation services in the public child welfare system. *Protecting Children* 10: 3–6.

Pecora, Peter J., James K. Whittaker, and Anthony N. Maluccio. (1992). *The child welfare challenge: Policy, practice and research.* Hawthorne, NY: Aldine de Gruyter.

Sallee, Alvin. (1994). *Family preservation services integration.* Paper presented to the Texas Department of Protective and Regulatory Services, Austin.

Smale, Gerald. (1994, Fall). Innovations transfer and community-centered practice. *Prevention Report:* 6–12.

Stein, Theodore J., Eileen D. Gambrill, and Kermit Wiltse. (1978). *Children in foster homes: Achieving continuity of care.* New York: Praeger.

Weiss, Heather. (1981). Doing science or doing policy? *Evaluation and Program Planning* 4: 397–402.

Zigler, Edward, and Heather Weiss. (1985). Family support systems: An ecological approach to child development. In Robert Rapoport (ed.), *Children, youth and families: The action-research relationship.* Cambridge, England: Cambridge University Press.

INDEX